PaintShop Photo Pro X3 for Photographers

PaintShop Photo Pro X3 for Photographers

Ken McMahon

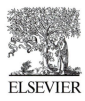

ELSEVIER

AMSTERDAM • BOSTON • HEIDELBERG • LONDON • NEW YORK • OXFORD
PARIS • SAN DIEGO • SAN FRANCISCO • SINGAPORE • SYDNEY • TOKYO
Focal Press is an imprint of Elsevier

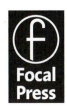

Focal Press

Focal Press is an imprint of Elsevier
The Boulevard, Langford Lane, Kidlington, Oxford, OX5 1GB, UK
30 Corporate Drive, Suite 400, Burlington, MA 01803, USA

First published 2010

British Library Cataloguing in Publication Data
McMahon, Ken.
   PaintShop Photo Pro X3 for photograhers.
   1. PaintShop Pro. 2. Photography—Digital techniques.
   I. Title
   006.6'86-dc22

Library of Congress Number: 2010925619

ISBN: 978-0-240-52165-7

For information on all Focal Press publications
visit our website at focalpress.com

Printed and bound in the United States

10 11 12 11 10 9 8 7 6 5 4 3 2 1

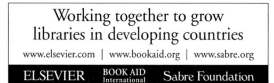

Working together to grow
libraries in developing countries

www.elsevier.com | www.bookaid.org | www.sabre.org

ELSEVIER   BOOK AID International   Sabre Foundation

Contents

Contents

Contents

Introduction

Why PaintShop Photo Pro X3?

If you're thinking about buying this book (or, better still, if you've already bought it!) the chances are that you own and use a digital camera. You're far from alone. Back in 2007 sales of digital cameras topped 100 million for the first time and have remained above that figure every year since.[1]

Digital photography is now the norm, and we're all familiar with the advantages that it has brought us. No more film to pay for, instant pictures that we can post online or email around the world, and virtually no limit to the number of shots we can take. Digital photography has also opened up countless new ways for us to work and play with our pictures.

Which is where PaintShop Photo Pro X3 enters the picture. This inexpensive, versatile application will allow you to do just about anything with your digital pictures, from correcting exposure problems and removing red-eye to making Christmas cards and event posters. It will also help you organize your growing collection of digital photos so that, in years to come, you'll easily be able to locate the ones you want without having to dredge through thousands of digital files. Dealing with the huge numbers of photos we now generate is such an important issue I've devoted an entire chapter to how you can manage it using PaintShop Photo Pro X3's Organizer.

Why This Book?

PaintShop Photo Pro X3 is a powerful image-editing application that's packed with sophisticated tools and features that will help you get the most from your digital photos. But all this power and sophistication comes at a price – you need to learn how to use it. This book is designed to help you do that.

In *PaintShop Photo Pro X3 for Photographers* I've tried to do much more than simply explain how PaintShop Photo Pro X3 works. In each of the chapters I've taken a practical approach to demonstrating tools and techniques so that you can learn how to use the program to do the things you want with your own digital photos. At the end of each chapter you'll find a series of step-by-step projects that demonstrate many of the techniques covered.

---

[1] According to the Camera and Imaging Products Association (CIPA).

Why Me?

The book is aimed at anyone who wants to get more from their digital photos and has a basic understanding of how to use their PC. You don't even need a copy of PaintShop Photo Pro X3! If you go to www.corel.com you can download a free, fully functional, trial version. The book is also suitable for those working with earlier versions of the software.

If you're new to PaintShop Photo Pro X3, I'd recommend you work through the book in a linear fashion as later chapters introduce more complex techniques. If you're keen to cover a topic dealt with later in the book, start by taking a look through the first two chapters, which provide an introduction to the workspace and basic feature set.

If you're already familiar with PaintShop Photo Pro X3, feel free to dip in wherever your interest takes you or where there is a gap in your knowledge. Chapter 1 covers features new to PaintShop Photo Pro X3.

Digital photography is here to stay and PaintShop Photo Pro makes getting the best from your digital images easier than it's ever been. With *PaintShop Photo Pro X3 for Photographers* you'll be able to get the best from PaintShop Photo Pro – and have some fun in the process!

A Note From Corel

Corel® PaintShop Photo Pro® X3 delivers a complete set of photo-editing tools to help you create professional-looking photos fast!

By combining Ken McMahon's ideas from a photographer's viewpoint and the powerful yet easy-to-use features within Corel® PaintShop Photo Pro X3, you will be able to: fix brightness, color, and photo imperfections; compose photos full of depth and imagination; give photos a unique and exciting look; plus organize and share all your photos.

Corel, Ken McMahon, and Focal Press have worked very closely to create a book for anyone who aspires to make good photos great and that puts the power of Corel PaintShop Photo Pro X3 at the fingertips of anyone who wants to create stunning photos right out of the box.

About Corel Corporation

Corel Corporation provides innovative software solutions that help millions of value-conscious businesses and consumers in over 75 countries improve their productivity. The company is renowned for its powerful software portfolio that combines innovative photo-editing and graphics creation, vector illustration and technical graphics applications, along with office and personal productivity solutions. Corel's flagship products include the

CorelDRAW® Graphics Suite, the WordPerfect® Office Suite, the Corel® Painter™ and Natural-Media® painting and illustration software, and the PaintShop™ family of digital photography and image-editing software.

Founded in 1985, Corel is headquartered in Ottawa, Canada. For more information, please visit www.corel.com.

CHAPTER 1

The Basics – Introducing PaintShop Photo Pro X3

What's Covered in this Chapter

- This chapter explains what PaintShop Photo Pro X3 can do and how it works. If you're new to the program I'd strongly recommend you start at the beginning and read this chapter right through; it'll put you in a much better position when it comes to some of the basic photo editing in Chapter 2. In fact, for beginners, taking things in a linear fashion chapter by chapter is the best way to use the book, as the simple stuff is dealt with early on and it gets gradually more advanced as you go along.
- Unlike the other chapters, there isn't a lot of hands-on stuff here, it's mostly an explanation of how PaintShop Photo Pro X3 works. All the same, I'd recommend you prop the book open in front of you while you're at your computer so you can play with the menus, tools, and features while you're reading about them.
- First off, the chapter covers PaintShop Photo Pro X3's basic tools, including the Learning Center and Organizer. If you're in a big hurry to get started on your own stuff, by the time you reach page 34 you'll know enough to download your photos from your camera and carry out basic guided tasks using the Learning Center.

PaintShop Photo Pro X3 for Photographers. DOI: 10.1016/B978-0-240-52165-7.10001-2

· Following on are brief descriptions of some of PaintShop Photo Pro X3's more advanced editing tools, then I take a look at the features Corel has introduced in this latest version of the program, so if you're using an older version of PaintShop Photo Pro and you want to know what you're missing, turn to page 14. In addition to the brand new stuff I also take a look at features that were introduced in earlier versions.

· Other than your camera, PaintShop Photo Pro X3 is probably the single thing that will help you get the most from your digital photos and enjoy the time spent doing it. But other things can add to the experience. The last part of the chapter takes a look at accessories for your 'digital darkroom'. It's not an exhaustive list, just a few words of practical advice on those things, like printer consumables, scanners, and memory cards, which can be hard to decide on.

· The four step-by-step projects (Exploring the Learning Center, Straightening an Image, Perspective Correction, and Cropping Pictures) can each be completed in just a few minutes with little or no previous knowledge of the program – a nice easy start!

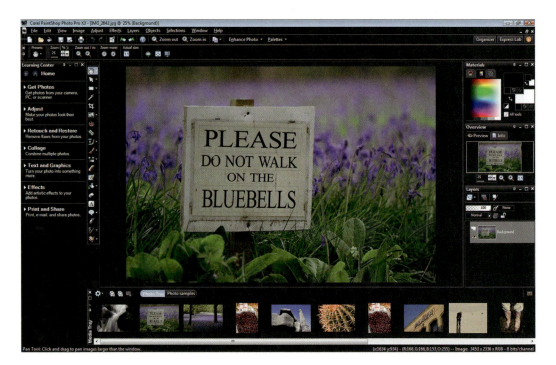

FIG 1.1 PaintShop Photo Pro X3's new-look workspace. The Learning Center on the left provides interactive guidance for photo-editing tasks and the media trays at the bottom of the screen help you to quickly locate and sort photos on your hard drive.

What you think when you first set eyes on PaintShop Photo Pro X3 will depend on your previous experience with the program and with digital photos in general. If you're a novice you may be a little intimidated by the array of toolbars, buttons, and menu options. Long-time users will be wondering what new features are to be discovered and how the revised workspace will affect the way they are used to working.

Whichever camp you fall into, you can be reassured. PaintShop Photo Pro X3's major strength is that it provides powerful image-editing tools and features on a par with more expensive applications, while at the same time being very easy to use.

One of the ways it does this is to make the interface customizable. Advanced users can turn off the helpful bits and make more space for palettes and toolbars. The other advantage of this is that as you learn more about the program, you can adapt it to suit your own level of experience.

Introduction: Basic Tools and Functions

Over the next few pages, I'll explain the various features of the PaintShop Photo Pro X3 workspace and how to use them to carry out basic photo-editing tasks. This part of the book is aimed squarely at beginners, so more experienced readers might want to skip to Advanced Features on page 11 or to the New Features section on page 14.

For those starting out, I'd recommend you read through the following section while in front of your PC, so that you can try things out and familiarize yourself with the basics of uploading, organizing, and editing your photos.

The Learning Center

The Learning Center, on the left of the screen, shows you how to get things done. If you can't see the Learning Center, select View > Palettes > Learning Center, or press the F10 key on your keyboard.

For simple tasks, like rotating photos, the Learning Center just does it for you. For more complex tasks involving several steps, the Learning Center walks you through, step by step, selecting the tools for the job at the appropriate moment.

Because the Learning Center selects the tools for you and tells you how to use them, after a while you'll find you no longer need it for common tasks like cropping, straightening, and rotating photos – when you know how, it's quicker and easier to do it yourself. When the time comes you can close the Learning Center palette (press F10 again) to make more room for your photos and other palettes.

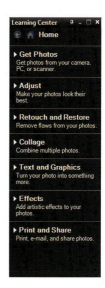

FIG 1.2 The Learning Center.

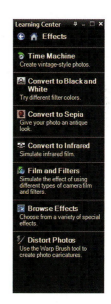

FIG 1.3 The Effects tab.

The Learning Center works like a website. The home page contains seven topics – Get Photos, Adjust, Retouch and Restore, Collage, Text and Graphics, Effects, and Print and Share. You can return to this page at any time by clicking the Home button at the top of the palette.

Each topic has a number of projects; click Effects and you'll find seven projects that demonstrate, among other things, how to use the Time Machine to create vintage-style photos, convert photos to black and white, and distort photos. Click either the Home or Back buttons at the top of the palette to return to the home page.

I'm not going to go through each of the projects in the Learning Center because they don't need any explanation. Try them out! Before we go any further, though, let's take a look at how to get your photos into PaintShop Photo Pro X3.

Getting Photos into PaintShop Photo Pro X3

When you install PaintShop Photo Pro X3 you also install another small application called Corel Photo Downloader. This starts up when you start your computer and runs in the background; if you look at your Windows task bar you'll see the Corel Photo Downloader icon. When you plug in your digital camera or card reader, Corel Photo Downloader handles the task of getting the photos off the card and on to your computer's hard disk.

You don't have to use Corel Photo Downloader, you can copy your photos to a folder on your hard disk using Windows, but Photo Downloader automates much of the job and makes the whole thing a lot easier. To change the default settings for Corel Photo Downloader, right-click the icon in the Windows task bar and select Default Settings from the menu.

The Default Settings panel allows you to specify a folder where the down-loaded photos are saved. It automatically saves them into a folder named with the current date and, if you want, it will also rename the files and rotate them if necessary. Finally, when the photos are downloaded, you can elect to start PaintShop Photo Pro X3, open the photos in the new Photo Express Lab, view them in Windows Explorer, or do nothing.

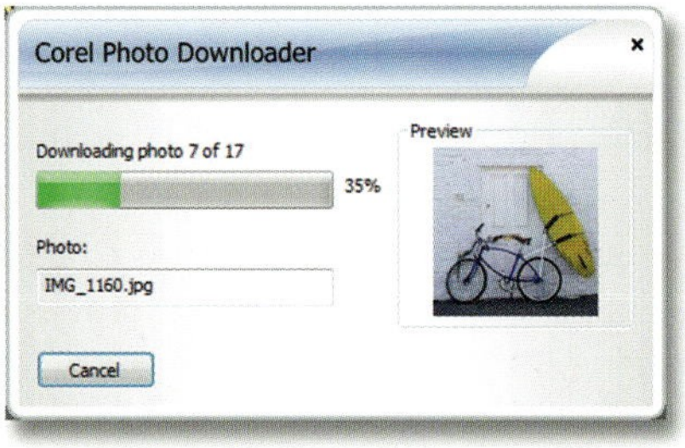

FIG 1.4 Corel Photo Downloader.

The Organizer

More likely than not, you already have some photos stored on your hard disk and you'll want to open these in PaintShop Photo Pro X3. There are a number of ways you can do this, but try to get into the habit of using the Organizer from the start. The Organizer button at the top right of the screen opens the Organizer and, when Organizer is open, it is replaced by a Full Editor button in the same location so you can easily switch between editing and organizing. Whichever screen – the Full Editor or Organizer – you have open when you quit PaintShop Photo Pro X3 is the one that appears when you launch the program.

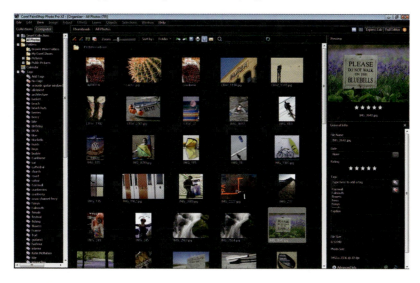

FIG 1.5 In earlier versions of PaintShop Pro the Organizer could be displayed as a palette in the Full Editor; now it appears as an independent module. You switch between the Organizer and Full Editor using the buttons at the top right of the screen. You can use the Organizer to display the contents of image folders on your hard disk, to organize and manage collections of images, and to view and add metadata (e.g. captions and keywords) to your photos.

Chapter 2 explains in more detail how the Organizer works; for now it will help you to know that the Organizer makes finding and opening photos much easier than selecting File > Open, though you're welcome to do it that way if you prefer. The Organizer, you won't be surprised to learn, can also help you organize your photos so that they are easier to find.

Initially, you'll probably want to point the Organizer at folders on your hard drive that contain photos. The Computer tab on the left displays all the drives attached to your computer; just navigate through the hierarchical folder structure in the usual way to locate the folders containing your photos. When you select a folder containing photos, thumbnails are automatically displayed in the Thumbnails panel in the center of the screen. The Organizer has two modes, selected by clicking the icons at the top right of the screen. Thumbnail mode displays thumbnails of all the images in a folder, Preview mode shows a bigger preview of an individual selected thumbnail.

The General Info panel on the right of the screen displays all of the metadata for a selected image. Metadata includes Exif information recorded by the camera about the the exposure settings used for the shot, the time and date, and other information you add yourself – captions, keyword tags and ratings, for example.

To open photos from the Organizer for editing you simply select them (Shift- or Ctrl-click to chose more than one) and click the Full Editor button.

The Menu Bar

PaintShop Photo Pro X3's menu system gives you access to most of the program's tools, commands, and features. There are other ways to access them, but the Menu bar lays them all out for you in a logical, organized fashion. If you're not sure where something is, a quick skim through the menus will usually reveal it. For example, if you want to apply a special effects filter there's a good chance you'll find what you're looking for somewhere in the Effects menu. Anything to do with making tonal and color adjustments is on the Adjust menu, and stuff to do with displaying toolbars, palettes, grids, guides and organizing the workspace is on the View menu (except work-space presets which, for some reason, are on the File menu).

Some menu items are nested in submenus. When I refer to these in the book they are denoted using the '>' character. For example, the Levels command on the Brightness and Contrast submenu of the Adjust menu is shown as Adjust > Brightness and Contrast > Levels.

Another useful piece of information you'll find on menus is keyboard shortcuts. After a while it will become second nature to you to press Ctrl + O to open a photo rather than selecting File > Open.

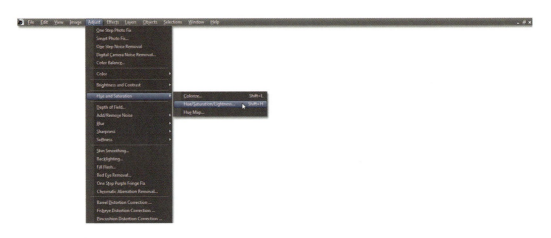

FIG 1.6 The Menu bar.

Toolbars

Now that you know how to use the Organizer to find and open photos into PaintShop Photo Pro X3 and you can carry out simple guided projects using the Learning Center, it's time to take a look at some of the other parts of the PaintShop Photo Pro X3 workspace.

The narrow strip of buttons running down the left side of the screen, between the Learning Center and the main picture window, is the Tools toolbar. If you need to select part of a photo, crop it, straighten it, retouch it, add text, or fix problems like red-eye, this is where you'll find the tools for the job.

PaintShop Photo Pro X3 displays tool tips when you hover with your mouse pointer over each of the tools and this is a good way to familiarize yourself with each tool's function. As well as the tool tips, the Status bar at the very bottom of the screen provides some guidance on how to use each tool.

There are several other toolbars; some of them, like the Standard toolbar, are visible in the default workspace and some need to be activated by selecting them from the Toolbars submenu of the View menu.

The different toolbars group together similar tools and functions that you're likely to need for a specific photo-editing task or that it seems logical to keep in the same place. On the Standard toolbar at the top of the screen you'll find tools for creating, opening and saving photos, scanning and printing, resizing, rotating, and displaying photo information.

Other toolbars include the Effects, Photo, Script, and Web toolbars. Some of these you'll use rarely, or possibly not at all, which is one of the reasons they're tucked away, so as not to clutter up the workspace. I've already mentioned that you can toggle the toolbars on and off by selecting them from the View > Toolbars menu (you can also hide toolbars and palettes by clicking their close box); you can also float or dock any of the toolbars by dragging the title bar. To dock a toolbar, drag it to one of the top, bottom or side edges of the main picture window, where it will snap into place. To float a toolbar, drop it anywhere away from one of the docking edges.

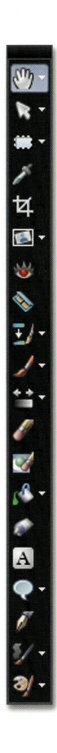

FIG 1.7 The Tools toolbar sits on the left of the main picture window. Hover over the tools to display a tooltip naming the tool and a brief explanation of its function in the Status bar at the bottom of the screen. From the top: Pan + Zoom tool, Pick + Move, Selection + Freehand Selection + Magic Wand, Dropper, Crop, Straighten + Perspective Correction, Red-Eye, Makeover – Blemish Fixer, Clone Brush + Scratch Remover + Object Remover, Paint Brush + Airbrush, Lighten/Darken + Dodge + Burn + Smudge + Push + Soften + Sharpen + Emboss + Saturation Up/Down + Hue Up/Down + Change to Target + Color Replacer, Eraser, Background Eraser, Flood Fill + Color Changer, Picture Tube, Text tool, Preset Shape tool + Rectangle + Ellipse + Symmetric Shape, Pen tool, Warp Brush + Mesh Warp, Oil Brush + Chalk + Pastel + Crayon + Colored Pencil + Marker + Palette Knife + Smear + Art Eraser.

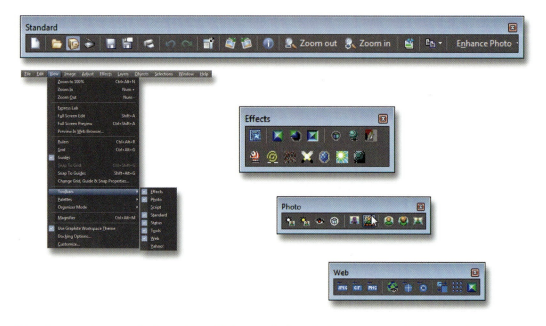

FIG 1.8 To activate toolbars select them from the View > Toolbars menu. The Standard toolbar appears in the default workspace and contains among other things filing commands, rotate buttons, undo and redo commands, zoom buttons, and access to the Express Lab and enhance filters.

Have a play around with showing, hiding, and rearranging the PaintShop Photo Pro X3 workspace elements. Before you do, though, first select File > Workspace > Save and save your existing setup as 'default_workspace' or something similar. When you've everything set up the way you want, save this new arrangement as 'favorite_workspace'. Now, to return the workspace to either of these arrangements you just need to select Workspace > Load and choose the one you want.

'Photo' Toolbar

If you deal with scanned or digital photos, this is the toolbar to get friendly with. The Backlighting and Fill Flash tools help to correct exposure problems caused by problematic lighting conditions, and the Chromatic Aberration and Digital Camera Noise Removal filters help reduce colored fringing and noise problems that can occur in digital photos. You can add tools for common photo enhance operations like Levels, for example, by right-clicking any of the toolbar buttons and selecting Customize from the contextual menu.

'Effects' Toolbar

If you have had no experience using PaintShop Photo Pro but are curious how its effects might look when applied to a picture, click the first button on the Effects toolbar – the Browse Presets button. This loads and displays the Effects Browser, a sophisticated program that displays all of the available adjustment and effect filter presets. Click on a folder to see the entire contents, all of the artistic effects for example, or choose an individual preset from within one of the folders.

This is quite an eyeful, even for a seasoned image-maker! Double-click the effect you like the look of in the Browser and PaintShop Photo Pro transfers it to the photo in the work area. In this way you can preview the filter effect and save time by only trying effects that you like the look of. Other programs provide a list of effects but little clue as to how long or how effective any, or each, might be on the opened picture file.

What else is there on the Effects toolbar? 'Buttonize', 'Drop Shadow', 'Inner Bevel', 'Gaussian Blur', 'Hot Wax', 'Brush Strokes', 'Colored Foil', 'Emboss', 'Fur', 'Lights', 'Polished Stone', 'Sunburst', and 'Topography'. All are preset filter effects that can be applied to a selection, or globally, depending on the application.

All can be customized through the displayed options window. Customized filter sets can also be saved in the same way as customized tools.

'Script' Toolbar

While strictly not a tool as such, scripting offers incredible power to anyone with a bit more than the most basic of photo-editing requirements. What's scripting all about? As the name might suggest, a script is a file of instructions that produce a series of actions or effects – much in the same way that a play's script, when followed by a group of actors, produces actions that result in a play (hopefully!).

PaintShop Photo Pro ships with a wide range of pre-recorded scripts, but the fun really begins when you start to record your own. The Script toolbar is set up just like a video recorder. Press 'Record', then perform the actions you want on the selected picture (e.g. rotate + change contrast + save). It's that easy. Once saved, the script can be run on other pictures in the work area. It's a great way to automate, and thus perfect your working style and throughput, so important in jobs that require repetitive actions applied to multiple pictures (for example, in website design).

'Web' Toolbar

Put together specifically for web designers, this small toolbar contains an 'Image Slicer' tool, an 'Image Mapper' tool, 'JPEG', 'GIF' and 'PNG' image optimizers, plus a 'Web Browser Preview' feature, 'Seamless Tiling', and a 'Buttonize' feature – most of the tools, in fact, needed to prepare images for your own website.

Tip

For lackluster digital photos start with the One Step Photo Fix. This versatile command applies six different processes to the image: Automatic Color Balance, Automatic Contrast Enhancement, Clarify, Automatic Saturation Enhancement, Edge Preserving Smooth, and Sharpen.

Tool Options, and Other Palettes

A tool wouldn't be very useful if it did only one thing, and PaintShop Photo Pro X3's tools are nothing if not versatile. The Tool Options palette is what gives tools their versatility, allowing you to change settings that modify the selected tool's behavior.

FIG 1.9 Tool Options for the Paint Brush.

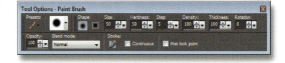

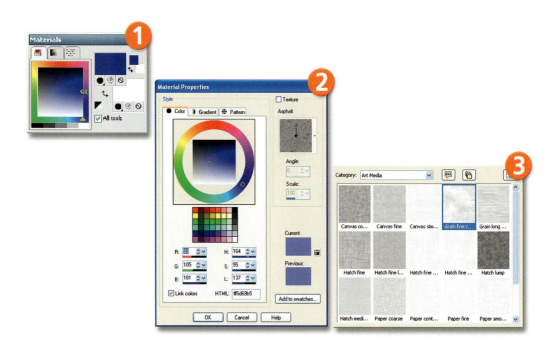

FIG 1.10 The Materials palette (1) is used for selecting foreground and background colors, gradients, and patterns for all the painting and drawing tools. The Material Properties dialog (2) is used to fine-tune color selection, create gradients, and choose pattern and texture swatches (3).

The Tool Options palette automatically displays the available settings for the selected tool. So, when you select the Paint Brush tool, the Tool Options palette displays size, shape, density opacity, and other options. Switch to the Selection tool and the Tool Options palette displays selection type, mode, feathered edge, and other selection options.

Try selecting a few different tools and looking at what aspects of their behavior can be modified using the Tool Options palette. Don't worry if it's not clear at this stage what they do or how they work. As you progress through the book, you'll discover how to use them in practice. Right now it's enough to know that, along with the Tools toolbar, the Tool Options palette is one of PaintShop Photo Pro X3's most useful assets.

We've already talked about two other palettes – the Learning Center and Organizer. PaintShop Photo Pro X3's other palettes include the Layers, Materials, Histogram, and History palettes. The Materials palette is used to select colors, gradients, and patterns for all of the painting and drawing tools.

PaintShop Photo Pro X3: Advanced Features

Tonal Controls

Most of the processes mentioned in the previous section deal with single-button operations that perform a logical, but not always controllable, function. These are often good for the bulk of your photo-editing tasks, like simple color and contrast corrections. However, there'll come a time when you need to make detailed changes to a photo – this is where PaintShop Photo Pro's advanced tools save the day. Most are simply expanded versions of the one-button-does-all toolsets discussed previously.

One of the most versatile is the Histogram Adjustment feature, found under Adjust > Brightness and Contrast > Histogram Adjustment menu. With this you can set shadow and highlight values, as well as all the tones in between (called the 'midtones'). A step up the sophistication scale is the Curves tool. Again, designed by professionals to get the maximum out of camera and scanned files, Curves has almost limitless possibilities for tone control and creativity.

Color Controls

PaintShop Photo Pro X3 provides a range of color tools that enables you to make global changes to all of the colors in an image – for example, to remove a color cast – and to change some image colors whilst leaving others unaffected.

Tools like Color Balance, Hue/Saturation/Lightness, and Hue Map require some understanding of how color works to get the most from them, but even these sophisticated tools have something to offer the novice with features like Smart White Balance, warm/cool adjustment, and a range of presets for dealing with common color problems like color casts caused by fluorescent lighting.

Once you've got your head round the idea that all digital pictures require at least some tonal fix-ups, you'll begin to appreciate the power of selections. A selection allows you to isolate part of a picture so that you can then apply a change or filter effect to that selected area only. PaintShop Photo Pro not only has a wide range of selection tools but also a comprehensive range of modifier features (under Selection Edit mode) that are so good as to shame most other photo-editing programs.

Perhaps, after tonal fix-ups and learning about selections, you'll move on to layers. Layers offer the digital image-maker incredible editing capabilities. You can add disparate picture elements to a 'master' picture file, move them about, change their colors and contrast, and then move them some more to make the weirdest montage effects imaginable. The reason you'd keep all these elements on layers is that you can move everything else in the frame even after it has been saved in a layered format. Once saved in a flattened, non-layered format, you lose all editability. Layers can also be radically changed using layer masks or individual adjustment layers.

An extension of the layers concept brings us to the use of text. PaintShop Photo Pro has a text engine that allows you to add text, as a separate vector layer, to any document. Again, the advantage of this is that you can return to the picture at any time and edit the text layer, changing the size, font, kerning or other text-specific characteristics. Because this is done using a special vector layer (not pixel-based), there's no loss of quality. Vector text introduces us to the creation of vector shapes and art.

All digital scans and photographs are bitmap or raster files; they are made up from pixels, which explains, in some part, why a bitmapped image requires so much computing power to manipulate. An A4 photo contains more than 20 million pixels! Vector images, on the other hand, are made from mathematical calculations: dots and points on the canvas that are filled with flat or graded colors. An A4 vector illustration might only be a few hundred kilobytes at most. Besides a small file size, the beauty of vector art is that it's scalable. You can increase or decrease vector shapes to almost any dimensions with no discernible loss of quality. Enlarge a bitmapped file too much and it begins to look distinctly fuzzy around its edges. Vector images are created and edited using the Pen tool, one of the most sophisticated of all the tools. The Preset Shape tool and the Rectangle, Ellipse, and Symmetric Shape tools also create vector objects.

Other advanced features of PaintShop Photo Pro X3 include the use of layer and image masks, adjustment layers, gradients, the picture tube, sophisticated warping tools, a range of very cool printing aids, framing assistants, GIF and JPEG image optimizers, image mapping, and image slicing.

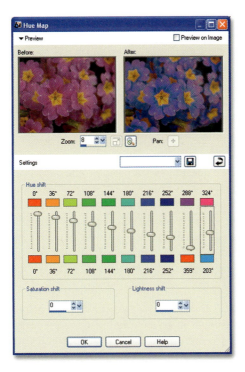

FIG 1.11 By adjusting the individual color sliders in the Hue Map dialog box, you can change specific colors in an image whilst leaving others unchanged.

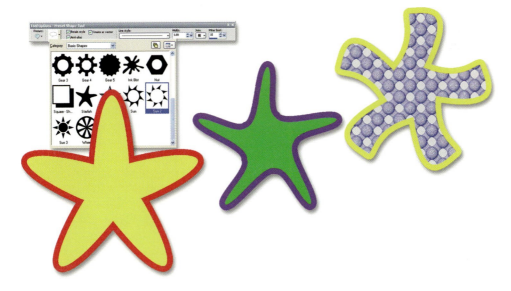

FIG 1.12 One of the advantages of vector graphics is that they can be resized with no loss in quality. Another consequence of their existence as mathematical constructs, rather than collections of dots, is that they can be easily modified. As well as changing the fill and stroke properties, the shape of these objects, created using the new Symmetric Shape tool, can be altered using Bezier handles to adjust the shape of the curve between two points.

New Features

Here's a brief overview of the new features that Corel has added to PaintShop Photo Pro X3. If you're an old hand with PaintShop Pro this is where to look to find out what's new and, in the following section, what's changed. You'll find more detailed descriptions of the new features, as well as practical examples of how to use them, throughout the book.

Multiple Photo Editing

PaintShop Photo X3 now provides an easy way to apply all of the edits you make to a photo to other photos in the Organizer. This is an extremely useful thing to be able to do and has the potential to drastically reduce the amount of time you spend editing. Let's say you've downloaded a card full of images from your camera and want to prepare them for a slideshow presentation. You select the first image, open it in Express Lab, apply the Smart Photo Fix, adjust the color using Color Balance, then sharpen it before saving the image.

These are general edits that you'd like to apply to every image, so back in the Organizer you select the image and click the Capture Editing button on the toolbar. Now you just need to select the photos you want to apply the same editing process to and click the Apply Editing button and you're done. There are other ways to apply a sequence of editing steps to multiple photos, but none is as quick and easy as this.

Smart Carver

The Smart Carver is like an intelligent Crop tool. It changes the dimensions of a photo without distorting the content by removing parts of the image that have little structural detail. You can also use the Smart Carver to target specific parts of the image that you want to remove. Used in this way, it's great for removing unwanted and distracting bits of photos like lampposts, cars, trees, or even people.

Object Extractor

The Object Extractor is a new tool that makes it easy to isolate and cut out part of an image from its background. While the conventional selection tools require some skill and patience to get a good result, using the Object Extractor is a much simpler process. You just paint an outline around the thing you want to extract, fill the area inside, then click Process to preview the result. You can then refine the result using Edit Mask.

Vibrancy

To adjust the saturation of colors in a photo you can use the Hue/Saturation/Lightness controls. The problem with increasing saturation, though, is that some colors can become over-saturated and unnatural looking. Vibrancy is a more subtle saturation controller – it increases saturation, but rather than a blanket increase only those colors that lack saturation are boosted. This makes it ideal for giving a boost to skin tones in portraits and in other images that have a mix of strongly saturated and more muted hues.

On-Image Text Editing

In previous versions of PaintShop Pro, when you clicked on a photo with the Text tool a Text dialog box opened into which you entered and edited your text. When you were done, you clicked OK and a text layer was added to the document. Now you can add and edit text directly on the image. It's a lot easier this way; with the text selected you can change the font, size, alignment, and other attributes from the Tool Options palette.

RAW Format Support

PaintShop Photo Pro X3 can open and edit images shot in your camera's proprietary Camera RAW format. For advanced photographers, there are many advantages to doing this, not the least of which is the potential to produce better quality images than if you shoot using the JPG file format to capture images.

The Organizer can display thumbnails for RAW images and when you open them they are initially processed using Camera RAW Lab. PaintShop Photo Pro X3 extends the range of Camera RAW formats supported; you can find a list of supported Camera RAW formats on the Corel website at www.corel.com. You can find out more about processing RAW files in Chapter 10.

HD Video Support

PaintShop Photo Pro X3 now supports HD video. You can import, make basic cuts, and export AVCHD video from a camcorder or digital camera. You can also create HD slideshows that include both video and still images.

Other Improvements

There are a number of other improvements that make this version of PaintShop Photo Pro faster and more flexible than its predecessors. The application is faster than it used to be, particularly on PCs equipped with multi-core processors. The Organizer is, well, better organized than it used to be and displays more information about your photos. Express Lab has some new tools for improving image quality and there are more options for sharing photos on Flicks, Facebook, and YouTube using the included Corel Paintshop Photo Project Creator application. Finally, PaintShop Photo Pro X3 is fully compatible with Windows 7, as well as Vista and XP.

Nearly New Features

These features were all added in previous versions – PaintShop Photo Pro XI and X2. I've included them here not just because they've only been around a short while (PaintShop Pro Photo XI was released in September 2006 and X2 in September 2008), but because they are among the most useful features of the program.

Express Lab

Express Lab allows you to apply quick edits to a folder of photos. It's designed to be used as a kind of triage station where you apply a bit of first aid to your photos when you've offloaded them from your digital camera. Among other things, you can rotate, crop and straighten pictures, fix red-eye, and use the makeover and clone brushes to sort out spots, blemishes, dust, and other ills. When you've fixed one photo, navigation buttons allow you to move on to the next one, or you can use the image strip at the bottom to switch between them.

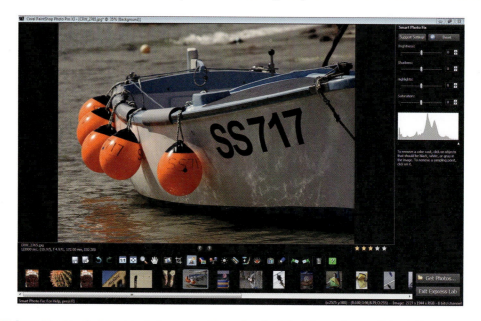

FIG 1.13 Express Lab – triage for digital photos. It allows you to quickly scan through a folder of photos and carry our basic tasks like rotating, cropping, and adding a rating.

HDR Photo Merge

HDR stands for High Dynamic Range, a process that allows you to capture the full range of tones in a scene, even though they may be beyond the range of your camera. The human eye is very good at registering a wide range of brightness, which is why you and I have little difficulty seeing things that are in bright sunlight as well as those that are in the shade.

Cameras aren't so good at this and if you're photographing such a scene you (or your camera's automatic exposure program) have to make a choice – to expose for either the sunlit or the shadow detail. If you go for the former option, everything in the shadow is so dark you can hardly make it out; expose for the parts of the scene that are in the shade and the sunny bits are blown out – everything is white.

This is where HDR comes in. It allows you to get good detail in both the shadows and the highlights of a scene with bright highlights and deep shadows by combining several photos of the same scene taken with different exposure settings into one image. It sounds complicated, but PaintShop Photo Pro X3 makes it pretty straightforward. If you want to find out exactly how to make an HDR image, take a look at the step-by-step project on page 150, which explains everything in detail.

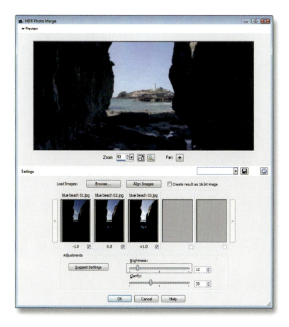

FIG 1.14 HDR Photo Merge.

Auto-Preserve Originals

It's always a good idea to back up your photos on to a CD or DVD so that, should the worst happen, you've always got the originals somewhere safe. Likewise, before you begin work on a photo in PaintShop Photo Pro X3 it's always a good idea to leave the original untouched and work on a copy. One way of doing this is to select 'Save As' from the File menu and save the photo with a different name and/or in a different location (I sometimes create a folder inside the folder containing the downloaded photos and call it 'edited').

17

PaintShop Photo Pro X3's Auto-Preserve Originals feature takes care of this for you by saving the original in a subfolder of the current folder. You can either use this in addition to the backup steps I've already suggested, or instead of using 'Save As' to create a copy. Auto-Preserve Originals is on by default; to turn it off select File > Preferences > General Program Preferences, select Auto-Preserve from the list on the left then uncheck the box and click OK.

Layer Styles

Layer Styles are live editable effects that can be applied to raster and vector layers. There are six Layer Styles – Reflection, Outer Glow, Bevel, Emboss, Inner Glow, and Drop Shadow. To apply Layer Styles, double-click a layer in the Layers palette and select the Layer Styles tab in the Layer Properties dialog box. Most of the Layer Styles have basic controls – to adjust the size, position, and opacity of a drop shadow, for example. You can edit Layer Styles at any time by reopening the Layer Properties dialog box and adjusting the settings. And when you edit a layer which has a Layer Style applied, the style automatically updates.

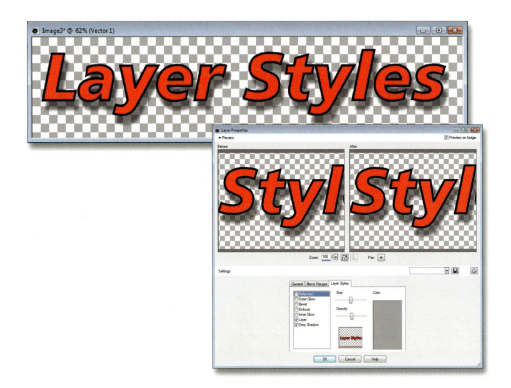

FIG 1.15 PaintShop Photo Pro X3 Layer Styles include Reflection, Outer Glow, Bevel, Emboss, Inner Glow, and Drop Shadow.

Visible Watermarks

Watermarking your images is one way of preventing copyright theft. Paint-Shop Photo Pro X3's visible watermarks make it easy for you to add a logo, or other text or graphic to your photos.

Save for Office and Copy Special

Save for Office and Copy Special automatically resize large photos that are intended for things like Powerpoint presentations or Word documents. You don't need megapixels of image data for photos embedded in these applications. Placing digital images at their original size in such documents has no advantages and creates big files that are difficult to email and take a long time to open. Save for Office and Copy Special create files of the right size for these applications without you needing to think about it.

Quick Review

Quick Review is an Organizer feature that displays a full-screen slideshow of the contents of a folder or selected images in the Thumbnail window. Slideshows can contain photos, video, and music. A toolbar provides controls to pause the show, apply rotation and other basic edits, rate images, and carry out organizational tasks.

> **Tip**
>
> If you forgot to set the date and time on your camera and your photos all have the wrong date and time (like midnight on 1 January 2000), you can correct it using the Organizer. Select the affected thumbnails, right-click, and choose Adjust Date Created from the context menu.

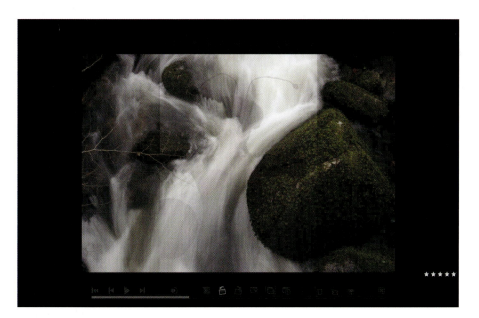

FIG 1.16 The Organizer's Quick Review feature can be used to scan through a folder of images, delete the ones you don't want and rotate, quick-fix, email, or otherwise edit and organize the rest. It's full screen, so you get a good look at the images, and it has transitions and, if you want it, audio too.

Media Trays

Formerly called 'photo trays', media trays are containers into which you can drop photos that you want to email, print, or upload. Media trays appear in the Full Editor workspace and are a convenient way of storing a bunch of pictures that you plan on doing something with later. You might, for example, use a media tray to hold a collection of photos that you plan on using for a montage. When you add an image to a media tray, it stays in its original folder and the thumbnail in the photo tray links to the original file. This is a more efficient way of organizing photos than copying them and saves on disk space.

Color Changer Tool

The Color Changer tool lets you change pixel colors at a stroke and provides sophisticated, but easy to use, selection methods so that only those pixels you want to recolor are affected. You can use the Color Changer tool to change the color of clothing, paintwork, or pretty much anything at a stroke. There's a step-by-step project using the Color Changer tool on page 244.

Skin Smoothing

Removing wrinkles and blemishes is one of the most difficult retouching tasks there is; even professional retouchers find it a challenge. PaintShop Photo Pro's Skin Smoothing feature makes it easy to remove wrinkles and skin blemishes, taking years off your portrait subjects.

Riff File Format Support

You can save PaintShop Photo Pro files in the Riff file format used by Corel Painter and Corel Painter Essentials. These programs provide natural media painting effects and tools that can be used to simulate traditional media.

Time Machine

Some photo applications have an 'antique' effect; PaintShop's Time Machine filter goes much further, providing a range of effects that simulate historical photographic processes such as the Daguerrotype and Platinotype.

Film and Filters

Film and Filters does two things. Firstly, it allows you to simulate the particular look of some color film stock. In the days of film, photographers

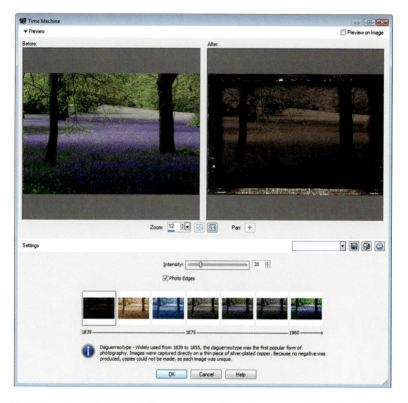

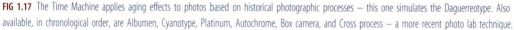

FIG 1.17 The Time Machine applies aging effects to photos based on historical photographic processes – this one simulates the Daguerreotype. Also available, in chronological order, are Albumen, Cyanotype, Platinum, Autochrome, Box camera, and Cross process – a more recent photo lab technique.

would choose a particular emulsion for the look. Portrait photographers would choose a film for the way it rendered skin tones; for landscapes an emulsion that rendered rich earth tones and natural-looking blue skies would be appropriate. Photo Paint Photo has seven film looks to choose from, including Muted Reds, Vibrant Foliage, and Glamour. Additionally you can apply creative filters from a range of six, including Night Effect, Warming, Orange, Champagne, and Sunset. You can also create your own custom filters.

Depth of Field

Creating artificial depth-of-field effects to simulate using a wide aperture and throwing the background out of focus isn't difficult, but it takes time and a little skill. To find out how you can do it manually see page 146. Alternatively, Corel PaintShop Pro's Depth of Field effect makes it a lot simpler.

FIG 1.18 The Depth of Field effect simulates narrow depth of field achieved in-camera by shooting with a wide open lens aperture.

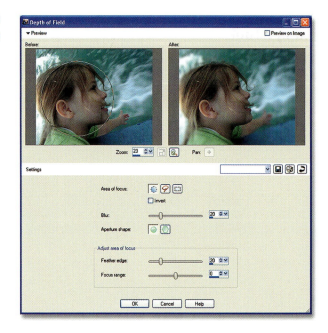

Other Features

There are numerous other innovative features that were introduced in previous versions of the program. Brief details of their function are given here; you'll find more detailed descriptions of how they work, as well as practical examples, throughout the book.

Interactive Learning Center

The Interactive Learning Center provides step-by-step guidance for common photo-editing and retouching tasks like rotating, cropping and straightening images, as well as advice on how to use PaintShop Pro's tools and effects to complete more involved projects. It's invaluable for beginners but is also useful for experienced users who aren't sure about a particular feature or technique.

Smart Photo Fix

Like One Step Photo Fix, the Smart Photo Fix feature provides a one-click method of 'toning up' lackluster images, but it also provides a degree of control over the process. Sliders provide control over tonal adjustments, saturation, sharpening, and color balance, all in an easy-to-use panel with big before and after thumbnail previews.

Makeover Tools

The Blemish Fixer, Toothbrush, and Suntan Brush can give your portraits an instant lift with very little effort. The Blemish Fixer can also be used where a more subtle effect than the Clone Brush is needed.

Red-Eye Tool

This is a much more straightforward tool than PaintShop Pro's previous red-eye removal tool; just set the tool size and click on the eyes.

Object Remover

Like the Clone Brush, but easier to use, the Object Remover seamlessly replaces unwanted detail in a photo, such as a lamppost, tree, or other distracting background detail, with another part of the image.

One Step Purple Fringe Fix

A common problem with digital cameras, purple fringing is caused by lens aberrations and the limitations of digital camera sensors. Purple fringing usually shows up as a thick purple fringe around high-contrast edges like tree branches against a bright sky. The One Step Purple Fringe Fix does exactly what it says.

High Pass Sharpen

High pass sharpening is a professional sharpening technique that has some advantages over conventional unsharp masking – mainly, it's less likely to exaggerate noise and produce haloing.

Color Balance

If you don't know your additive from your subtractive primaries, then PaintShop Pro's new Color Balance tool is the one for you. It automatically adjusts the white balance to remove color casts, then all you need to decide is whether you want to warm the colors up or cool them down. There's also an advanced mode.

Black and White and Infra-Red Conversion Filters

These effects allow you to easily convert your images to black and white and to simulate shooting with infra-red and black and white film with colored filters for enhanced tonal reproduction.

One Step Noise Removal

PaintShop Pro's existing Digital Camera Noise Removal provides powerful tools for cleaning up noisy images providing you have the time and know-how to use it effectively. For everyone else, there's One Step Noise Removal.

16-Bit Support

You can open, edit, and save 16-bit images in PaintShop Pro X onwards. The advantage of this is that you have more tonal and color information, so images have a higher dynamic range and are less prone to degradation, like highlight and shadow clipping and posterization, when you make color and tonal adjustments. Some PaintShop Pro features require you to convert 16-bit images to 8-bit before you can use them. These adjustments are best left until last in your editing workflow.

Color Management

PaintShop Pro's new color management engine lets you work with embedded image color profiles to improve screen-to-print color matching.

IPTC Metadata Support

Most metadata that's saved with images when you shoot them – the camera model and exposure settings, for example – isn't editable. But IPTC fields are designed to allow you to record information about the photographer, the location of the scene, and searchable keywords. You can add and edit IPTC metadata in PaintShop Pro.

Pick Tool

The Move tool has been replaced with a Pick tool, which works like a combination of the old Deform and Object Selection tools.

File Open Pre-Processing

This feature allows you to run a script on files as they are opened. It's a time-saver if you want to automatically apply the same process to all images you open, such as the One Step Photo Fix. Or you might use it to automatically downsample 16-bit images to 8-bit, or anything else you have, or can write a script for.

Equipping Your Digital Darkroom

Having made it this far through Chapter 1, it would be fair to assume that you own a digital camera and have decided to use PaintShop X3 to organize and edit your digital photos. These two essentials will get you a long way, but there's a world of gadgets and accessories out there that will make your digital photography easier, more productive, and more fun.

Cards, Readers, and Portable Storage

When you bought your digital camera it probably included a memory card in the box. If you didn't buy a second one at the time, go out and buy one now. It's the one single purchase that will make the biggest difference to your photography.

Let's go off at a tangent for a second. You won't find a lot of advice in this book on how to take great pictures – that's another book, but here are a couple of tips. The best way to get good pictures is to take a lot of them. Why shoot one or two when you can shoot 10 or 100? It doesn't cost you any more, the chances of getting a good one go up with every additional shot you make, and you can always delete all the rubbish ones.

Tip number two: always keep your camera on the highest quality setting. Why pay for high-quality optics and a megapixel sensor only to cripple your camera by using a lower resolution than it's capable of, or compressing your photos so much that they look like they were taken on your phone?

Many cameras are sold together with a card that will store only a few dozen images at the camera's highest quality setting. If you buy one or two additional cards of at least 1 or 2 GB capacity you'll be able to take as many best-quality photos as you want without fear of filling them up.

Which brings us on to card readers. You can, of course, plug your camera directly into your PC with a USB cable to transfer photos, but using a dedicated card reader has a number of advantages. Card readers are small and inexpensive so won't take up much space in your camera bag. They're easy to use – you just plug them in to a USB port on your PC and insert the card, then you can copy the files to a folder on your hard drive using Windows Explorer, Corel Photo Downloader, or your preferred method. A good card reader can usually transfer images faster than your camera and, providing you have spare cards, you can continue shooting while you download the full card.

Digitizing Tablets

For most photo retouching tasks you'll find that you can get good results using the mouse and your keyboard. But some tasks, like retouching using the Clone Brush or the Makeover tool, you'll find you can get much better results using a graphics tablet and stylus. A stylus allows you to use drawing and painting tools in a more natural fashion and provides much greater accuracy for making freehand selections. Many of PaintShop X3's brush tools are designed specifically to take advantage of stylus features, responding to tilt and pressure changes by, for example, changing opacity or brush shape and size.

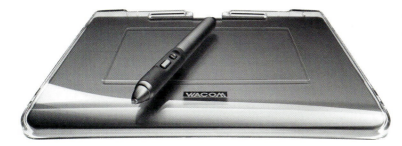

FIG 1.19 If you spend a lot of time making selections or creating digital art using a photo-editing program such as PaintShop, you'll find a graphics tablet essential in providing ease of use and incredible accuracy.

Scanners

Most people these days are as familiar with flatbed scanners as they are with photocopiers. If you have a lot of pre-digital photos in the form of prints, a flatbed scanner provides a simple and inexpensive way to digitize them and get them on to your computer, where you can manipulate them, add captions and keywords, put them into slideshows, and do anything with them that you can with regular digital photos from your camera.

FIG 1.20 Desktop scanners, whether film or flatbed, are also becoming part of the landscape, producing impressive results.

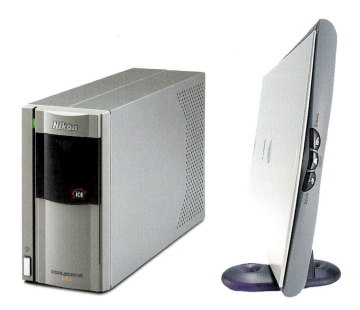

Many flatbed scanners can also scan slides and negatives. They have a small light box built into the scanner lid that provides illumination to scan transparent materials. For occasional scanning of slides and negatives, flatbed scanners do a reasonably good job, but the resolution is often insufficient to enlarge a 35 mm frame up to a reasonable size. Also, at these magnifications, shortcomings in the scanner's light source, optics, and CCD sensor, combined with any dust or scratches on the film, can result in quite poor-quality results.

If your pre-digital photography days were largely occupied with shooting color transparency film, you should consider investing in a dedicated film scanner. The sensor, optics, and light source in these devices are designed specifically for scanning film and produce far superior results than a flatbed scanner, which is designed primarily for scanning reflective material. Most film scanners also include, or offer as an option, a feeder tray that allows you to scan multiple slides in mounts and negative strips.

Printers, Ink, and Paper

I'm not going to give you advice on buying a printer; in all probability you already have one. Regardless of the make and model of your printer, one of the biggest factors affecting the quality of your prints will be the paper and inks you use.

After many years of experimenting with manufacturers' own brand products and ink and paper produced by independent manufacturers, I've come to the conclusion that the only way to be sure of getting consistent good-quality results is to use the ink and paper produced and recommended by your printer manufacturer.

Yes, manufacturers' branded products are expensive, but you'll find that cheaper alternatives are a false economy as you'll waste a lot of material trying to get acceptable quality results. Another factor to consider is that printer profiles for use in color management systems are produced using the manufacturer's materials and will be useless with anything else. If you want to use third-party ink and paper in a color-managed workflow you'll need to produce your own profiles, which is a complicated, time-consuming, and expensive business requiring a high degree of skill.

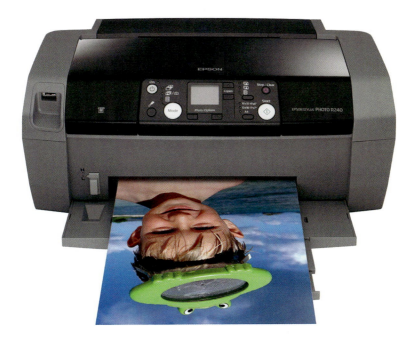

FIG 1.21 A photo-quality inkjet printer is another essential; picture quality is exceptional and long-lasting.

PC

A question that frequently comes up a lot on digital photography forums is 'what kind of PC should I buy to edit my digital photos?' The truth is that pretty much any budget PC is capable of running PaintShop Photo Pro X3 and managing a sizeable collection of digital Photos. The recommended system requirements for PaintShop Photo Pro X3 are fairly modest and even if your PC is a few years old it will probably be more than up to the task. Here are the recommended system requirements:

- Microsoft® Windows® 7, Windows Vista® or Windows® XP with latest service packs installed (32-bit or 64-bit editions)
- 1.5 GHz processor (2 GHz or higher recommended)
- 1 GB of RAM (2 GB or higher recommended)
- 3 GB of free hard drive space
- Minimum display resolution: 1024 × 768 (24-bit color)
- Windows-compatible DVD-ROM drive for installation
- Internet connection required for online features.

Depending on the kind of photography you do, you might want to splash out on some extras. With large image files, you'll find that processing edits, filter effects, and so on will happen much more quickly if you install additional RAM. And if you shoot a lot of images and like to keep them accessible on your hard drive (backed up, of course), an additional external or internal large capacity hard drive is worth considering.

FIG 1.22 A range of photo-quality inkjet papers is essential for all photo-editing enthusiasts.

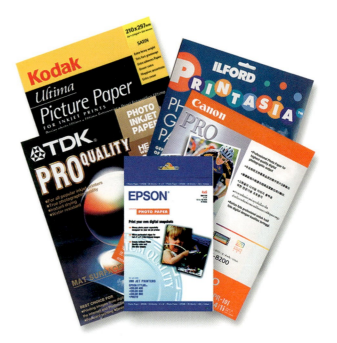

Step-by-Step Projects

Exploring the Learning Center

Whether you're new to PaintShop Photo Pro X3, or an old hand, it's worth taking a little time to explore the Learning Center and see what it has to offer. As well as taking you step by step through basic editing techniques, like cropping and rotating images, the Learning Center can help you with more ambitious projects, like producing a photomontage and advanced editing techniques like digital camera noise removal.

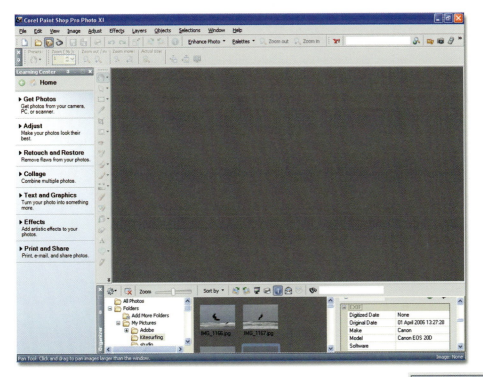

STEP 1 If the Learning Center isn't on the home page, click the Home button. Topics are divided into seven categories: Get Photos, Adjust, Retouch and Restore, Collage, Text and Graphics, Effects, and Print and Share. Click on any of these to view the list of available projects. You can get back to the home page either by clicking the Home button or the Back button at the top of the Learning Center palette, just like in a web browser.

STEP 2 Click the top option, Get Photos, and on the next page click Organizer. This panel gives basic instructions on how to use the Organizer. You can find out more from the relevant section in the Help file, which you can read by clicking the 'More details…' at the bottom.

Learning Center ⇤ ⨯

← 🔧 **Organizer**

Lets you view thumbnails of all images on your hard drive. Images are cataloged, so you can quickly search by folder, date, keyword, caption, or other image data, which you can view and edit in the Organizer. You can also create slide shows, print contact sheets, and more.

More details...

STEP 3 Follow the instructions to open an image from your hard disk using the Organizer, then click the Home button to return to the home page.

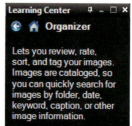

Straightening an Image

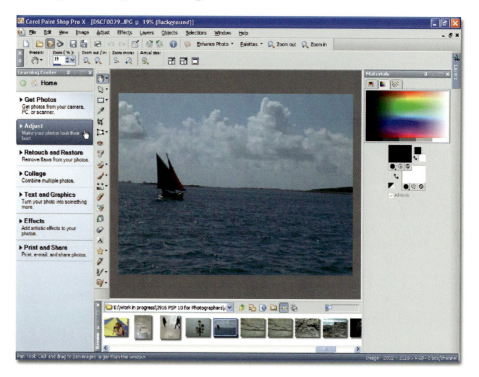

STEP 1 It's often not until you get to look at your photos on screen that you realize the horizon isn't level. Deliberate tilting of the camera to create a dynamic angle is one thing; a horizon that runs downhill, whether due to a tilted camera or skewed scanning, is generally to be avoided and can easily be fixed. Use the Organizer to open the offending image and click the Adjust button on the home page of the Learning Center.

STEP 2 Click the Straighten button in the Learning Center. The Straighten tool is automatically selected for you (it's the sixth tool from the top of the toolbar and looks like a tilted rectangle) and a line appears in the center of your image.

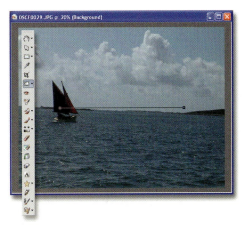

STEP 3 The panel in the Learning Center tells you exactly what you need to do to straighten the image. Move the endpoints of the line until it lines up with a horizontal or vertical line in the image – in this case the horizon.

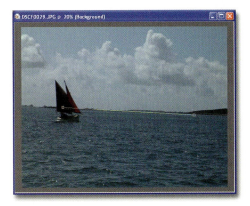

STEP 4 Then click the Apply button, or double-click the photo to apply the straightening.

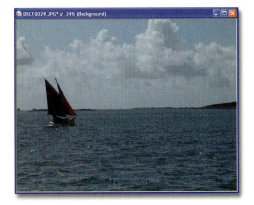

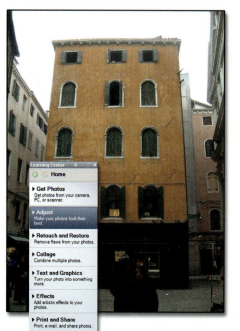

Perspective Correction

STEP 1 As well as straightforward editing tasks like opening and straightening images, the Learning Center can help you with more advanced techniques. The Perspective Correction tool can be used to straighten 'converging verticals' – the tendency for tall buildings to appear to be falling backwards when you tilt the camera upwards. Start by opening the problem photo and selecting the Adjust button on the Learning Center home page.

STEP 2 Click the Advanced Adjustments button at the bottom of the panel, followed by the Perspective Correction button. The Perspective Correction tool is selected and a rectangular box appears in the center of the image window.

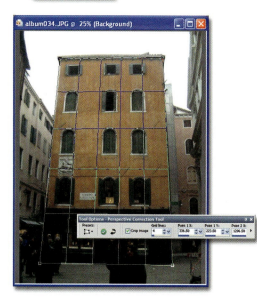

STEP 3 Follow the instructions in the Learning Center to align the box with the edges of the building. If the building shape is irregular and you find alignment difficult, enter a number of around 4 to 8 in the Grid Lines box in the Tool Options palette. This applies a grid to the perspective rectangle, making it easier to align it with what should be vertical features on the building.

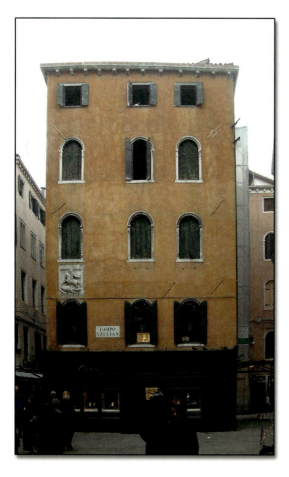

STEP 4 Click the Apply button to correct the perspective distortion. If you check the Crop Image box the edges of the photo will be cropped to remove the white space that appears as a result.

Cropping Pictures

After a while you'll find you can do without the Learning Center for simple and even more advanced editing tasks. Most pictures need cropping for aesthetic reasons and there are very few pictures that can't be improved by removing some of the detail around the outside to focus attention on the central subject. You might also want to crop a picture to change its proportions for printing, for example so that it will fit a 4 × 6 inch or 5 × 7 inch frame, or a space on a web page.

Tip

Select the Crop tool, click the Presets button on the Options palette, and select one of the preset crop sizes from the pull-down menu. You can save your own crop settings to this list, enabling you to quickly apply custom crop settings to any number of images.

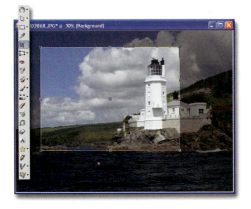

STEP 1 Open a picture and choose the Crop tool from the Tools toolbar. The image area outside the crop rectangle is shaded. Adjust the crop area size or position.

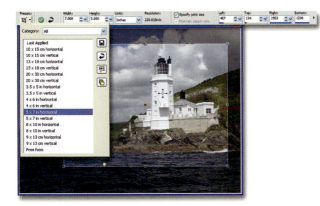

STEP 2 Click inside the crop area and drag to reposition it. You can constrain the crop area to its existing proportions by holding down the Shift key. If you're cropping for a standard-sized photo frame choose a preset from the Options palette.

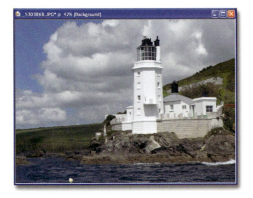

STEP 3 When you're satisfied with the area you've chosen, double-click in the crop area, or click the Apply button (the green check mark) on the Tool Options palette to crop the image. The inside section of the marquee remains while the image contents outside the crop area are discarded. Care must be taken so as not to crop off too much! If it is not right, choose Edit > Undo or Ctrl + Z.

If you know the dimensions that the picture is to be cropped to, click the Specify Print Size checkbox and enter the dimensions in the Width/Height and Units fields provided. The crop area automatically appears in the correct proportions for the desired crop. If you have many photos to be cropped for, say, a web gallery, this is a very productive tool. Click-drag any of the corner 'handles' or edges to expand or contract the crop dimensions while maintaining proportions.

You can also snap the Crop tool to a previously made selection in the image, its layer opaqueness, or a layer's merged opaqueness. Once the cropped image is saved, the discarded area cannot be recovered. As a general rule you should click File > Save As to save a copy and make sure you have the originals safely backed up on a CD!

The Organizer – Managing Your Photos

What's Covered in this Chapter

PaintShop Photo Pro X3's Organizer is where you keep track of all your photos, organize them into collections, rate them, and apply caption, keyword and other metadata. You can open images from the Organizer into PaintShop Photo Pro's Full Editor or go straight to Express Lab for editing, and you can view and prepare Camera RAW images.

In this chapter you'll discover how to do all of those things. As well as helping to manage your growing digital photo library, the Organizer has some great productivity features. You'll learn how to quickly rate, caption and add keywords to multiply images and in the step-by-step projects at the end of this chapter we'll show you how to process Camera RAW files and how to apply a sequence of edits to multiple images.

When you first open the Organizer what you see will most likely look like Figure 2.1. The default view is arranged over four panels. On the left is the

PaintShop Photo Pro X3 for Photographers. DOI: 10.1016/B978-0-240-52165-7.10002-4

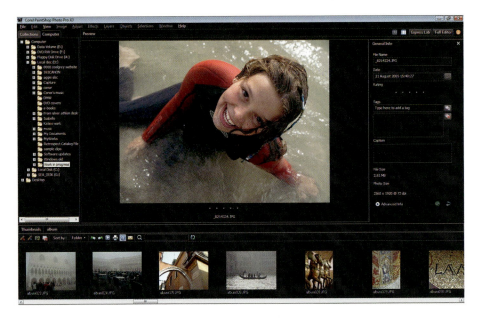

FIG 2.1 The default view of the Organizer is Preview mode, which arranges the Tree, General Info, and Thumbnails panels around a central Preview panel.

Tree panel, which shows the structure of folders and files on your computer; use it to navigate to where you keep your photos and the contents of any folder will be displayed in the Thumbnails panel at the bottom. A preview of any thumbnail you select is displayed in the preview window and

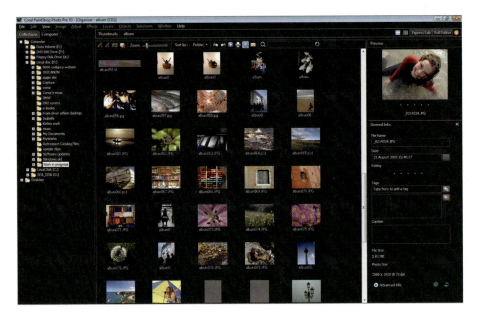

FIG 2.2 Use Thumbnail mode to get an overview of the contents of a folder, searching and sorting.

information about the selected image, including its filename, file size, caption and associated keyword data, is displayed in the General Info panel on the right of the screen.

The Organizer is customizable and you can change the layout to better suit the way you like to work. It's currently in Preview mode, which is good if you want to get a look at each of your photos; for more of an overview switch to Thumbnail mode by clicking the Thumbnail mode button at the top right next to the Express Lab and Full Editor buttons. You can switch back to Preview mode at any time by pressing the Preview mode button.

In Thumbnail mode the preview window shrinks to a small panel on top of the General Info palette and the Thumbnails panel expands to fill the central space. Atop it the Organizer toolbar has controls for, among other things, changing the thumbnail size, sorting thumbnails, rotating them, printing a contact sheet, and emailing photos. There's also a search field, which you can use to search image metadata, for example, to locate an image from its caption.

You can further customize the workspace in either of these two modal layouts (Preview and Thumbnail) by changing the size of the panels and windows by dragging the boundaries between them. Hover over the line dividing two panels until the cursor changes to a double-bar with a double-headed arrow and drag to expand one panel and contract the other.

The Tree Panel

Take a closer look at the Tree panel and you'll see that it has two tabs. The default view – the Computer tab – shows the structure of folders on your computer, but this isn't always the best or easiest way to organize your photos. The Collections tab allows you to arrange your images in a way that isn't tied to the way you keep them on your hard drive – it's not bound by the folder and filename conventions used by windows.

Using the Computer Tab

If it isn't already selected, click the Computer tab at the top of the Tree panel to display a Windows-style list of all of the disk drives and folders on your PC. Click the plus symbol next to a drive or folder to expand the list and reveal its contents. The Thumbnail panel remains empty until you click on a folder that contains images or video.

You can organize your images using only the Computer tab of the Tree panel, locating folders of pictures on your computer and carrying out all of the Organizer functions, such as captioning and rating, described later, but then you'd be missing out on one of the Organizer's best features. The problem with the Computer tab is that it shows you all of the disks and folders on your PC, whether they contain photos or not. Most people keep all of their photos

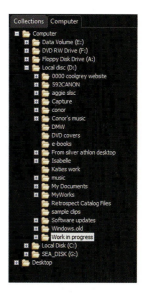

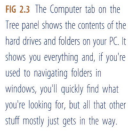
FIG 2.3 The Computer tab on the Tree panel shows the contents of the hard drives and folders on your PC. It shows you everything and, if you're used to navigating folders in windows, you'll quickly find what you're looking for, but all that other stuff mostly just gets in the way.

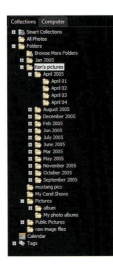

FIG 2.4 The Collections tab provides
a much less cluttered way to view
and organize your photos because it
shows only those folders you choose,
in other words only those containing
photos and video.

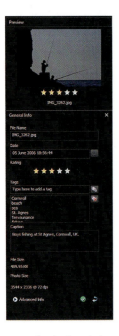

FIG 2.5 In Thumbnails mode the
General Info panel sits underneath
the Preview panel.

in one place and all that other stuff – folders containing applications, text
documents, spreadsheets, stuff downloaded from websites, your personal
finances – all just gets in the way. The Collections tab lets you concentrate
only on the folders containing your photos and videos.

The other really useful thing the Collections tab can do is group together
photos on the basis of their content, rather than where they happen to be on
your hard drive.

Using the Collections Tab

Click the Collections tab at the top of the Tree panel and you'll see a list that
contains five items, each of which can be expanded by clicking the plus icon
next to it. For now, click the plus icon to expand the folders list. If this is the
first time you've used the Organizer, you'll see two folders in here – My Corel
Shows and Public Pictures. Within the Public Pictures folder you'll find
another folder containing some sample photos.

There's one other item in the list that looks like a folder, but isn't. Click the
Browse More Folders button and a dialog box opens that you can use to
search for folders on your hard disk and add them to the Folders list. If you
select a folder containing subfolders, all the subfolders are added too. So, if
you keep all of your photos in a folder on your hard drive called 'Pictures',
which contains subfolders called things like 'summer holiday 2010' and 'Joe
and Anna's wedding', just select the Pictures folder and everything else will be
added automatically, neatly arranged in subfolders just like on your hard drive.

We'll come back to the Collections tab of the Tree panel after we've taken
a look at some other aspects of the Organizer, including how to add captions,
keywords, and other metadata to your photos.

Using the General Info Panel

The General Info panel displays metadata – information about your
photos – which you can edit and add to. Adding metadata like caption
information and keywords tells you and others more about your images
than the picture data alone can and it also helps when it comes to
finding particular photos, computers being much more adept at recog-
nizing words than pictures.

Adding a Rating

Below the image preview and in the General Info panel you'll see a Rating
section with five stars. If you haven't rated any of your images the stars will
appear white. Hover over them with your mouse and they turn gold; click on
one of the stars to apply that rating to the selected image. That's all there is to

it. If you change your mind, just click on one of the other stars to change the rating, and to remove the star rating click to the left of the first star.

As you'll discover in the section about searching and Smart Collections, rating your images is one of the best ways to sort them, allowing you to quickly locate your best shots. It's quick and easy to do (you can also apply ratings in Express Lab) and the rewards are more than worth the effort.

Adding Keyword Tags

Underneath the Rating section is the Tags section, which is where you assign keywords to your images. To add a new tag to an image, type the tag in the top field, then click the Add Tag button to the right and it will appear in the Tags list below. To add further tags just keep typing them in and adding them to the list.

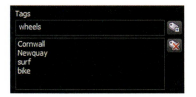

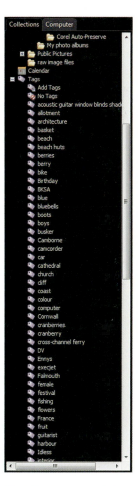

FIG 2.6 To add a tag to a photo, select the thumbnail, type the keyword into the tag field, then click the Add Tag button to the right.

Is there an easier way to add keywords than typing them individually for each and every image? Yes there is. Each time you add a keyword to a photo it is added to the Tags list in the Collections tab of the Tree panel. Once you've added a few keywords, click the plus sign next to Tags in the Collections tab of the Tree panel to expand the Keyword list – you'll see all of the keywords you just added in addition to every keyword tag you've ever previously added to a photo.

To add these tags to other images, first select the images in the Thumbnail panel then drag and drop them on to the keyword you want to apply.

The way to get all your keywording done quickly, without it turning into a tedious chore, is to start with the most generic keywords and work your way down to more specific ones. For example, let's say you've spent a day at the beach with your family. You'll want to add the tag 'beach' to most, if not all, of those shots, so select the first thumbnail, then press Ctrl + A to select them all and drag them on to the word 'beach' in the Tags list.

A lot of your photos are of the sandcastle competition, so Ctrl-click to select those thumbnails and drag them on to the 'sandcastle' tag, then on to the 'competition' tag. Remember, to get these words into the Tags list you'll first need to apply them to a single image by adding them in the Tags section of the General Info panel.

FIG 2.7 Every image tag is added to the Tags list in the Collections tab of the Tree panel. Click the plus icon next to Tags to expand it and see them all.

EXIF	
Digitized Date	10 July 2007 19:23:08
Original Date	10 July 2007 19:23:08
Make	Canon
Model	Canon DIGITAL IXUS ...
Software	Paint Shop Pro
X Resolution	180.000
Y Resolution	180.000
Resolution Units	Inches
Exposure Time	1/80 second
F-stop Number	2.800
Flash	Flash did not fire
ISO Speed	
Shutter Speed	1/79 sec. (6.31)
Lens Aperture	2.969
Max Aperture	2.969
Focal Length	7.41 mm
Focal Length in 35...	
Color Space	sRGB
Digital zoom ratio	1.000
Exposure Bias	F/1.0 (0.00)
Exposure Index	
Exposure Mode	Auto
Exposure Program	
White Balance	Auto white balance
Image Width	
Image height	
Scene capture type	Standard
Image sensor type	One-chip color area se...
Contrast	
Saturation	
Sharpness	
Subject distance ra...	Unknown
IPTC	

FIG 2.8 The Advanced Info section of the General Info panel is divided into two subsections – EXIF and IPTC. The EXIF subsection shown here displays camera make and model, exposure details, and other metadata recorded by the camera at exposure time.

Keep on going in this fashion, selecting and tagging batches of images with common keywords – family members, etc. Eventually, you'll be dealing with small groups and eventually single images that you can keyword tag from the General Info panel.

Once all your photos are tagged, finding photos that contain a particular tag is easy: just select the tag from the list in the Tree panel and all of the photos tagged with that word are displayed in the Thumbnails panel.

Adding a Caption

Like keyword tagging, captions can be applied to batches of photos. Shift- or Ctrl-click to select the photos you want to caption, then type the text into the Caption field in the General Info panel. If you can't be bothered to individually caption your images, give them all a more general caption – 'Beach trip, Cornwall, UK, August 2010', for example. You can always go back and edit them later if you have time.

Advanced Info

Click the Advanced Info toggle to display all the metadata information associated with a selected image, or group of images; the General Info panel expands to display the information. The Advanced Info panel is split into two sections – EXIF and IPTC. These are simply standards defining how image metadata is organized. EXIF (it stands for Exchangeable image file format) data is usually recorded by your camera at the same time as the image data, i.e. when you press the shutter.

EXIF data can tell you a lot of things, including the date and time the image was taken, the camera model, exposure settings, the lens focal length, the exposure mode, and whether a flash was used.

Generally, EXIF data isn't editable – there's no reason you'd want to change it – but the Organizer does allow you to change one EXIF item and that's the date and time stamp. Let's take a brief look at that before going on to look at the other kind of metadata – IPTC.

Changing the Date and Time Stamp

Every digital camera records the date and time an image was taken to the EXIF information stored along with the image data. Some digital compacts can also stamp this information onto the image if you so wish – but here we're concerned with the EXIF metadata that you can view in PaintShop Photo Pro Organizer's Advanced Info panel.

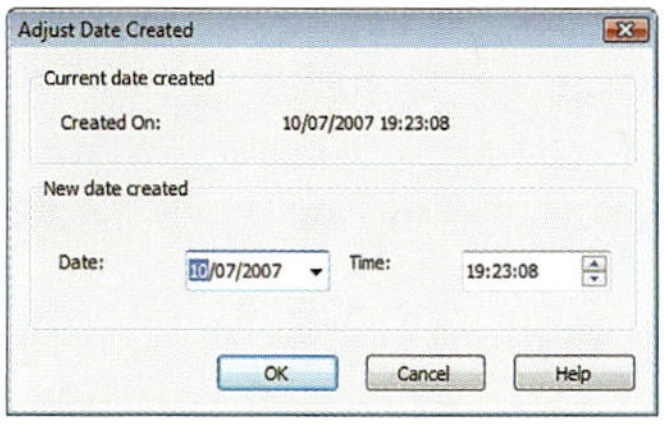

FIG 2.9 Click the Edit Date button in the General Info panel to change the recorded date and time for an image.

The date and time will only be accurate if your camera's clock is set correctly. If you didn't bother to set the clock when you first got your camera, or you went on holiday to a different time zone and forgot to change it, all of your photos will be stamped with the wrong time. But it's a problem that's easily fixed.

In the Organizer, go to the General Info panel and click the button next to the Date field. In the dialog box that appears enter the new date and time for the selected image and click the OK button.

IPTC

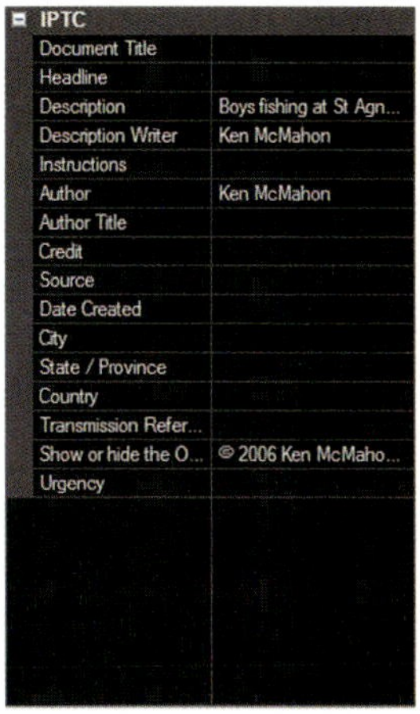

Unlike EXIF, the IPTC section of the Advanced Info panel contains information that is added after the event, by the photographer or others. IPTC stands for International Press Telecommunications Council, the body that defined the standard. The IPTC standard for this kind of information was developed so that newspaper picture desks, stock photo libraries, and other organizations dealing with lots of photos from lots of different sources would find it easier to manage them. But that doesn't mean IPTC data isn't useful to everyone else.

FIG 2.10 Use the IPTC subsection of Advanced Info to add and edit caption (description), title, and author credits.

If you've added captions to your photos you'll notice that they appear in the Description IPTC field, where you can edit them. Your changes will be updated in the Caption field of the General Info panel – it's the same information, it just appears in two different places with a different label.

Other IPTC fields that are useful include Author and Credit, which you can use to state your ownership as the photographer and to add a copyright notice – useful if you apply to competitions or send your images for potential use in publications.

Earlier we looked at how to add folders of photos to the Collections tab of the Tree panel. Then we saw how you can add keywords and other metadata to the existing metadata recorded by your camera and stored with each individual image file. Now we'll see how all this organization pays off by making it easy to quickly locate your photos and organize them into meaningful collections.

Searching and Smart Collections

Click the plus icon next to the Smart Collections item at the top of the Collections tab to reveal the list of existing Smart Collections. Click the Smart

Selection called 'Last 12 Months' and, provided you've cataloged a folder of recent images (see 'Using the Collections Tab' earlier), the Thumbnails panel will display all of the shots taken during the last 12 months. If you've rated your photos, selecting the 'Highest Rated' Smart Collection will display all photos with a keyword rating of five stars.

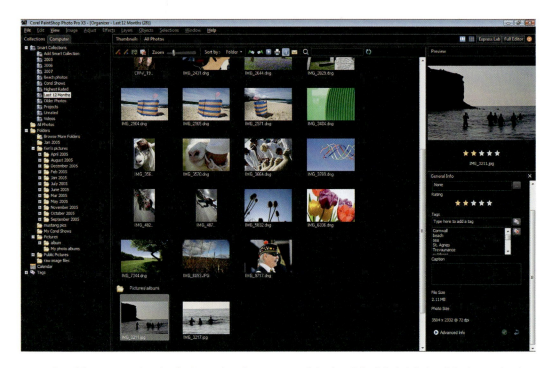

FIG 2.11 Smart Collections are saved searches. The Organizer has a few preset ones, including 'Last 12 Months', which displays all the photos you've taken in, that's right, the last year.

Using Search and Advanced Searching

We'll come back to Smart Collections in a minute. There's another way to search for photos using the metadata they contain. The Organizer toolbar (on top of the Thumbnails pane in Thumbnail mode) has a Search field. Type anything in here and the Organizer will show you thumbnails of all the images that contain what you type in any of the metadata fields or the filenames of your images. Before using search, select All Photos from the Collections tab to search all of your cataloged images. Alternatively you can search within a folder – either in the Collections tab or the Computer tab.

For more advanced search options, click the magnifier icon next to the search field in the Organizer toolbar to open the Smart Collection dialog. Use the left pull-down menu to select the search criteria; you can search by image name, caption, date, size, file type, keyword tag, or rating. The next pull-down menu defines how the search engine matches the search term. Normally you'll set this to 'contains', but 'starts with' and 'ends with' can be useful, or you might want to search for images that don't contain a particular search term. Next, type your search term into the field on the right.

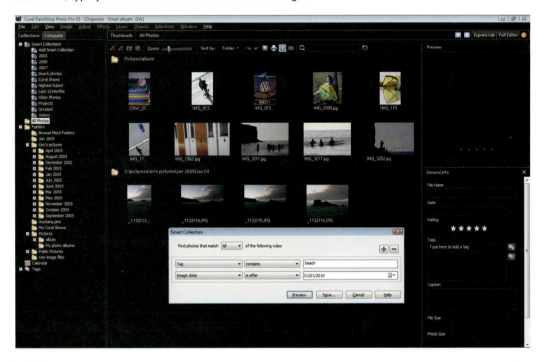

FIG 2.12 Click the magnifier to perform advanced searches. Using the Smart Collection dialog you can search for images that match all or any of multiple search criteria.

If you want to search for more than one term, click the plus icon to add another line. For example, you might want to search for images that contain the keyword 'beach' that were taken after 1 January 2010. In this case the first line of your advanced search would read 'Tag contains beach' and the second line would read 'Image date is after 01/01/2010'.

There's one final thing you need to consider before applying the search criteria. The pull-down menu at the top of the Smart Collection dialog has two settings. The default position is 'Find photos that match *All* of the following rules'. This means that if you select multiple criteria, like our beach example, only photos that comply with all of them will be displayed, i.e. they must contain the tag 'beach' and be taken after 01/01/2010. Changing this to 'Find photos that match *Any* of the following rules' means that only one of your criteria need be matched for images to be displayed. With *Any* selected, all photos tagged with the keyword 'beach' will be displayed, regardless of when they were taken. Likewise, all photos taken after 01/01/2010 will be displayed, even if they aren't tagged with the 'beach' keyword.

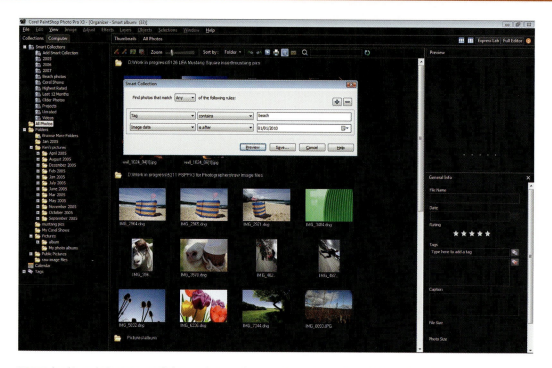

FIG 2.13 Searching multiple criteria using find any results in a wider range of images that match any of the search criteria.

Saving Searches as Smart Collections

When you've entered your search criteria and rules, click the Preview button to see all of the images that match. Click the Save button and enter a name to save your advanced search to the Smart Collections list in the Collections tab of the Tree panel. Now you can access the same search simply by clicking its name in the Smart Collections list. You can also duplicate and edit existing Smart Collections.

The Highest Rated Smart Collection displays all images with a five-star rating, but supposing you want to display all images with a three-star rating and higher? First, right-click the Highest Rated Smart Collection in the Collections tab of the Tree panel, select Duplicate from the contextual menu, and enter 'Rated three stars and above' in the Save as a Smart Collection dialog. Click OK to add the new Smart Collection to the list.

FIG 2.14 You can duplicate and edit Smart Collections to create new ones. In this case the Highest Rated Smart Collection has been edited to produce a more useful 'Rated three stars and above' one.

Now right-click your new 'Rated three stars and above' Smart Collection and select Edit from the contextual menu. The Smart Collection dialog shows 'Rating is five stars' – the setup for the Highest Rated Smart Collection that we duplicated. Change it to 'Rating is greater than three stars' and click the Save button – you'll be prompted with another dialog containing the name of the Smart Collection; as you've already renamed it, just click Save. Now when you select the 'Rated three stars and above' Smart Selection you'll see all images in the selected folder that have a three-star or higher rating.

Smart Selections are live – whenever you catalog new folders of images by adding them to the Collections tab your Smart Collections will automatically update to include them. So from now on any new images that you assign a three-star or higher rating to will appear when you choose the 'Rated three stars and above' Smart Selection.

Working with Camera RAW Images

PaintShop Photo Pro X3 now supports Camera RAW image file formats for a wider range of camera manufacturers and models. To see if your camera is supported go to www.corel.com, click support, on the support page click knowledge base and from the search by product drop-list choose PaintShop Photo Pro, then type RAW in the search box and click the search button.

What are Camera RAW files and why should you use them? Camera RAW is a proprietary format that's available on most digital SLR cameras and some advanced compacts. If you're not using RAW, your camera processes the information collected by the sensor and saves it as an RGB image file with JPEG compression (see Chapter 10 for more details about how JPEG compression works). As well as compressing the file, in the process of con-verting the RAW file to a JPEG a lot of the original image data is discarded. By shooting and recording the RAW data, then doing the conversion yourself in PaintShop Photo Pro X3, you can make your own decisions about how best to perform the conversion and get a better quality image than if you'd left it to your camera.

One of the main advantages of shooting and processing RAW files is that you can import them into PaintShop Photo Pro X3 for editing as 16-bit RGB files – retaining all of the bit data for each pixel that the camera was capable of recording. When you shoot JPEG images the files are automatically down-sampled to 8 bits per pixel, giving you much less scope when it comes to making tonal and color corrections and other edits.

The downside to this is that, with more bits per pixel and no JPEG compression applied, RAW files are much larger than JPEGs and eat up your memory card and hard disk space more quickly. With the falling cost of storage, this isn't the big issue it used to be though. And, when you've finished editing, you can always down-sample files to 8 bits per pixel (select Image > Decrease Color Depth > RGB – 8 bits/channel), just remember to keep a backup of your original RAW files.

The Organizer displays thumbnails for RAW files in the Thumbnail pane. Camera RAW files are processed by PaintShop Photo Pro X3 in the Camera RAW Lab; to open a file into the RAW lab, double-click its thumbnail. To process more than one image at a time, Shift- or Ctrl-click to select several thumbnails, right-click, and select Open from the contextual menu.

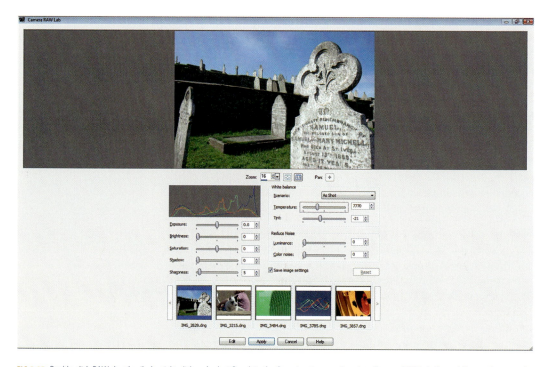

FIG 2.15 Double-click RAW thumbnails (or right-click and select Open) in the Organizer to open them into Camera RAW Lab. Several files can be opened into the Lab for editing at the same time.

The Camera RAW Lab window displays a preview image at the top; to get a better look maximize the window. It's important to understand that what you're looking at is an RGB interpretation of the RAW data. By adjusting the controls in Camera RAW Lab you can interpret the data differently to produce different results, finally outputting an RGB file for editing in the Full Editor, or saving the settings to a 'sidecar' file that's associated with the original RAW file.

Two things about this approach are radically different to the way you might be used to working with image files. First, you can't make changes to and save RAW files; RAW files are in effect locked. Because the data in a RAW file isn't in RGB format, it can't be edited in the conventional way. Instead, any changes you apply in the Camera RAW Lab are saved in a 'sidecar' file and applied when you next open the RAW file in the Camera RAW Lab.

The second thing is that these changes in interpretation aren't destructive in the same way that editing an RGB file can be. You're not manipulating pixels, but reinterpreting the information in the RAW file to produce a different outcome. When you're happy with that interpretation you can output the file in RGB format for further editing in the PaintShop Photo Pro X3 Full Editor, or simply export it in any RGB format such as TIFF, JPEG or PSPIMAGE.

So let's take a look at the controls in the Camera RAW Lab. The panel in the top right contains the 'White balance' controls. Ordinarily white balance is applied in the camera – all you need to do is set the white balance to automatic or one of the available presets. But, as we've seen, none of this in-camera processing occurs when you shot RAW and the white balance can be applied later. This is hugely advantageous as it allows you to easily remove color casts caused by incorrect setting of the white balance or the camera's auto white balance getting it wrong – it happens.

There are three white balance controls. A drop-down menu provides presets, one of which is the camera's white balance setting. Others include common lighting setups like Daylight, Tungsten, Flash, and Fluorescent Lighting. More control is provided via two sliders below. The main one sets the color temperature – you can enter it numerically in the adjoining field. Dragging it to the left or entering a lower value makes the image cooler or more blue; in the opposite direction the image becomes warmer or more yellow.

If you know anything about color temperature this may seem a little counter-intuitive. On the Kelvin scale used to represent color temper-ature the higher the color temperature, the bluer the light, so why does setting a higher color temperature make the image warmer? The answer is that the setting represents the color temperature of the prevailing lighting conditions when the photo was taken. By dragging the slider to a higher color temperature you're telling Camera RAW Lab that the light used to create the image was cooler (more blue) than the currently specified setting and therefore the result is a warmer (more yellow) image.

The Tint slider below the Temperature sliders is used to eliminate green/magenta casts. Drag it to the right to add green (remove magenta) and to the left to add magenta (remove green).

49

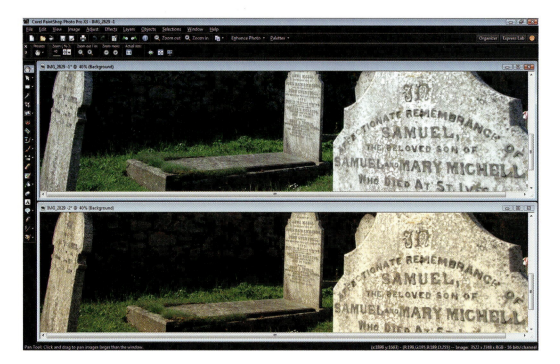

FIG 2.16 These two images show the same RAW file saved to RGB using different white balance settings in Camera RAW Lab. The one on top was saved with the 'As Shot' white balance of 7770, the one below with the white balance adjusted to 12,500.

The next panel down provides noise reduction controls. There are two sliders, one each for Luminance and Color noise. As we will see in Chapter 4, PaintShop Photo Pro X3 has an excellent tool for removing noise from RGB images in the Digital Camera Noise Removal filter. These controls in the Camera RAW Lab, however, can give you a head start removing some of the digital noise from high ISO shots. As most of the noise that occurs in high ISO shots is luminance noise, you'll find the Luminance slider the more effective of the two.

Moving over to the left panel you'll find a range of sliders designed for fixing exposure problems underneath a histogram that shows overlaid RGB channels. The Exposure slider controls highlight detail and you can use it to recover blown highlights in overexposed shots. Brightness controls shadow and midtone ranges, and can be used to recover detail in underexposed images. Shadow increases contrast in the shadows and is another useful tool for rescuing overexposed images and images lacking contrast.

Finally, there's a Sharpness slider. This control isn't like the Unsharp Mask filter, but is designed to reduced some of the softness that's inherent in all Camera RAW images due to a process called 'demosaicing', which converts the grayscale information in the RAW file into color pixel values.

Step-by-Step Projects

Technique: Using Camera RAW Lab to Restore Detail in Overexposed Photos

This shot of a horse's head is overexposed by around one stop. If you'd shot this as a JPEG you might be able to recover the lost highlight detail in the front of the horse's head and the sky in the background, but with only 8 bits per channel of pixel information the chances are the image would begin to look harsh and contrasty before you recovered as much detail as you'd like.

Making the exposure corrections in Camera RAW Lab gives you much more scope – you can recover more detail without causing the kind of image degradation that editing pixels inevitably results in. Remember, what we're doing here is simply interpreting the raw data to give us a more acceptable starting point. Once the corrections have been made you can output the image as a 16-bit RGB file. Then, there's nothing to stop you making further improvements in the Full Editor or Express Lab. With a rock-solid 16-bit RGG file you'll still be in a better position to make further improvements than you would have been with an 8-bit JPEG from the camera.

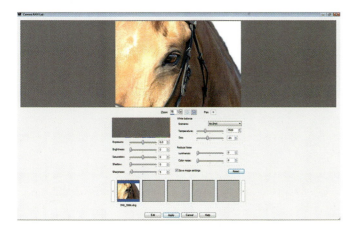

STEP 1 Double-click the RAW file thumbnail in the Organizer to open it into Camera RAW Lab and click the Maximize button at the top right to fill the screen. This is your first chance to get a look at the image as interpreted using Camera RAW Lab's default settings. As well as suffering from overexposure the white balance is on the cool side – both problems easily dealt with in Camera RAW Lab.

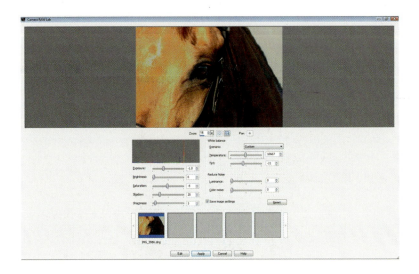

STEP 2 First, deal with the exposure by dragging the Exposure slider to the left. In this case we've dragged it to −1.0, effectively reducing the exposure by one stop. It doesn't matter if you can't drag the slider to precisely −1.0, but if you do want more precise control use the nudge buttons on the Exposure numeric field next to the slider.

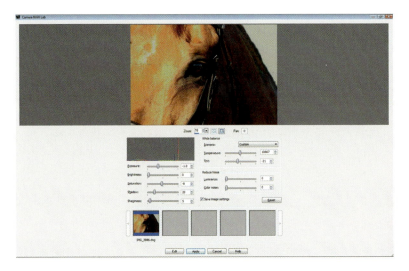

STEP 3 The exposure is looking better, but now the shot looks dull and murky. To increase contrast in the shadows, drag the Shadow slider to the right. As you drag, the preview will update and you need to make a visual assessment of how much Shadow to apply. You want to increase contrast in the shadows without losing any detail. Here we're aiming to make the horse's bridle black without losing detail in the neck and eye.

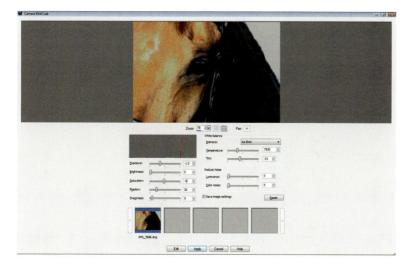

STEP 4 Increasing the contrast in the shadows has led to slight over-saturation at the front of the horse's head. Drag the Saturation slider to the left to reduce the saturation a little. Don't overdo it; small movements of the Saturation slider have quite a large effect. Use the nudge buttons for precise control. Around −5 on the Saturation is enough to return things to a more natural-looking state.

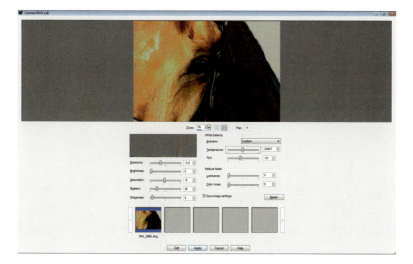

STEP 5 Now we can address the color cast. The 'As Shot' white balance is 7520, but produces too cool a result — notice the blue highlight running down the horse's neck at the back. Selecting one of the presets — for example, Daylight or Cloudy — won't help as these are both lower and will result in more blue (see the section on white balance earlier in the chapter for a description of how this works). The simplest way to deal with most color casts is simply to drag the Temperature slider whilst assessing the result in the preview window.

Because this shot was taken quite late in the evening, the light was getting very blue and the color temperature setting required to eliminate the cast is 10,667.

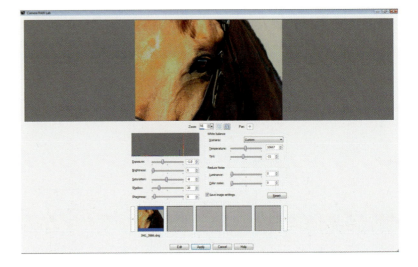

STEP 6 Notice how changing the color balance has once again increased the saturation of the yellows and browns? Use the nudge buttons to knock them back again – in this case to −8 is enough.

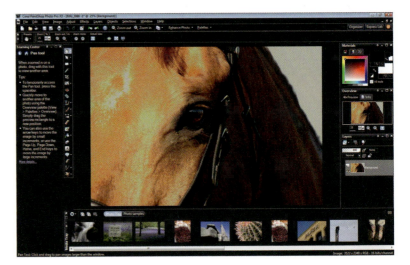

STEP 7 Check the Save image settings checkbox if you want these settings to be retained next time you open the RAW file in Camera RAW Lab. Now you have two options. Click the Edit button to open the image in PaintShop Photo Pro's Full Editor. You can now make any further edits to the image that you want before saving it in the file format of your choice. Remember that this is a 16-bit per pixel image and if you want to retain it as such, you'll need to save it in a format that supports it, such as PSPIMAGE, PSD, or TIF.

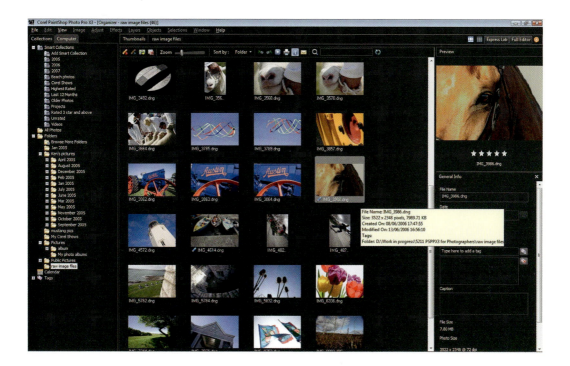

STEP 8 If you don't want to edit the image in PaintShop Photo Pro, clicking the Apply button will close Camera RAW Lab. If you take a look at the thumbnail in the Organizer, you'll see that it has been updated to reflect the changes you just made and has a small pencil icon next to the filename to indicate it has been edited. These changes are stored in a separate 'sidecar' file on your hard drive in the same folder as the RAW files.

STEP 9 To export the RAW image to an RGB file without opening it again in Camera RAW Lab, select it in the Organizer and click the Convert RAW button on the Organizer toolbar. Select an image type and choose a location on your hard drive where you want the image saved. The Modify button allows you to add text or sequence numbers to the filename for batch conversion.

Technique: Using The Organizer to Apply a Series of Image Edits to Multiple Photos

One of PaintShop Photo Pro's hot new features is the ability to capture a whole editing session from one image and apply it to many others. This feature is particularly useful for applying image edits to Camera RAW edits, but can be applied to any image that you've already edited in PaintShop Photo Pro.

When dealing with RGB files, you can only capture and apply an Edit list from photos that have been edited during your current session (the changes don't need to have been saved though). PaintShop Photo Pro X3 keeps lists of all the edits you make to images (it uses these lists for the Undo command), but once you exit the program the lists are deleted.

If you recall, when you make changes to a Camera RAW file they're not saved to the RAW file itself, but as a list of edits in a sidecar file. This means that those lists are always available to PaintShop Pro (it applies them each time you open the program and view thumbnails for RAW files in the Organizer). This means the current session limitation doesn't apply to RAW files; you can capture the settings you applied to them in Camera RAW Lab at any time and apply them to as many other RAW files as you like.

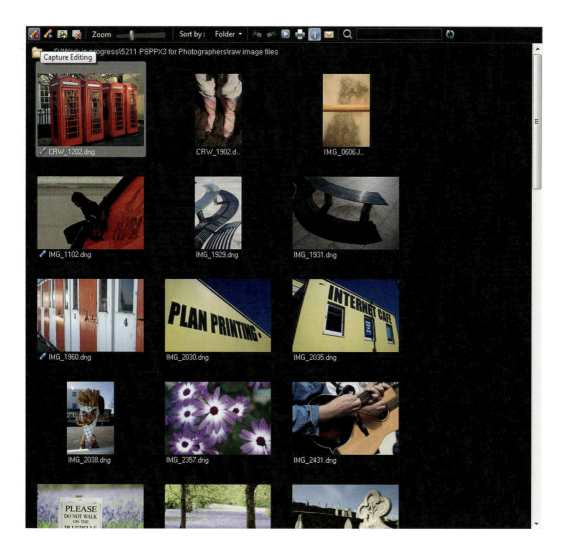

STEP 1 Launch PaintShop Photo Pro X3 and open the Organizer. Select a RAW thumbnail that you've previously edited in Camera RAW Lab and click the Capture Editing button on the Organizer toolbar.

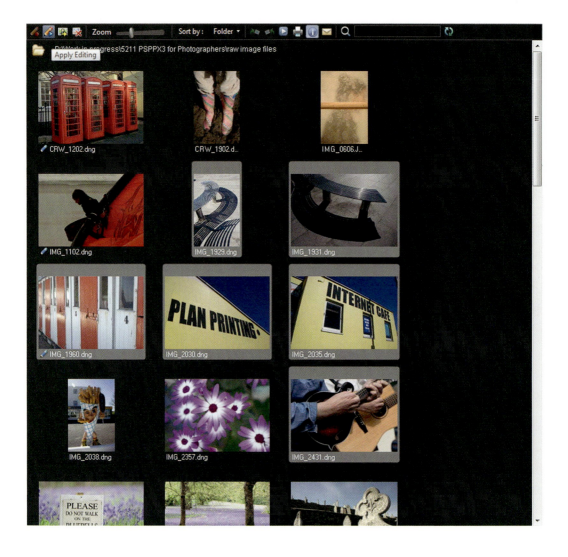

STEP 2 Now select all the other RAW image thumbnails that you want to apply the same settings to and click the Apply Editing button. If you selected more than a handful of images, it may take a short while for them all to be processed. You'll be warned that this can't be undone, and for RGB files this is the case, so make sure you have backups! For RAW files though, all you're doing is changing the settings in the sidecar file that determine how the RAW data in the original file is interpreted. And you could always open up one of the changed files, reset everything back the way it was, then capture that file's editing and reapply it to the others to get back to where you started.

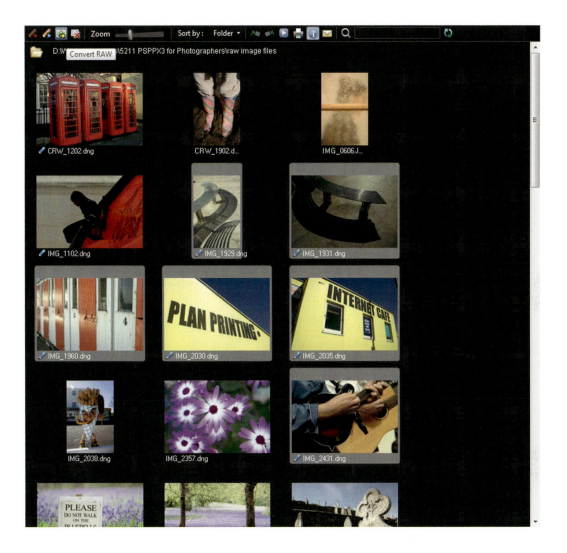

STEP 3 That's it! It really is that simple. I probably don't need to reiterate that all you've done is changed the RAW settings that are applied when you create an RGB file. To do that you'll need to click the Convert RAW button on the Organizer toolbar.

CHAPTER 3

Improving Your Photos – Basic Editing

What's Covered in this Chapter

- This chapter explains how to use PaintShop Photo Pro's tools to improve digital photos that suffer from common problems like incorrect exposure, or are simply a bit dull and lifeless and need polishing up. PaintShop Photo Pro X3 has a selection of tools like One Step Photo Fix, Smart Photo Fix, and Color Balance that do most of the work for you and make it easy to get good results with very little effort. There's also Express Lab, which has a range of tools that you can apply to make an instant difference to lackluster shots. We'll take a look at these first of all.
- Later in the chapter we'll look at some of the more advanced tools for enhancing image quality, like Hue/Saturation/Lightness, Levels, Histogram Adjustment, the Unsharp Mask filter, and High Pass Sharpen filter.
- There are so many tools in PaintShop Photo Pro X3 that it's sometimes difficult to know where to start, but if you work through this chapter you'll discover one of PaintShop Photo Pro's biggest strengths; you can start with the simple tools like Smart Photo Fix and, if you can't get good results, move on to the more advanced tools that target specific exposure and color problems.

PaintShop Photo Pro X3 for Photographers. DOI: 10.1016/B978-0-240-52165-7.10003-6

61

- It's not all about fixing pictures. Tools like Hue/Saturation/Lightness, Curves, and the Hue Map can be used creatively to replace colors. This chapter also touches briefly on how to do this.
- Sharpening digital photos is something that can hugely improve picture quality, but there's more to it than simply whacking on the Unsharp Mask filter. Towards the end of the chapter I'll show you how to do it properly and, for those who want to squeeze every last drop of sharpness out of their photos without introducing other problems like noise and haloing, there's a step-by-step project that covers advanced sharpening using the High Pass Sharpen filter.
- The other step-by-step project goes into detail on how to use Smart Photo Fix. Though this is covered comprehensively in the text, it's such a useful tool that I thought a hands-on walk-through would be a big help if you haven't used this tool before.

PaintShop Photo Pro X3 has a bewilderingly large array of tools for fixing up photos, so many, in fact, that it can be a problem knowing where to start. If that's the case, then the short answer is probably the Express Lab. Express Lab contains all the tools you need to sort out most of the common problems that affect digital photos from bad exposure to red-eye removal.

You can use Express Lab on a single image, or on an entire folder; to get started select the photos you want to edit in the Organizer then click the Express Lab button in the top right corner of the screen. The first image appears in the preview window and the others are arranged in a strip along the bottom. Just above the thumbnail strip you'll see the Express Lab tool strip, which contains numerous tools for enhancing and editing. When you first open Express Lab the Smart Photo Fix filter is selected. This versatile tool is described in more detail a little later in this chapter, so if you want to know what the individual settings are for and how to use them, read on. For now, you can usually get quite good results, or at least a good place to start, by clicking the Suggest Settings button.

If you hover over the tools a tooltip will tell you what the tool is for and the Status bar at the bottom of the screen will tell you a little more about it. Among others, there are tools for rotating, cropping, straightening, sharpening, and adjusting the tonal (contrast and brightness) and color balance in photos. You'll also find these tools in the Full Editor workspace, but in the Express Lab they are much simpler and you'll find it easier to work through a batch of photos applying the same or similar edits to each.

For example, if all you have is a batch of photos that you want to rotate, crop and enhance, you can open them in Express Lab, apply your edits to the first image, then click the Next button to process the next file, and so on. It's also much easier to see what you're doing without the clutter of the Full Editor workspace getting in the way.

You can also rate images in Express Lab – just click on the stars in the bottom left corner to apply a one- to five-star rating to each photo. Before you exit Express Lab make sure to save your changes by clicking the Save or Save As button on the left of the tool strip.

It's rarely the case that you'll need to apply exactly the same edits to a folder of photos, even if they were all taken at the same time. If you're cropping photos, for example, you obviously won't be selecting exactly the same area in each one. And even when making tonal and color adjustments, different images usually require slightly different settings to get the best results. Sometimes, though, you'll want to do exactly the same thing to a batch of images. For example, you might want to prepare some images for your website by reducing the size, you might have a folder of photos that were taken at a high ISO setting and are in need of noise removal, or you might want to convert a folder of photos to black and white and apply an Effects filter.

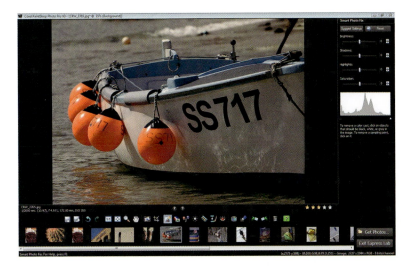

FIG 3.1 If you're not sure where to begin with photo-editing, take a look at Express Lab. It provides a set of tools for everyday photo-processing tasks that are easy to use and can be applied to a series of photos in quick succession.

This is where PaintShop Photo Pro X3's new multiple photo-editing feature proves useful. Once you've made your edits in Express Lab or the Full Editor, save the image and switch to the Organizer. You can close the image. PaintShop Photo Pro keeps track of all the edits in the current session for both opened and closed images; only when you quit the application are these Edit lists lost. Next, select the image you've been editing in the Organizer and click the Capture Editing button at the top left of the screen. Now select the image or images you want to apply the same edits to and click the Apply Editing button. A dialog appears warning that you can't undo the changes (they are applied and then the edited image is resaved, so make sure you have the original backed up); click OK and you're done.

63

One Step Photo Fix

One of the central tools in the Express Lab's arsenal is One Step Photo Fix. It's also available on the Adjust menu in the Full Editor workspace. As the name suggests, One Step Photo Fix applies a 'one-step' correction to improve overall image quality. What One Step Photo Fix actually does is make tonal adjustments to improve image contrast, boost (or in some cases reduce) the color saturation, sharpen the image, and correct the color balance.

There's nothing for you to do other than select Adjust > One Step Photo Fix and wait for a second or two for the filter to do its work. For most photos you'll see a marked improvement in image quality.

Tip

Don't forget that you can use PaintShop Photo Pro X3's new Express Lab to perform basic editing on an entire folder of images. Get into the habit of doing this when you first download your photos and you'll have less work to do on them later.

Smart Photo Fix

If the One Step Photo Fix doesn't quite do the job, or you just like to tinker, you'll get more satisfaction, and quite probably a better result, using Smart Photo Fix – it's the next option down on the Adjust menu.

Smart Photo Fix does exactly what One Step Photo Fix does, only you get access to the individual controls that determine the degree of correction applied. In other words the smart component is supplied by you.

Like most PaintShop Photo Pro filters, Smart Photo Fix has 'before' and 'after' preview thumbnails so you can see the effect your changes make before applying them. Click the Maximize button at the top right of the dialog box to get the best possible view or, if you don't have much screen space, click the Auto Proof button to see changes previewed in the image window.

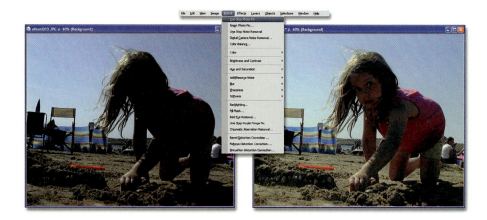

FIG 3.2 One Step Photo Fix does all the work for you – just select it from the Adjust menu, sit back and await the transformation.

Advanced Options

The first thing you should do when using Smart Photo Fix is click the Advanced Options checkbox. This reveals the histogram and Color Balance tools. The histogram provides important information about the tonal range in the photo – see the 'Histogram' section later in this chapter to find out why this is important.

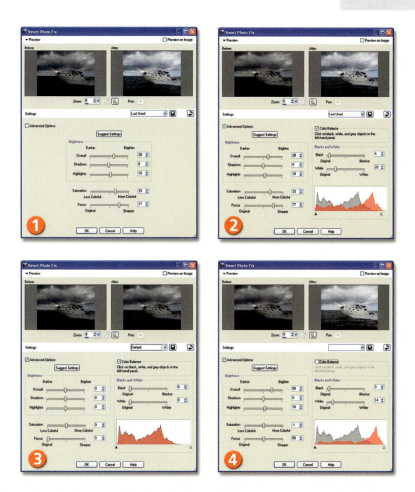

FIG 3.3 Select Adjust > Smart Photo Fix to open the Smart Photo Fix dialog box. (1) On opening, the image is automatically analyzed and suggested settings applied, which you can see in the preview thumbnail on the right. No changes are actually made to the image until you click the OK button. (2) Click the Advanced Options checkbox to display the Histogram, Color Balance, and Black and White controls. The histogram is a graphical display of the tonal distribution in the image and provides indispensable feedback when making tonal adjustments. (3) Click the Suggest Settings button to get back to the original situation, or select Default from the Presets pull-down menu to remove all corrections and start from scratch. Incidentally, in this mode you can see the typical histogram for an underexposed photo with all the pixels on the left (shadow) side of the histogram and nothing on the right (highlight) side. (4) For this image, the suggested settings were improved upon by increasing the overall brightness, reducing the saturation, and unchecking Color Balance as there is no cast. The amount of sharpening has been reduced to avoid exaggerating the noise that will become more visible as a result of the large brightness adjustment. Note the adjusted histogram (pink), which now shows a more even distribution across the tonal range from shadows to highlights.

When you open the Smart Photo Fix dialog box it automatically analyzes the photo and sets all of the controls to where it thinks you will get the best improvement in image quality. This is exactly what happens when you use One Step Photo Fix, except in this case the settings aren't applied and you can use them as the starting point for further refinement. If at any point you feel that you've gone too far with the sliders and want to get back here, just click the Suggest Settings button. Alternatively, if you select Default from the Presets pull-down menu you can start from the original uncorrected image and make your own adjustments. When you've arrived at settings that work well for a particular kind of problem, for example underexposed photos, save the settings as a preset so that you can easily apply them to other problem images.

Brightness

The Brightness panel contains three sliders – Overall, Shadows, and Highlights – which allow you to adjust the brightness individually in these areas. If the shadows in your photo are very dark you can use the Shadows slider to bring out some detail in them without making the highlights too bright. If a photo is just generally too dark, use the Overall slider to brighten it throughout the range.

The best way to judge whether you're doing the right thing is to take a look at the 'after' thumbnail preview on the right and compare it with the original on the left. Sometimes, though, it can be hard to tell whether you're making things better or worse and this is where the histogram can help.

Using the Histogram

The histogram is a graph of the values of all the pixels in the image. Dark pixels have low values and light pixels have high values. Black is 0, white is 255, mid-gray is 128. So the histogram shows the distribution of pixels in the image from black to white, with darker pixels on the left and lighter ones on the right.

The shape of the histogram depends on the nature of the subject, but generally it should show a reasonably even distribution from black to white. Typical problems like under- and overexposure have very characteristic histograms. In an underexposed image there's a predominance of dark pixels and few, if any, white ones so the histogram tends to be bunched down at the left-hand end. In overexposed photos the histogram is bunched at the right-hand end, with no black or very dark pixels.

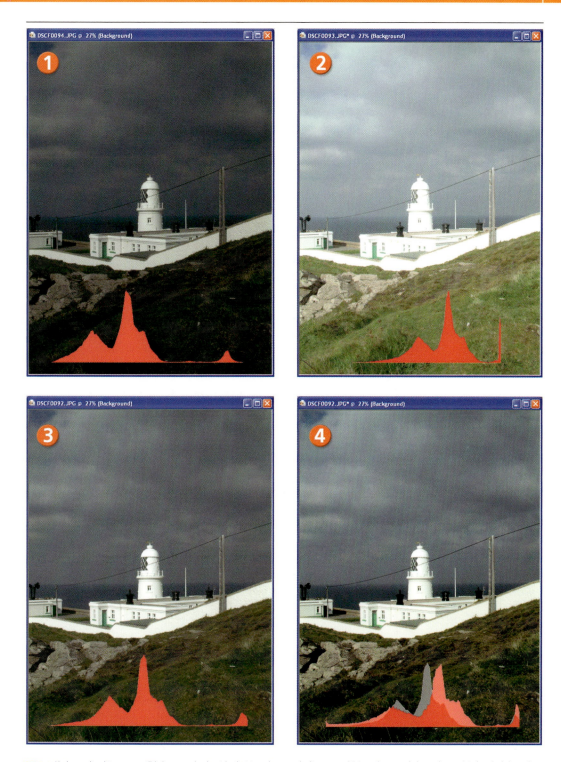

FIG 3.4 Understanding histograms will help you make the right decisions about tonal adjustments. (1) In underexposed photos the graph is bunched down the left-hand side. (2) The histogram for overexposed photos is squeezed up on the right-hand side. (3) The correct exposure shows most detail in the central area of the histogram, but the image lacks contrast. (4) Smart Photo Fix improves things by 'stretching' the histogram to produce true blacks and whites, but be careful: using these settings will lose some highlight detail in the lighthouse building – note the clipped bunch of pixels on the far right of the histogram.

Another problem that is easily confirmed by a quick look at the histogram is lack of contrast. Images that lack contrast look flat and dull. They lack punch due to the absence of pure black and pure white pixels. The tonal range starts at light gray and ends at dark gray, and the histogram this time is all in the middle of the range with no pixels at either end.

In the Smart Photo Fix dialog box when you make an adjustment with the Brightness sliders the histogram displays a pink overlay, which shows you how the tonal distribution of pixels changes; the original histogram appears in gray. If you drag any of the sliders towards the right (brighter) direction you'll see the histogram move the same way. Dragging the Shadows and Highlights sliders moves the histogram at the ends, while the Overall slider moves the whole thing, but the middle more than the edges.

The important thing to remember when making adjustments with the Brightness sliders is not to let the histogram slip off either end of the chart – it should taper off just before reaching the end. If you allow pixels to drop off the end of the histogram, you are losing image detail – in the case of highlights remapping light gray pixels to pure white and, in the shadows, turning darker detail pure black. This applies to all dark and light colors that are represented by gray pixels in the red, green, and blue channels.

Blacks and Whites

To quickly fix contrast problems use the Blacks and Whites sliders. Remember, a flat image lacking in contrast has a histogram that's bunched in the middle and doesn't make it to either end of the histogram. Drag the Black slider until the black triangle under the histogram is underneath the leftmost edge of the graph, then do the same with the White slider, positioning the white triangle under the rightmost edge. Smart Photo Fix 'stretches' the histogram, mapping the darkest gray to black and the lightest gray to white and adjusting all the tones in between.

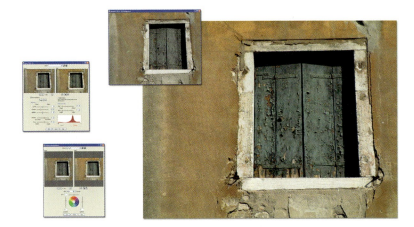

FIG 3.5 Sometimes, all a photo needs to give it a lift is to boost the color saturation. In this case, the saturation has been increased by +30. You can do this using the Saturation slider in either the Smart Photo Fix dialog box or the Hue/Saturation Lightness dialog box.

Saturation

The Saturation slider makes colors more vivid when you slide it to the right and less vivid when slid towards the left. Depending on your camera settings you may find increasing the saturation by up to 20 gives you punchier colors, but beware of going too far.

Color Balance

To correct an overall color cast in your pictures, check the Color Balance box and click on areas of the image that should be neutral in color – i.e. pure blacks, whites, and grays in the left-hand thumbnail. Smart Photo Fix places a cross-hairs target where you clicked and automatically adjusts the colors in the image. Often you'll find one target is sufficient; you can place as many as you like but, at most, three or four will do the job. To remove a target, just click it with the eyedropper.

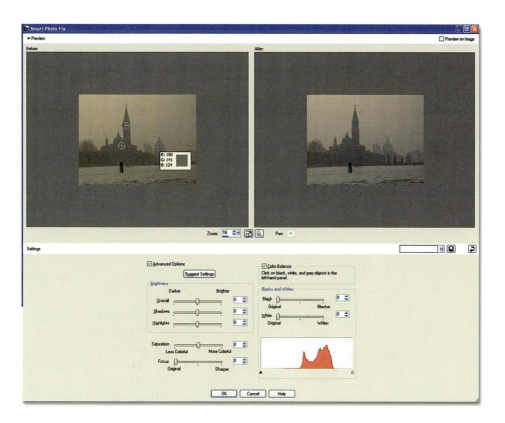

FIG 3.6 Check the Color Balance box in the Smart Photo Fix dialog to remove an unwanted color cast from a photo. Click in the left thumbnail image to place cross-hair targets where the color should be black, white or neutral gray.

Focus

The Focus slider applies the Unsharp Mask filter. For most images, the suggested setting, which will be around 30, is plenty. Be wary of applying large amounts of sharpening to photos that have had a lot of tonal adjustment as you can end up exaggerating noise. You should also make sure to look at the preview thumbnail at 100% magnification (there's a special 1:1 button for this underneath the thumbnails).

Color Balance

To use PaintShop Photo Pro X3's Color Balance tool, select Adjust > Color Balance. Like the Smart Photo Fix dialog box, Color Balance has Basic and Advanced modes. In Basic mode it couldn't be simpler to use – you just drag the slider to the right to make photos warmer and to the left to make them cooler. If you simply want to neutralize a color cast, check the Smart White Balance box and set the slider in the center.

For more control over color balance check the Advanced Options box. This divides the dialog box into two panels. The tools in the White Balance panel are used to identify the original conditions under which the photo was taken; you then use the sliders in the Enhance Color Balance panel to make further minor adjustments.

This can be a little counter-intuitive if you're not used to it because dragging the Temperature slider in the White Balance panel towards warm actually makes the image cooler, or more blue. This is because you're telling the program that the original lighting conditions were warmer than those depicted in the unadjusted image.

For example, if you set your camera's white balance for indoor use, and then go and take photos outdoors without resetting it, all of your pictures will have a blue cast. This is because daylight is much cooler (or more blue) than the artificial indoor light that you've set the camera up for.

In the Color Balance dialog box, by dragging the White Balance Temperature slider towards cool, you're saying that the actual color temperature of the light this picture was taken in was much cooler than what the camera was set up for and recorded – and the blue cast is eliminated.

There's another way to get rid of unwanted color casts in the Color Balance dialog box and that's to use the Smart Select button. This works in a very similar fashion to the Color Balance option in the Smart Photo Fix dialog box, except that you only get to place one target on a black, white, or neutral gray area. This isn't as much of a limitation as it might seem as one sample is all you really need. If it doesn't produce the desired results just click somewhere else in the image and carry on sampling until you hit somewhere that does. When you're happy that the color cast has been neutralized you can use the sliders in the Enhance Color Balance panel to fine-tune the result.

Tip

In the Color Balance dialog box, clicking either side of the slider makes a fixed increment adjustment. The Color Temperature sliders increase or decrease by 100 and the Tint sliders go up or down by 10. Alternatively you can enter a figure in the Number field or use the toggle buttons to increase or decrease the amount by one.

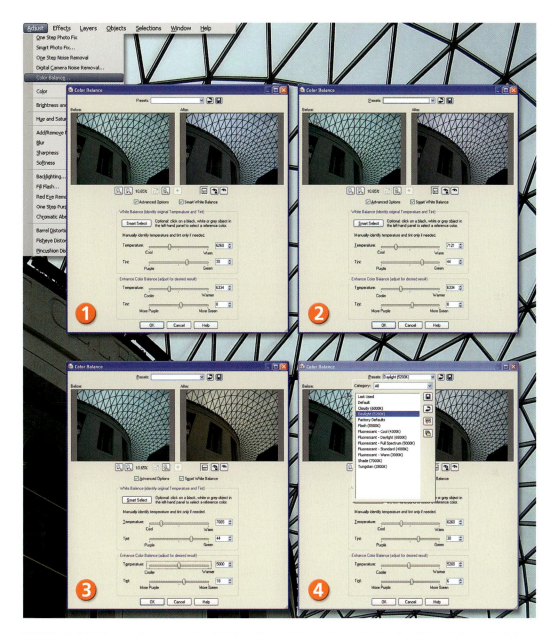

FIG 3.7 Nearly all digital cameras have an automatic white balance feature, which in most circumstances works well to assess the prevailing lighting conditions. It's not foolproof, however, and in this instance has resulted in a blue/green cast. (1) When you select Adjust > Color Balance the image is automatically assessed and the preview thumbnail on the right shows you what the corrected image will look like. These settings are based on an automatically selected neutral area indicated by the cross-hair target. (2) To select a different neutral area click anywhere in the left thumbnail; keep trying different locations to see if you can improve the result. (3) You can nearly always improve things by making your own adjustments using the sliders – in this case to produce a more neutral, slightly warm result. (4) The Color Balance dialog is one of the few to offer a useful set of ready-made presets – just pick the one that most closely resembles the lighting conditions under which the photo was taken. Here, the Daylight (5200K) preset produces near perfect results.

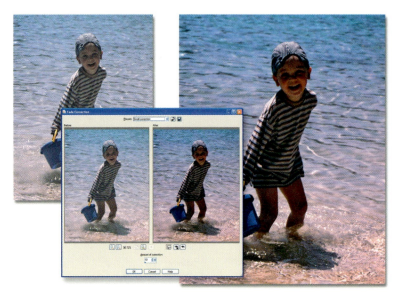

FIG 3.8 You can use Fade Correction on pictures that have faded through age, like this color slide, or those that just suffer from poor contrast.

Other Tools for Correcting Color Problems

For most situations Smart Photo Fix provides all the tools you'll need to sort out exposure problems and remove unwanted color casts from your photos. But it's not the best way to deal with every problem, and it's always good to have alternatives. The following tools not only provide an alternative route to sorting out problem photos, but they can be used creatively to introduce new color and tonal effects. Chapter 4 shows you how to introduce color into black and white images using some of these tools.

Channel Mixer

Although it appears under the Adjust > Color menu, the Channel mixer isn't the best tool with which to make color changes to photos. The most practical use for the Channel mixer is to produce black and white images – this is covered in Chapter 4.

Fade Correction

The Fade Correction tool is intended for use on, you guessed it, faded photos. The inks and dyes used in photographic printing processes aren't permanent and, as anyone with prints more than a few years old will know, they tend to fade with age. Exposure to the air and light accelerates this process but, even if you keep your photos in a sealed box, after a few years they won't look as good as the day they were printed.

The Fade Correction tool is a one-step solution to this problem. There's only one setting – use the Amount slider to vary how much correction is applied. Fade Correction boosts the saturation and makes a levels adjustment, so if you're confident about making those changes individually, you'll have more control using Smart Photo Fix, or Hue/Saturation/Lightness and any of the tonal adjustment tools. It'll take a little longer, but you'll have more control and obtain better results.

Red/Green/Blue

Red/Green/Blue allows you to add or subtract color from the individual RGB channels in the image. It works a little like the Channel mixer, only slightly more intuitively. The trick with Red/Green/Blue is to make sure all your adjustments add up to zero, otherwise you'll affect the brightness of the image. For example, if you add 20 to the red channel you should subtract 10 from both the blue and green channels (or two other amounts that add up to 20).

Red/Green/Blue has a few useful presets, like 'Sun exposure', which produces a color cast simulating the warm tones of late afternoon sun. And you can of course save your own presets.

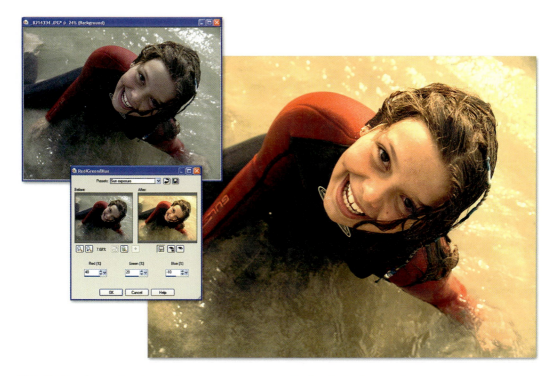

FIG 3.9 Red/Green/Blue can be tricky to use for color correcting, but it's good for effects like this 'Sun exposure' preset.

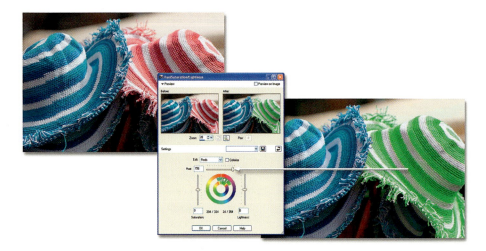

FIG 3.10 By matching a subject color with one of those displayed under the 'Master' drop-down menu and then shifting the Hue values, you can radically change the color in one part of the picture while not affecting anything in the rest of the picture.

Hue/Saturation/Lightness

While it's simple enough to change contrast and color in a photo using the histogram and Color Balance tools, not all picture-makers take the time to adjust the color hue and its intensity or 'saturation'.

PaintShop Photo Pro's Hue/Saturation/Lightness or 'HSL' tool (Adjust > Hue and Saturation > Hue/Saturation/Lightness) is a specialized feature that encompasses controls to change specific color values within a picture, rather than by simply increasing or decreasing its color shades.

What this means, in English, is that you can choose the yellow values and shift them to blue. When this is done, all other colors shift the same amount. So reds shift to green, blues to yellow, and so on. The outer color circle in this dialog represents the original color while the smaller inner color circle represents where that original color has been shifted to.

This tool can be used to remove slight color casts in a picture or to add specific color effects that you might not be able to achieve using one of the Color Balance tools. For my money, the real power in this feature is its ability to shift color values in individual color channels. On some pictures this works as if you have custom-made selections built into the picture.

For example, if it's a snap of a green-colored car, you'll be able to select Green from the 'Master' drop-down menu and change the Hue values so that only the car color changes. How neat is that? If there are other green objects in the frame, these will also change color proportionally; while the selection concept works OK, it's important to note that it's color-specific, not pixel-specific. Options include Reds, Greens, Blues, Cyans, Magentas, and Yellows.

What else can be done using this tool? While hue is an expression of color values within a picture, saturation refers to the intensity of those colors. Saturation is often where we come unstuck! If a photo looks a bit dull you might naturally reach for the Saturation slider and crank it up fully in an attempt to make the photo more attractive.

Superficially this might work quite nicely and will certainly produce seriously attractive colors on screen. However, the trouble with radical saturation increase is that often it becomes unprintable because so much color has been added to the image it's impossible to match using regular inkjet printer inks. The machine will keep firing ink at the paper without any apparent color change. Care must be taken at all times not to overdo the saturation and make an unprintable result.

You can also use this dialog to change the lightness of the image – although I'd choose the Levels dialog for this. The only exception to this rule might be if you are using the tool to make backgrounds – in which case the picture integrity is not paramount. Another neat effect is to colorize the picture by clicking the Colorize checkbox and increasing the Saturation slider. Colorize essentially applies an old-fashioned tinting effect to the picture: the higher the saturation, the stronger the tint. The result is a beautifully tinted light blue/red/yellow/green picture. You see this type of effect a lot in advertising, as it's particularly effective in evoking a mood or specific period in a picture. Click the Colorize checkbox and move the Hue slider, noting how the color in the tint changes. Move the Saturation slider more to increase or reduce the intensity.

If colorizing as a special effect is all you are after, use the Colorize dialog (Adjust > Hue and Saturation > Colorize). This is faster and less complicated than the full-on HSL tool, plus it has the additional benefit of having vari-colored 'Amount' sliders that display the part of the spectrum that the sample is taken from. This is a nice touch.

Hue Map

The Hue Map is another slightly off-center tool used to change specific colors within a picture. This is similar to applying a color change using the HSL tool on a specific channel, as just described. You can select a particular color, move the appropriate slider to choose another hue for that color only, and check the results live. If you then want to change that second color, you must remember to go back to the original slider to make the change, rather than selecting a color that matches the changed state. PaintShop Photo Pro used the original color information as the source for its changes. Check the preview window to locate the (original) color source. Try the Color Replace tool to get a similar result.

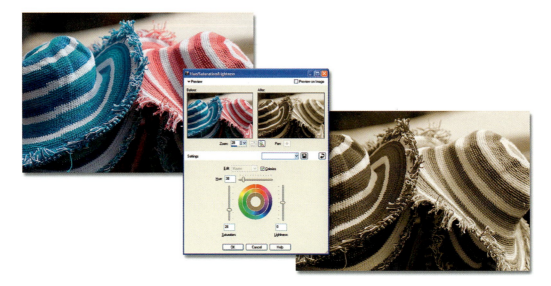

FIG 3.11 In the Hue/Saturation/Lightness dialog, check the Colorize box and watch as PaintShop Photo Pro tints the entire image. Use the Saturation slider to temper the effect.

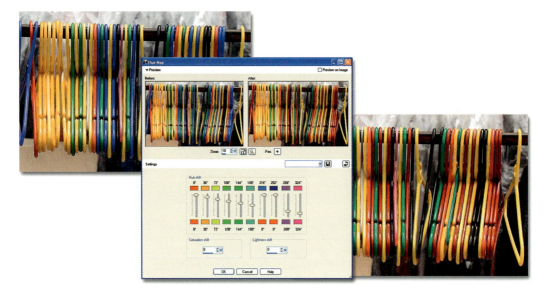

FIG 3.12 The Hue Map works like a graphic equalizer for colors. Use the sliders to change only colors in a specific band of the hue spectrum; here the blue hangers have been changed to red. Fine-tune the effect using the two fields at the base of the dialog for Saturation.

Other Tools for Correcting Exposure Problems

On the Brightness and Contrast submenu of the Adjust menu you'll find no fewer than nine tools for adjusting the tonal values in your pictures. Why so many? Well, many of these tools do the same thing in a slightly different fashion. As you become more experienced you'll no doubt find your own personal favorite. For some people, Levels is the only way to make tonal adjustments to an image; others swear by Histogram Adjustment. There is at least one tonal adjustment tool that's probably best avoided, so we'll deal with that first.

Brightness/Contrast

This is the first option on the Adjust > Brightness and Contrast menu – give it a rearward glance every time you flash past it on your way to more useful tools. The problem with Brightness/Contrast is that it applies a blanket adjustment across the tonal range – there's little that's sophisticated or subtle about it.

When you drag the Brightness slider to the right, each and every pixel value is increased by the same amount and the result is that the highlights in your image quickly disappear. The same happens to the shadows when you go in the opposite direction. Let's waste no more time on it.

Clarify

Clarify applies a contrast boost to photos and sharpens them. As a one-step method for cleaning up photos that lack oomph it works pretty well but, once you've read the section on sharpening later in this chapter, you'll probably want to take a more hands-on approach.

Curves

In some ways, Curves is the most versatile of the tonal adjustment tools because it allows you to experiment with altering pixel values in any one part of the range without affecting the rest. The curve is also a simple concept to grasp. Input values are displayed on the horizontal axis and output values on the vertical axis, so initially the curve is in fact a straight diagonal line running upwards from left to right at 45 degrees.

Dragging the top end of the line horizontally to the left has the same effect as dragging the Highlight Input slider in the Histogram Adjustment or Levels tool to the left. If you click in the center of the line a control point is added and dragging this is akin to moving the Gamma slider in Histogram Adjustment or Levels.

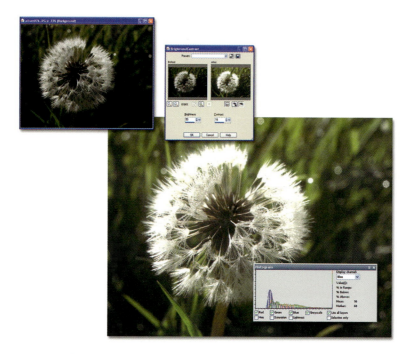

FIG 3.13 OK, this is the last word on Brightness/Contrast. A quick glance at the histogram reveals the damage – no more highlights and shadows turned to mush. You have been warned!

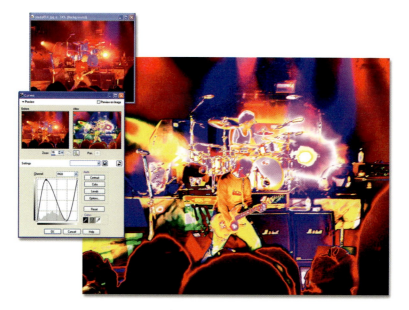

FIG 3.14 Use Curves for ultimate control over specific parts of the tonal range, or special effects. Create a solarization effect using an S-shaped curve or reverse the slope for a negative.

But neither of those tools can match Curves when it comes to tweaking a narrow range of tones. By adding additional points to the curve and adjusting them, you can tweak the shadows whilst leaving the highlights untouched. You can also use Curves for extreme tonal effects. You can create a solarization effect (traditionally achieved in the darkroom by momentarily switching the lights on halfway through processing) by making the curve S-shaped.

Highlight/Midtone/Shadow

This could be quite a useful tool as it provides individual control over the highlights, midtones, and shadows in your photos. However, it is complicated by the fact that, instead of pixel values, it uses percentages. It also has two different ways of applying the figures – an absolute and a relative method – which makes it even more difficult to work out what's going on. There are other tools, namely Histogram Adjustment and Levels, that are more versatile, provide better feedback, and are easier to use.

Histogram Adjustment

The Histogram Adjustment dialog box can be a little intimidating at first glance, but if you've read the earlier section on using the Smart Photo Fix histogram, you'll already be well on your way to getting the most from this versatile tool.

As we discovered earlier, the histogram is a graphical representation of the tonal values of all of the pixels in an image. Black pixels appear on the far left, getting lighter as you move towards the right on the horizontal axis. The more pixels there are of a particular value, the higher the line appears at that point.

The three most useful controls in this dialog box are the triangles that appear beneath the histogram, which allow you to remap the black point, white point, and gamma. To produce an image with good tonal distribution and contrast you should drag the Highlight Input slider (the white triangle) to the right edge of the histogram and the black triangle to the left edge. Use the central Gamma slider to make overall adjustments to the brightness.

There are other controls, like the slider on the right that allows you to expand or compress the midtones for solarization-style effects, but Curves is better suited to making these kinds of adjustments.

Histogram Equalize and Histogram Stretch

These two are essentially one-step applications of specific histogram (or levels, or curves, depending on how you want to look at it) adjustments. Equalize is the least useful of the two as it averages out all the pixel values across the histogram (try pressing F7 to display the Histogram palette, then applying Histogram equalize and you'll see).

Tip

You can apply any of these histogram adjustments to selections. Make the selection first, save it, and then run the tone adjustment, as described.

Histogram stretch automatically sets the black and white points to the values of the darkest and lightest pixels in the image. It's exactly the same as selecting Histogram Adjustment and dragging the triangle controls explained in the previous section to the ends of the histogram. As such, it's an excellent one-step contrast fix.

Levels

The controls in the Levels dialog box work in a similar way to those of the Histogram Adjustment tool. You can use the Output Levels controls to reduce contrast in the shadows and highlights. This is the best way to produce a 'knocked back' image tint for a panel on a website or printed publication that has text running over the top. By dragging the black Output Levels slider to the right, you can lighten the dark pixels in the image and still retain detail in the midtones and highlights.

Threshold

Threshold converts an image to pure black and white – what used to be called 'lineart'. Enter the value that determines whether pixels are converted to black or white in the Threshold dialog box. The default is 128 – any pixels darker than a midtone gray are turned black and any lighter are turned white. As with desaturation, Threshold removes the color, but doesn't change the image mode, making it possible to add color back in and produce interesting graphic effects.

Using Fill Flash and Backlighting

While the Histogram Adjustment tool provides ultimate control of image tonal values throughout the entire range, sometimes that can be its biggest drawback. Often you'll want to change tonal values in one part of the range – the shadows or the highlights. The difficulty with using the Histogram Adjustment tool in such circumstances is that, more often than not, while you can make considerable improvements in one part of the image it's at the cost of lost image detail elsewhere in the tonal range.

For example, in trying to get back shadow detail in underexposed areas you'll often find that you lose detail in the highlights. Likewise, attempting to restore detail in overexposed areas, the sky for example, you'll find that shadow detail disappears into the darkness.

You can get around this problem by making careful feathered selections, but PaintShop Photo Pro X3 has two filters aimed at precisely this problem: the Fill Flash filter and the Backlighting filter.

Tip

Though not all the tonal adjustment tools have their own histogram display (Levels being the prime example), the new live Histogram palette can be used instead. Prior to selecting Levels (or Curves, or Highlights/ Midtones/Shadows), press F7 to display the Histogram palette. Now, when you click the Proof or Auto Proof button the Live Histogram palette will automatically update.

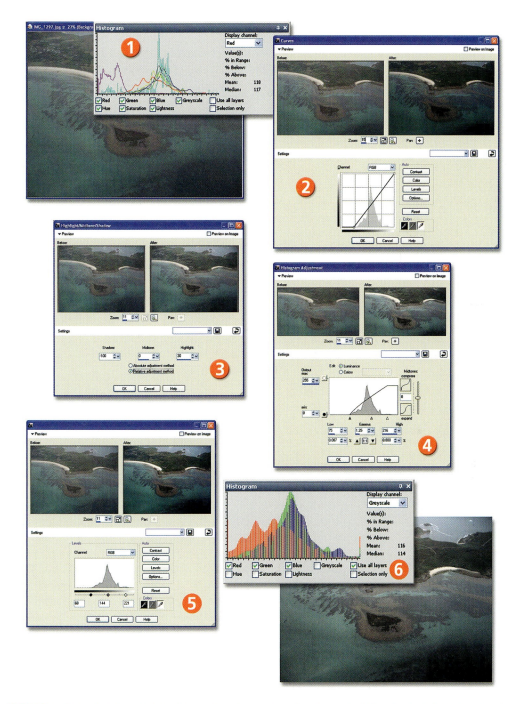

FIG 3.15 Each of the tonal adjustment tools has their strengths and any can be used to achieve a straightforward contrast adjustment as shown here. (1) Press F7 to display the Histogram palette and confirm the problem. (2) Curves. (3) Highlight/Midtone/Shadow. (4) Histogram Adjustment. (5) Levels. (6) The adjusted image with new histogram covering the entire tonal range.

The Fill Flash Filter

As its name suggests, the Fill Flash filter provides the digital equivalent of fill-in flash – a photographic technique that uses flash in daylight conditions to provide fill-in lighting for shadow detail.

The kind of situation where you might use fill-in flash is where the subject is strongly backlit, for example in front of a window or on a beach. Typically, camera automatic metering systems select an average exposure setting for such situations, resulting in very dark shadows. The Fill Flash filter allows you to lighten the tones in the shadows while leaving the midtones and highlights unaffected.

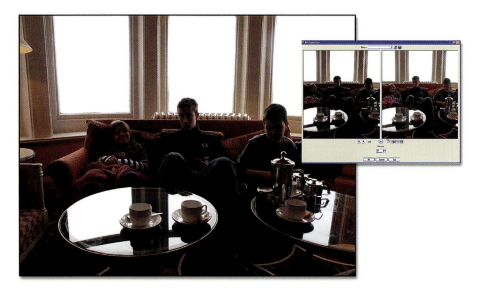

FIG 3.16 Use the Fill Flash filter to restore detail in shadow areas of strongly backlit subjects.

To use Fill Flash click the Fill Flash button on the Photo toolbar or select Fill Flash from the Adjust menu. Maximize the Fill Flash dialog box so you can see a generously sized before and after preview and use the Zoom tools so that most of the photo is in view. You can adjust the amount of fill flash applied by entering a value in the Strength field, or by using the slider just below it. The default setting of 40 works well with all but very underexposed images. If you need to apply more than 60 keep an eye out for noise – a speckled grainy appearance in areas of flat color or tone. The Fill Flash filter also includes a Saturation slider that can be used to add or remove color.

The Backlighting Filter

The Backlighting filter solves the opposite problem to Fill Flash. Where the camera has made a suitable exposure to capture good shadow detail in an image with a wide tonal range, the highlight detail will be overexposed. This often happens to the sky detail on photos taken in the shade on bright sunny days. The Backlighting filter can help restore highlight detail without affecting shadow areas. Select the Backlighting filter by clicking its button on the Photo toolbar or from the Adjust menu (Adjust > Backlighting).

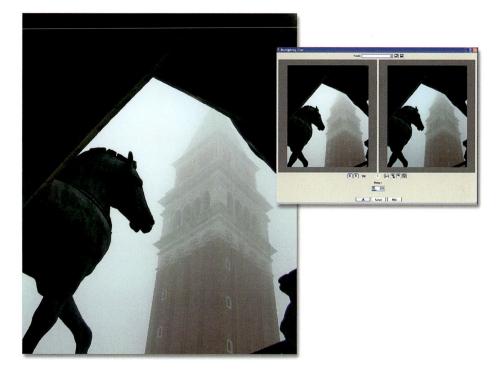

FIG 3.17 Use the Backlighting filter to restore burnt out highlights.

Making Photos Appear Sharper

Sounds too good to be true? While it's acceptable to change color, contrast, or saturation in a digital file, changing the sharpness is a little trickier.

PaintShop Photo Pro has several tools designed to make pictures appear sharper than when they were scanned or shot using a digital camera. For some this might seem a godsend, but it's important to note that you can never really change an out-of-focus picture to one that looks pin-sharp. Even well-focused digital shots can look a little soft, however, and that's something that can be fixed.

How does this magic work? Most sharpness tools act on picture contrast. You might have noticed this using the Histogram tools. A general contrast boost usually makes a picture appear sharper.

PaintShop Photo Pro has several sharpness filters. Clarify is a one-button filter used to add a quick bump in contrast and image sharpness. Most times this works well; however, for total control you have to use the perversely named Unsharp Mask filter. What this does is apply a selected contrast boost, at pixel level, to parts of the picture with varying lightness levels.

The reason that this is the best picture-sharpening tool is that it has three adjustable controls written into the equation: Radius, Strength, and Clipping. Radius selects the number of pixels around the point of contrast difference. Strength controls the amount of contrast added to those pixels, while Clipping affects the lightness of the chosen pixels.

One of the disadvantages in sharpening digital pictures is that the filter is non-discretionary; it has a habit of sharpening the bits you don't want to sharpen as well as the bits you do. This includes any digital noise, film grain, or other electronic imperfections that have been added to the file along the way. So, the more it's sharpened, the more noticeable the imperfections (the digital noise) become. Help is at hand, though, because the main reason for the dialog controls is to help in minimizing this inevitable noise increase.

- Too much Radius creates a nasty-looking whitish halo throughout the high-contrast sections of the picture.
- Too much Strength adds an equally fiendish grittiness that looks particularly bad once in print.
- Too much Clipping makes the picture appear soft, destroying the sharpness effect entirely.

Like all sophisticated photo-editing tools, unsharp masking requires practice to get right. There's no 'perfect' setting because some pictures need more sharpening than others.

The picture's application also has a profound impact on how you sharpen its pixels; inkjet prints need less sharpening than those designed for commercial printing. If you are submitting pictures to a third-party publication, call the relevant art department first to check on that publication's specific material (sharpening) requirements, if any.

As a general rule start with:

- A Radius of 1 or 2 pixels
- A Strength of between 100 and 200
- A Clipping value of 'zero'.

If nothing seems to improve in the picture with these settings, increase the Strength value. Then try increasing the Radius value (a bit at a time). If the Unsharp Mask effect is applied to a high-contrast picture, you'll need to enter a small Clipping value to soften its impact. The beauty of this is that you see what you are getting instantly and can make changes live before applying them to the full-resolution version.

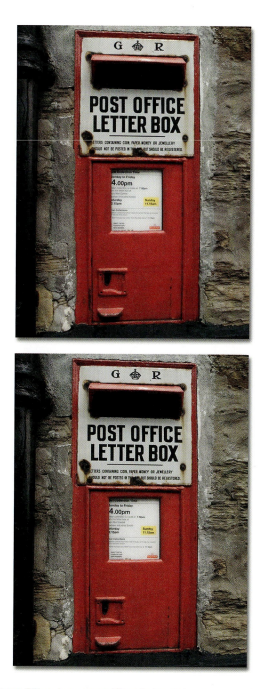

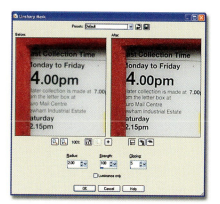

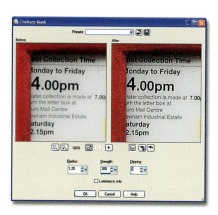

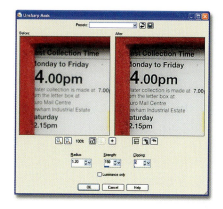

FIG 3.18 Different images require different Unsharp Mask settings, so a trial and revise approach is required. The trick is to increase overall sharpness without introducing sharpening 'artifacts'. Reducing the Radius from its default setting of 2 and increasing the Strength to 300 introduces unwanted white specks. You could eliminate these using the Clipping slider, but it's better just to reduce the Strength until they disappear. A final setting of Radius 1.20, Strength 150, and Clipping 5 results in a sharper image with minimal sharpening artifacts.

PaintShop Photo Pro comes with two other no-brainer sharpen tools: the Sharpen and the Sharpen More filters. The Sharpen filter is a good place to start; it applies a preset contrast boost to a selected range of pixels. This might be enough to give most digital snaps a nice sharpen. For a stronger filter effect, try the Sharpen More filter. This is slightly more radical, though still by no means as radical as the Unsharp Mask filter can be. The good thing about these effects is that they are repeatable. If the effect isn't strong enough, repeat it using the keyboard shortcut Ctrl + Y till it is.

High Pass Sharpening

As we've already mentioned, one of the problems with unsharp masking is that it can sharpen parts of the image you just don't want to sharpen. PaintShop Photo Pro X3 includes a method of sharpening that doesn't suffer from these drawbacks because it confines sharpening only to edge detail and other high-contrast areas within an image.

High pass sharpening isn't new, but previously it was a complicated business that involved duplicating layers, applying a High Pass filter, or creating an edge mask and using Layer blend modes. While all this was great fun, the new High Pass Sharpen filter makes things much easier. See the step-by-step work-through at the end of the chapter to find out how to get the best from High Pass Sharpen.

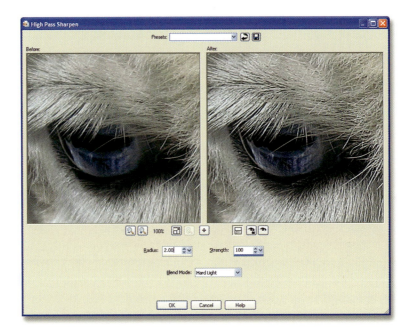

FIG 3.19 Use PaintShop Photo Pro's High Pass Sharpen filter to sharpen edge detail without exaggerating noise and other unwanted detail.

Tips for Making Digital Files Appear Sharper

- If using a digital camera, make sure that the picture is exposed correctly and that the focus is correct for the subject. It's possible to enlarge the image on the camera LCD screen to check this focus closely. If you think that there's a problem, erase that frame and reshoot.
- In Shutter (Tv) or Manual (M) shoot modes, pick a faster shutter speed (a higher number) to 'freeze' action, essential if the subject is fast-moving.
- Learn to use the AF lock in the camera. This works by half-depressing the shutter button that activates the AF system. Once the in-camera audio 'beep' confirmation sounds, you can then either press the shutter fully or reframe to position a subject off-center and then take the picture. The most obvious cause of out-of-focus snaps is from the subject not being in the camera's AF focusing area when the shutter button is pressed.
- Scans normally require unsharp masking to compensate for the scan process, which can make things appear slightly unsharp.
- Most scanner software comes with inbuilt Unsharp Mask filters to compensate for quality loss. Most will not be as good as PaintShop Photo Pro's Sharpen tools. You might want to leave that feature switched off and sharpen the files using PSP later. It's always preferable to have an untouched 'Master' file on your hard drive. Once an effect like unsharp masking has been added to a file, it's impossible to remove.
- The same can be said for in-camera sharpen functions. Switch this off and apply it using your software.
- Use PaintShop Photo Pro's Overview palette to move the view around the preview picture. Sharpening never has the same effect across all sections of a picture, so it pays to check the important bits up close.
- If you just don't have a clue where to start, try the Randomize tab. It's a good starting place and one that's likely to come up with an answer in a matter of a few clicks.

Adding Soft Focus Effects

In a digital file, regular blur filters never produce as nice a result as you'd get using film and real glass soft focus filter screwed to the front of a lens.

PaintShop Photo Pro addresses this problem with a Soft Focus filter. The difference between this and the straight 'blur everything' filter set (Average, Blur, Blur More, Gaussian Blur, Motion Blur, Radial Blur) is that the former applies more blur to the highlights than to the other tones. This produces an effect similar to the effect that you'd get using a regular glass photographic filter – only PaintShop Photo Pro offers a wealth of controls over how you can influence the way that the blur looks.

You can vary the overall softness of the filter, as well as the edge importance (edge sharpness), plus there are three controls for adjusting the blur halo (Amount, Size, and Visibility).

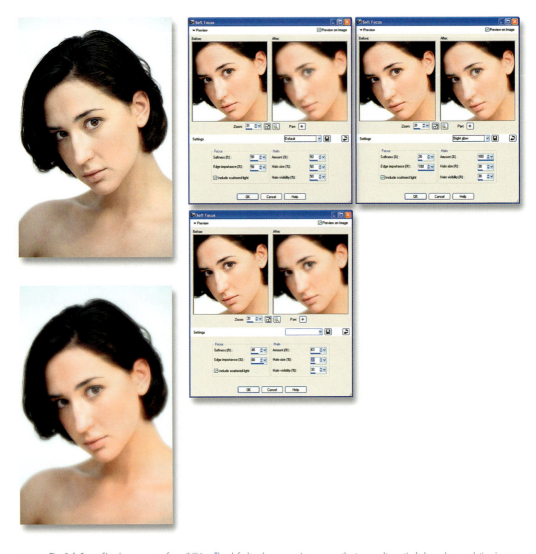

FIG 3.20 The Soft Focus filter has a range of possibilities. The default values may give an over-the-top result, particularly on low-resolution images. The presets provide good results, though, and you can experiment with the sliders to get the exact effect you're after.
Picture: Nathan Blaney, iStockphoto 1790776

Much time has been put into creating this filter and it works extremely well, emulating the precise look of a glass filter costing more than PaintShop Photo Pro itself. As with most filters, it's possible to try a combination of effects using the Randomize tab. You can also save a particular combination for use any other time via the Preset tab.

Step-by-Step Projects

Technique: Improving Your Photos Using Smart Photo Fix

Often, you can make big improvements to photos that lack contrast, look a bit washed out, are a little on the dark side, or slightly substandard in some other way using One Step Photo Fix.

Sometimes, though, One Step Photo Fix doesn't result in a big improvement and you need to take matters into your own hands. If you don't feel confident about dealing directly with tools like Histogram Adjustment and Color Balance, then Smart Photo Fix is the tool for you. It has automatic features that can improve contrast, saturation, color balance and sharpness, but it also gives you control over what's happening, so if things don't look quite right, you can tweak the results.

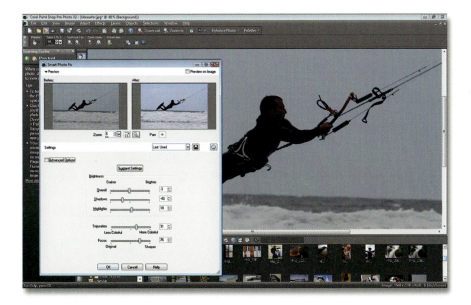

STEP 1 Open the image you want to fix and select Smart Photo Fix from the Palettes menu on the Standard toolbar, or by selecting Adjust > Smart Photo Fix.

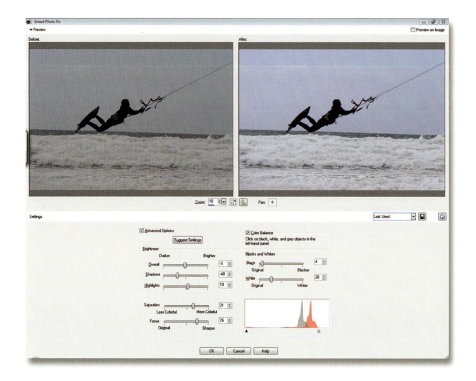

STEP 2 Maximize the Smart Photo Fix dialog box to fill the screen, then check the Advanced Options box to display the histogram, Black and White point sliders, and the Color Balance checkbox. You'll notice that some or all of the sliders have moved from the zero positions. Smart Photo Fix has analyzed the photo and these are its suggested settings. Half the time this will work just fine, but this picture is in the other category. You can see the effect in the 'after' preview thumbnail on the right. The suggested settings have improved things a little, but some problems have been ignored and some things have actually been made worse.

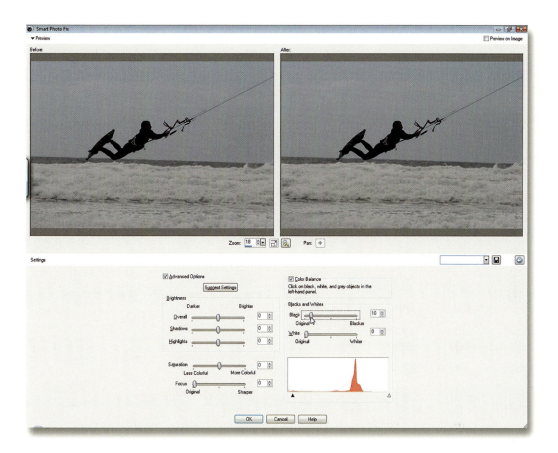

STEP 3 Select default from the preset menu to return all the settings to zero. The first job is to set the Black and White point sliders so that the darkest and lightest pixels in the photo reach either end of the histogram. Drag the Black slider to the right and watch the black triangle under the histogram – it too moves to the right as you drag the slider. Stop dragging when you reach the first peak or bump in the histogram – in this case there's a small group of pixels at around the 10 mark.

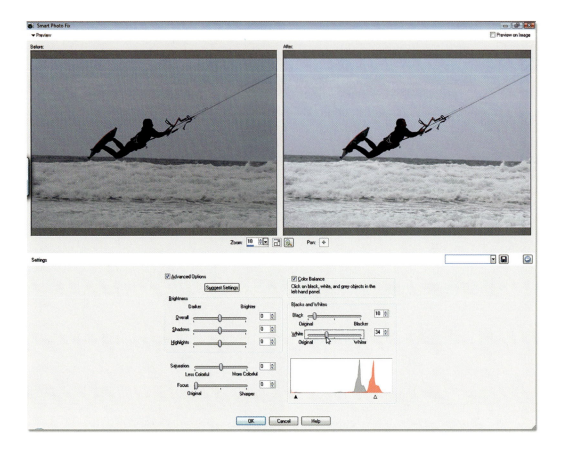

STEP 4 Now drag the White slider until the white triangle reaches the first bump or peak on the right side of the histogram – in this case there's a shallow plateau that starts at 34 – before the big peak nearer the middle. What you've just done is remap the darkest and lightest pixels in the photo to pure black and white. The new histogram is overlaid in red on the old gray one. You can see the improvement in the 'after' preview, but if you're still not quite sure how you've managed this, take another look at 'Using the Histogram' on page 66.

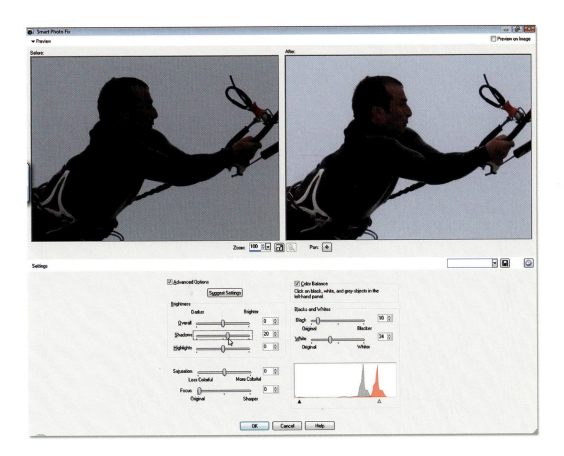

STEP 5 Often, adjusting the Black and White sliders will be all that's needed, but the Brightness controls can be used to add detail to the shadows and highlights and to brighten or darken the image overall. Click the 'Zoom image to 100%' button under the thumbnails and use the Pan tool to center the kitesurfer. Drag the Shadow slider to 20 to bring out the detail in his face and wetsuit.

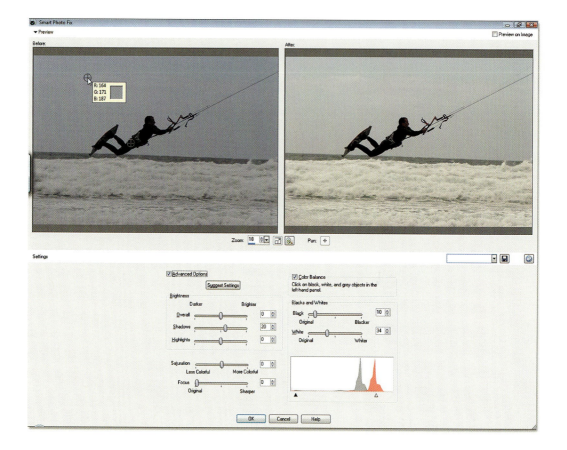

STEP 6 The next problem is the color balance. This photo looks much bluer than the actual conditions in which it was shot. Click the 'Fit image to window' button and correct the blue cast by checking the Color Balance box and clicking with the eyedropper to place a color sampler on any part of the photo that should be neutral, i.e. black, white, or gray. Here I've placed markers on the kitesurfer's black wetsuit and a white cloud. If positioning a marker produces unexpected or undesirable results, click on the marker again to remove it.

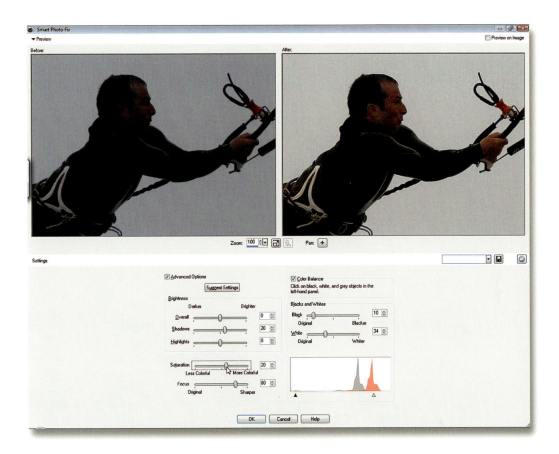

STEP 7 Before sharpening the photo, click the 'Zoom image to 100%' button under the thumbnails. Drag the Focus slider to the right to sharpen the image, but don't go too far or you'll exaggerrate noise and make the photo look 'grainy'. Finally, drag the Saturation slider to the right (again, be careful not to overdo it) to give the color a bit of a boost and click OK to apply the changes.

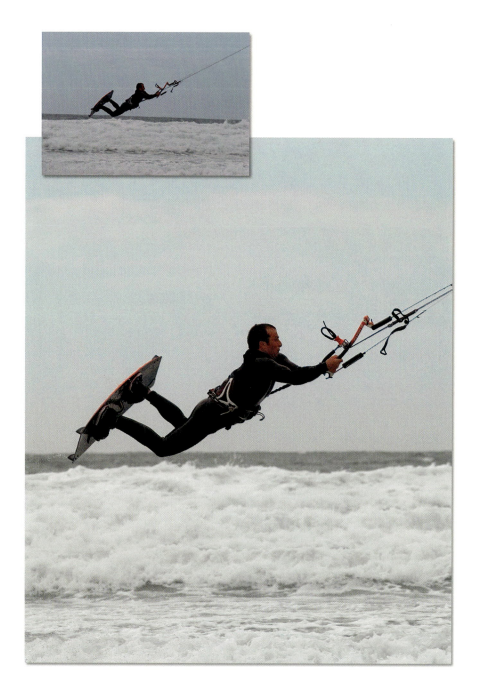

STEP 8 It doesn't end with Smart Photo Fix; there are lots of other simple things you can do to improve photos and give them more impact. Here I've used the Crop tool to remove some of the background, change the aspect ratio, and straighten the horizon.

Technique: Sharpening Photos Using the High Pass Sharpen Filter

The High Pass Sharpen filter is a real lifesaver with certain kinds of images. While Unsharp Mask does a fantastic job 90% of the time, as we've seen, it's indiscriminate and can create problems, or at least make existing ones more obvious.

The kinds of photos you should avoid unsharp masking include:

- Those taken on a high ISO setting (400 and above) which will, depending on how good your camera is, display at least some visible noise.
- Photos that were badly exposed and have had a large tonal correction applied using Smart Photo Fix, Histogram Adjustment, or one of the other tonal adjustment tools.
- Photos with high JPEG compression applied, either because they were taken using a low-quality camera setting, or have subsequently been recompressed using a low-quality JPEG setting.
- Photos that are well exposed, of a high quality and fine in every other respect, but have large areas of flat color, such as an expanse of clear blue sky.

For all of these images and anything else that fails to come up shining using the Unsharp Mask filter, follow these steps.

STEP 1 Open the image to be sharpened. If you plan on using 'Preview on Image' to preview the effect then first make sure to zoom in to 100% view (keyboard shortcut Ctrl + Alt + N). Always view sharpening adjustments at 100% magnification as it's the only way you can really see what's happening to the individual pixels in the image.

STEP 2 Select Adjust > Sharpness > High Pass Sharpen to open the High Pass Sharpen dialog box and use the Pan button to select a representative part of the image. To preview the sharpening in the image window check the Preview on Image checkbox having first zoomed to 100% view as described in Step 1.

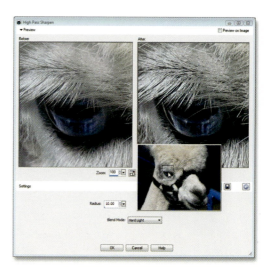

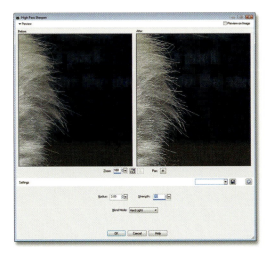

STEP 3 The High Pass Sharpen dialog box has three settings – Radius, Strength, and Blend Mode. The default values for these are 10, 70, and Hard Light respectively. The Radius setting determines the distance within which the filter looks for dissimilar pixels to sharpen. A larger Radius value will result in more of the image being sharpened, a smaller one will sharpen less. With zero Radius none of the image is sharpened. Use the Pan button to find part of the image you don't want sharpened (the sky, or out-of-focus background) and adjust the Radius to a value just below that at which you can see a change.

STEP 4 Now use the Pan button to center a part of the image that's representative of what you want to sharpen. If necessary adjust the Amount slider to increase or decrease the amount of sharpening applied.

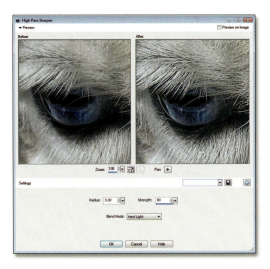

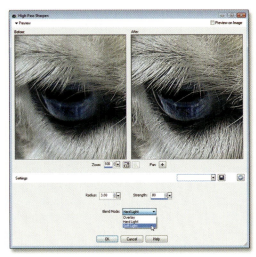

STEP 5 The Hard Light blend mode produces the most dramatic sharpening. To reduce the effect change the blend mode to Overlay and for even gentler sharpening use the Soft Light blend mode.

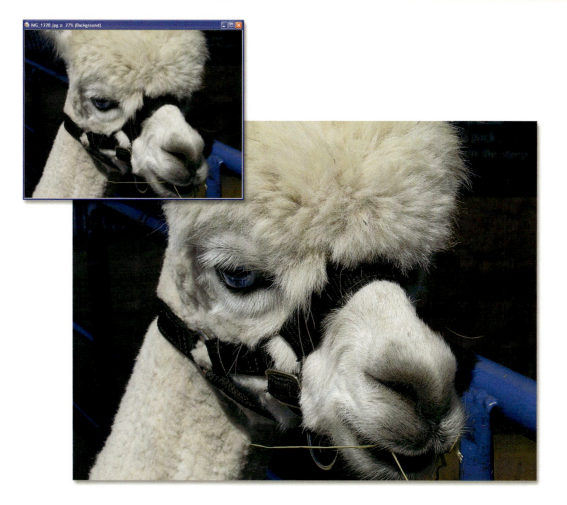

PaintShop Photo Pro X3's High Pass Sharpen filter makes a fantastic job of sharpening edge detail in images like this, without affecting out-of-focus areas or compounding common digital image problems like noise.

CHAPTER 4

Image Manipulation – Beyond the Basics

What's Covered in this Chapter

- So far we've looked at what PaintShop Photo Pro X3 has to offer in terms of features and tools for organizing and editing your photos, and covered some of the basics of image editing. We've also looked at how to fix photos that have a problem with brightness or color.
- This chapter is called 'Beyond the Basics' because we're going to look at some more complex features than the 'one-step' fixes and tonal and color adjustment tools covered in the previous chapters.
- The chapter begins by looking at some of the methods for removing scratches and blemishes from your photos. This is a particular problem with scans of prints, slides and negatives, and also when using digital SLRs, which can get dust on the sensor leading to blotchy photos.
- The same techniques can be usefully applied to removing other things that you don't want in your photos, such as lampposts, trees, and people you're no longer on speaking terms with. You'll learn how to become an expert retoucher with the Clone tool and about some other tools for fixing damaged photos.

PaintShop Photo Pro X3 for Photographers. DOI: 10.1016/B978-0-240-52165-7.10004-8

- As in the last chapter, it's not all about fixing things. Later on in the chapter you'll discover how to produce black and white photos from color originals using Black and White Film photo effects, and how to produce tints and color overlay effects to add extra depth and tone to black and white photos.
- Digital noise can be a real problem when shooting in low-light conditions using a high ISO setting on your camera. PaintShop Photo Pro X3 has one of the best tools around for dealing with this problem and I'll go into detail on how to get the most from it. I'll also show you how to add noise to your photos to create atmospheric grain effects.
- Finally, there's a brief introduction to PaintShop Photo Pro's Scripting features. Scripts are one of PaintShop Photo Pros's most powerful features, allowing you to automatically record and apply a sequence of editing steps to any number of photos.
- The step-by-step projects at the end of the chapter guide you through the process of restoring badly damaged photos and applying a hand-colored effect to black and white pictures.

No matter how careful you might be when scanning film or prints, dirt always gets in the way and inevitably ends up on the scan. PaintShop Photo Pro has a good range of filter-based tools designed for cleaning up or removing these problem areas, however bad they might appear. Dirt isn't only a problem with scanned photos. If you use a digital SLR you may have noticed slight dark blotches on your photos. These are caused by small particles of dust that find their way into the camera body and settle on the sensor. Eventually, you will need to clean the sensor, or have it done for you, but in the meantime you can use the techniques described below to fix the problem.

Removing Scratches and Blemishes from Scans

You might never realize quite how dirty scans can be unless they are magnified to a size that reveals the mess. If you only enlarge your snaps to about 6 inches × 4 inches, the worst dust blemishes may ever become apparent. If you print to 20 inches × 16 inches, however, you might get a shock when you see the dirt and surface scratch marks picked up by the scanner!

Tip

Don't use filters to remove large blemishes; they aren't that effective and will degrade the overall picture quality. Use the Clone or Scratch Remover tool instead.

The first thing to do is rescan the print or negative. Clean the flatbed scanner's glass platen, the place where the print is positioned. Use a mild window cleaner and a soft, lint-free cloth (i.e. linen). Finger grease, however minimal, is a great dust attractant so don't forget to gently wipe the surface of the print as well. If scanning film, use an appropriate film-cleaning solution and soft cloth.

Once the scan is made, open the file in PaintShop Photo Pro and enlarge the file to between 200% and 400%. Do you see dust specks that weren't there in the original? They probably were there, but were just too small to be noticed. If you are planning to enlarge and print to A3, or bigger, you might need to run one, or more, of PaintShop Photo Pro's clean-up filters over the file to improve the quality.

Here's how: open the picture and crop to suit. Many scanners are more than generous with their flatbed scan areas, adding extra 'real estate' to the edges of the print or transparency. Select the Crop tool from the Tools toolbar and, when the Crop Box appears, drag it to the required dimensions and click the Apply button (to maintain the aspect ratio use the Maintain Aspect Ratio checkbox in the tool's Options palette).

Assess the damage. Enlarge the file to 400% or 500% by clicking on the picture with the Zoom tool (keyboard shortcut 'Z'; left-click or push your mouse wheel forward with your index finger to zoom in on the affected area) and, using the Pan tool (keyboard shortcut 'A'), move the picture around the screen for a closer inspection. Increase or decrease the magnification according to the amount of detail you might want to retouch. If it's a high-resolution scan (i.e. scanned for A2 output), you'll have to zoom in on the image further, say up to 400%, to see the same (scratch) detail as if it were scanned to A4 and magnified only to 200%.

A quick way to remove dust spots blanket fashion is to run a filter over the entire picture. Zoom to 100% view (Ctrl + Alt + N) and select the Automatic Small Scratch Removal filter from the Adjust > Add/Remove Noise menu (Adjust > Add/Remove Noise > Automatic Small Scratch Removal). To preview the effect check the Preview on Image checkbox in the Filter dialog box. Most filters and effects have this option; though it takes a while longer to display, you get a much clearer picture of the result than with the dialog box thumbnail previews.

Try the default settings first. The reason there are many variants is to cover the multiple quality situations scanning introduces. Note that there are check-boxes for 'light' and 'dark' scratches, a contrast inhibitor (move the sliders to the center to limit the contrast range), as well as three filter strength settings. It's important to remember that, with this and most of PaintShop Pro's other filter-based tools, the dialog window offers multiple options so that you can customize all actions to suit whatever image you have open. If the filter effect doesn't work fully first time, try another combination. With some filters you can use the Randomize button to get the program to make the decision for you.

Scratch Removal filters apply their effects globally. For specifically difficult or large blemishes, use a scratch removal tool locally first. This is a more effective technique because you can limit the filter's softening action to a small area of the scan only. There is no point in softening the entire picture to remove one or two scratches.

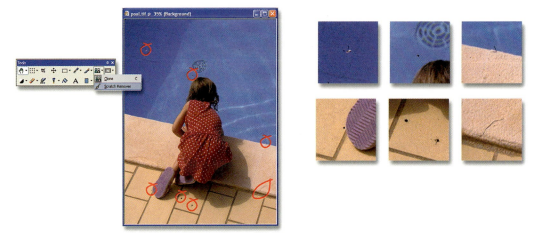

FIG 4.1 Color negatives and transparencies are among the worst culprits for attracting dirt and scratches. Although they may look OK to the naked eye, the high degree of scanning enlargement necessary to produce a decent-sized digital image also enlarges the dirt. A global filter won't do the job – you will need to individually retouch these marks out with the Scratch Remover and Clone tools. The same applies for blotches caused by dust on the sensor of a digital SLR.

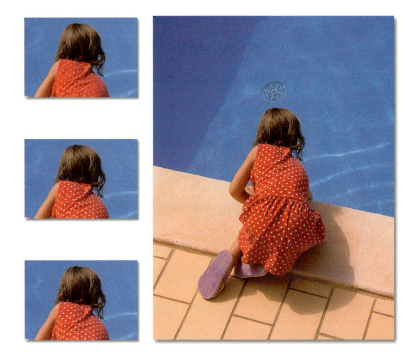

FIG 4.2 The Salt and Pepper (top), Median (middle), and Edge Preserving Smooth (bottom) filters can be used for removing dust or subtly softening skin blemishes, but the filter strength required to remove larger spots and scratches results in unacceptable loss of overall image quality. The best result (right) is achieved by repeated application of the Scratch Removal and Clone tools.

Click the small black triangle next to the Clone Brush and choose the Scratch Remover tool from the fly-out. Drag the cursor over the blemish to remove or soften it. PaintShop Photo Pro clones/blurs out the damaged pixels. This is quite a fast tool to use and, like most of the tools in PaintShop Photo Pro, it has a preset save function allowing you to create your own customized scratch remove brushes. Once satisfied that Paint-Shop Photo Pro has removed/diffused enough of the small scratches to make the scan appear credible, save the file under another name before continuing with further editing (always keep the original file untouched, where possible).

Other smoothing filters to try:

- Salt and Pepper filter
- Despeckle filter
- Median filter
- Edge Preserving Smooth filter.

(All of these are found on the Adjust > Add/Remove Noise menu.)

Controlling Digital Noise

Photos taken with a digital camera all suffer, to a greater or lesser extent, from a phenomenon called 'digital noise', which gives digital photos a speckled, grainy appearance. Noise is generated by a camera's electronic circuitry, mostly when the electrical current generated by the image sensor is amplified before being digitally sampled.

If you've owned a film camera, you'll be familiar with film grain (clumps of silver in a photographic emulsion that become visible when enlarged) and you'll also be aware that fast films (those with higher sensitivity to light) exhibit more grain than slow ones.

With digital cameras it's the same story; if you set your camera to a higher ISO rating, to capture images in low-light conditions, the digital noise becomes worse. Depending on your camera, you may not notice noise on images

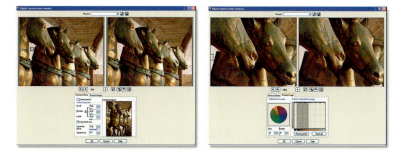

FIG 4.3 The Digital Camera Noise Removal filter allows you to remove noise from some areas of the image whilst protecting others.

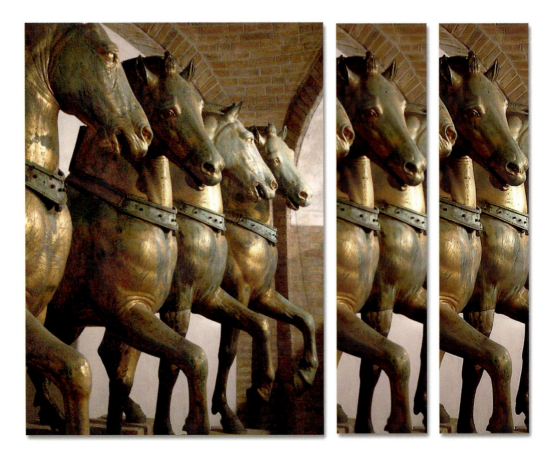

FIG 4.4 Noise-wise, this is about as bad as it gets. The original image (left) was shot with the camera set to 1600 ISO. The center section shows the results of the DCNR filter on the default settings and, on the right, the same settings with 70% sharpen.

taken at an ISO setting of 200 or lower, but at settings above 400 ISO, particularly at larger image sizes, noise can become very intrusive.

Digital noise can also occur as a result of long exposures – shots taken at night are often prone to noise because of the high ISO setting used, combined with long exposures.

In some circumstances you can live with noise. Like film grain it can provide a gritty atmospheric realism. Mostly though, it's something you'd rather do without. You can't get rid of noise entirely, but you can reduce it. Before version 9, PaintShop Pro users had to rely on techniques using the Salt and Pepper, Median, Texture Preserving Smooth, and other filters on the Adjust > Add/Remove Noise menu. Now we have the Digital Camera Noise Removal filter, which, for the sake of brevity, I'll call the DCNR filter.

Select Adjust > Digital Camera Noise Removal, or click the DCNR button on the Photo toolbar. The DCNR filter provides a quite sophisticated dialog box with the usual 'before' and 'after' preview windows and two tabbed panels labeled 'Remove Noise' and 'Protect Image'. Maximize the dialog box to get the biggest preview possible so that you can see the noise and what the filter is doing to the image detail. Use the Pan tool (it appears automatically in most of the Filter dialog boxes when you mouse over the right-hand 'after' preview) to select a representative area of the image.

In the Noise Correction pane, the three input boxes and sliders control the degree of noise removal for small, medium, and large noise artifacts. Clicking the Link Detail Sizes box locks these three together, maintaining the relationship between them – so if you increase one of them by, say, 5, they all increase by 5.

In practice, you'll get better results by using a higher value in the small field than in the other two, but much depends on the image and you'll need to experiment. When you apply the DCNR filter it combines the corrected image with the original one and the value in the Correction Blend field determines the proportions of the two; 100 is all corrected image and no original. By lowering this value you lessen the degree to which the correction is effective, but also minimize overall loss of image detail. Finally, you can sharpen, which will help restore detail softened by the noise reduction process.

On the left of the Remove Noise tab there's a thumbnail preview with, initially, two cross-hair targets on it. These are the sampling regions; they appear in the 'before' preview window as rectangular marquees with resize handles. You can move and resize the existing sampling regions (by clicking and dragging them) and create new ones (by clicking and dragging anywhere in the left preview window). Try to sample image areas where noise is particularly bad, or that are representative of noise in large areas of the picture. Careful sampling will help the DCNR filter to distinguish noise from genuine image detail.

Tip

You can save DCNR filter settings as a preset and easily reapply them to other images taken on the same camera with the same ISO settings.

(a) **(b)**

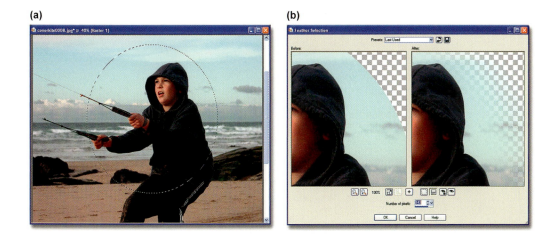

FIG 4.5 (a) Adding noise can transform a photo into something quite special. Here I have drawn an elliptical selection. (b) The next stage is to apply a feather to this selection to soften the edges (in this example, by 143 pixels).

FIG 4.6 Use Levels to brighten the center of the picture (i.e. the bit that's selected), then press Ctrl + D to select None and add the grain effect to the entire image using the Add Noise. The final stage involves adding a blur effect using the Radial Blur filter in Zoom mode. You can restrict the effect to the outside of the image — keeping the center sharp either using the filter's Protect center controls, or by making a selection.

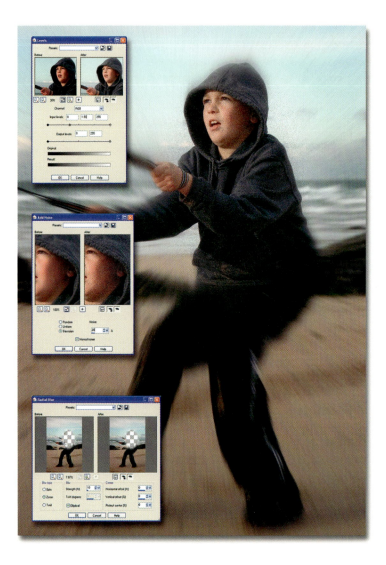

Another way to protect parts of the image from the unwanted attention of the DCNR filter is to use the Protect Image tab, where you can select a range of colors from within the image that you don't want processed by the filter. The simplest way to use this feature is to Ctrl-drag the area you want to protect in the left preview window.

PaintShop Photo Pro also has a filter that is ideally suited for adding noise (Add Noise). Why add noise to a digital photo? For several reasons.

All retouching, whether you are using a filter effect or a specific retouching tool (like the Clone or Scratch Remover tools), smooths out textures. This is an excellent result for portraits, glamor, fashion, and any other applications where flattery pays.

But if one area of the picture has had too much retouching, it will look smoother than the rest of the image. Add noise to the retouched section to make it appear more like the rest of the photo rather than attempt to smooth out the entire picture. You can also add noise to increase the grittiness and overall impact in a picture (see illustration). There are several ways to do this:

- Add noise to the retouched section using one of the textures from the Materials palette.
- Copy the Background layer, make sure that the new layer is selected, and use PaintShop Photo Pro's Add Noise filter to add a suitable quantity of noise to match the rest of the image. Then, using the Eraser tool, rub out the bits of the top layer that have had no retouching done to them.
- Apply noise using a selection.

Retouching Using the Clone Brush

The Clone Brush is possibly the most useful of all PaintShop Photo Pro's retouching tools because it can be used for repairing damaged pictures and for improving photos with distracting background, or other unwanted detail. Learn how to use this tool with skill and it'll open up potential you never thought possible with your current photo-retouching skills.

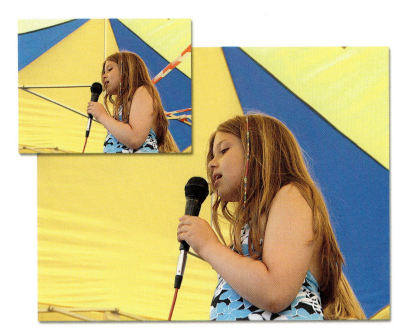

FIG 4.7 The Clone tool can do a lot more than remove a few spots and scratches from old photos. Use it to remove distracting background detail, unwanted objects, and even people from your pictures.

There's no big mystery to the Clone Brush. What it does is simply to copy one part of a picture into the clipboard or temporary memory (this is called the 'Source') and paste it over another part of the picture (called the 'Target'). Typically this tool is used for repairing damaged prints. Tears, scratches, blemishes, and dust spots picked up by a scanner can all be things of the past using the Clone Brush. Where the Clone Brush has a distinct advantage over dust and scratch removal filters (discussed earlier in this chapter) is that it has a local effect. You only retouch the bits that need retouching. Filters, on the other hand, apply a blanket effect, softening the entire picture rather than just the blemishes.

In Use

Choose the Clone Brush from the Tools toolbar (keyboard shortcut 'C'). This is shared with the Scratch Remover and Object Remover tools so you might have to click the latter's icon and reselect Clone from the fly-out menu. Make sure that the Tool Options palette is also open by right-clicking on the Menu bar and choosing Tool Options from the palette's submenu. Pressing F4 toggles the Tool Options palette on and off.

To make the Clone Brush work properly you must select a Source area. First off, find a spot in the picture that is tonally close to the tone in the section to be replaced. There's no point in trying to copy a dark patch over a light patch. The light patch goes dark with the copied pixels and ends up looking unconvincing.

Move the brush over this area and right-click once with the mouse. This sets the Source point and copies the pixels that are under the brush. Move the brush to the target section of the picture, left-click and drag to paint. This pastes or 'clones' the copied pixels over the damaged pixels. You should see the target section disappear or, at least, reduce in intensity.

The Clone Brush has several options designed to fine-tune the brush performance. These include brush Size, Shape, Step, Density, Thickness, Rotation, Opacity and Blend mode. The most important controls to try first are the brush Size, its Opacity and, finally, the Blend mode.

Setting brush size is important. If there are huge scratches, large fade spots or ripped sections in the picture, choose a brush size that's smaller than the damaged areas. Do this because building up the repair gently is preferable to trying to do it with a single brush stroke, and besides, there might not be enough of the Source area to copy from. Several softer brush strokes always produce a smoother finish and inevitably a more convincing result.

Tip

To replace larger sections of an image with background detail, try making a feathered-edged selection and copying and pasting it.

Change the brush size during the retouching operation as well as the Source area. So many novices copy and paste with such enthusiasm that they don't notice the tell-tale step-and-repeat tracks left across the print surface because they have not reselected the Source area. This is something to be avoided. Moving the Clone Source point often is the best way of avoiding these tell-tale marks and (usually) produces a more convincing retouched result.

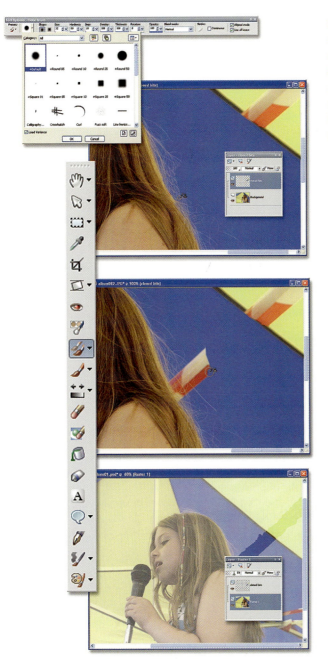

FIG 4.8 The Clone tool Options palette provides a wealth of brush presets and other settings so that you can adapt the tool to the job in hand. Before you do anything, create a new Raster layer to clone into, keeping all your changes in one place and keeping the original unmarked. Be sure to check the Use All Layers box on the Options palette so that you can clone from one layer to another.

Start with a small brush and use lots of small strokes so that if you make a mistake you can easily undo. Change brush size frequently to match the area being cloned and experiment with brush hardness, opacity, and blend mode to get the best result.

Here, the background layer opacity has been reduced so you can more clearly see the cloning on top. If you're not happy with your first effort, just erase the cloned sections from the 'cloned bits' layer and start again.

The Options palette also offers an Opacity setting. This affects the brightness of the pixels copied from the Source area. Effectively, this slows the retouching process noticeably as you end up trying to cover damaged areas with less dense pixels (reduced opacity). Several mouse-clicks might have to be made to achieve the same as one set at 100% opacity. However, it's always better to reduce the opacity to get a smoother tonal result. Top fashion retouchers use this technique to dramatically soften skin tones even if the model appears 'perfect'. Setting the opacity to a low value, say about 10–15%, and cloning again and again can produce a surreal, almost porcelain-like effect on skin tones, especially if the contrast is kept quite high (using the Levels tool for this).

Another control to experiment with is the Blend mode. Blend modes, which we discuss in detail in Chapter 6, influence the way copied pixels react with the underlying, original pixels. For example, click the default Normal drop-down menu in the Options palette and try cloning using Burn (darken), Dodge (lighten), or the Color blend mode.

Other Tools for Fixing Damaged Pictures

- Scratch Remover tool (to remove blemishes locally).
- Small Scratch Remover tool (to remove small blemishes only).
- Clarify filter (to make a picture sharper and clearer).
- Fade Correction (to rejuvenate contrast and color).
- Histogram Adjustment tool (to increase the contrast).

Other Tools to Try

Like many of PaintShop Photo Pro's tools, the Dodge and Burn Brushes perform the digital equivalent of a conventional darkroom technique. During print-making, areas of the paper exposed under the enlarger are held back, or given additional exposure using masking tools. In this way it's possible to bring out detail in parts of the print that would otherwise be over- or underexposed.

The Dodge and Burn Brushes do exactly the same thing. Dodge lightens the pixels to which it's applied and the Burn Brush darkens them – the equivalent of giving more exposure under the enlarger. You need to be careful not to overdo it with these tools, or your intervention will become obvious. With each application of the tool the effect becomes more obvious. It's a good idea to duplicate the Background layer before using the Dodge and Burn Brushes and apply the changes to the copy. Use large, soft-edged brushes and reduced opacity settings to avoid burning hard-edged holes. You can use the left and right buttons to switch between Dodge and Burn, but I wouldn't recommend this; if you've over-burned an area, undo, or use the History palette to get back the detail.

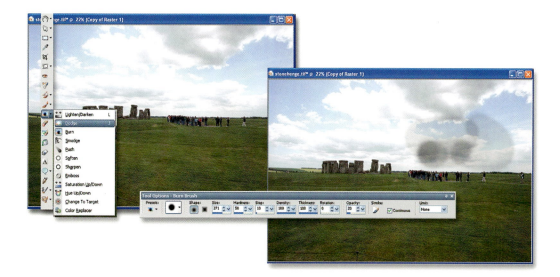

FIG 4.9 The Dodge and Burn tools provide, in the form of a brush, the power to add (or subtract) exposure to a photo. Before using any retouching tool, duplicate the Background layer and call it 'retouching', and make all your changes to this new layer. That way you can compare 'before' and 'after' versions by toggling the layer visibility; you can also go back to the original should things go badly wrong. The secret to successful burning (and dodging) lies in the Tool Options palette. Too much burning produces these tell-tale dark smudges. Use a large, soft-edged brush and reduce the opacity so that each brush stroke makes only a small difference. Then gradually build up the effect using multiple strokes. Just press Ctrl + Z to undo if something doesn't look right.

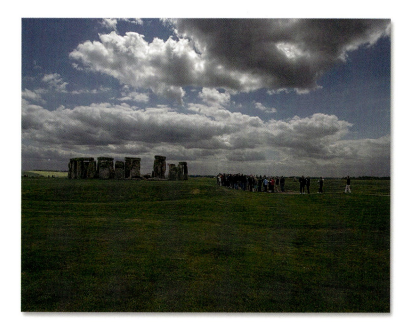

FIG 4.10 This is what the Burn tool can do for a photo – completely transform an image that would have otherwise perhaps found its way to the trash bin, but is now something worth showing to others.

113

Creating Black and White Pictures

Despite the fact that digital photography makes it no more difficult or expensive to shoot in color than black and white, monochrome images are proving as popular as ever. For some subjects removing the color altogether produces an aesthetically desirable result and digital image processing makes it easier than ever to produce toning effects like sepia, split toning, and cross-processing that, in the days of chemical processing, were messy, time-consuming, and often produced hit-and-miss results.

One of the simplest ways to produce black and white photos is to set your camera to Black and White mode but, other than in exceptional circumstances, I'd advise against this. Shooting with color in the camera and converting the images to black and white, as we shall see, gives you a much greater degree of control over the process and provides many more creative opportunities. It also gives you the option of keeping the color photo as well.

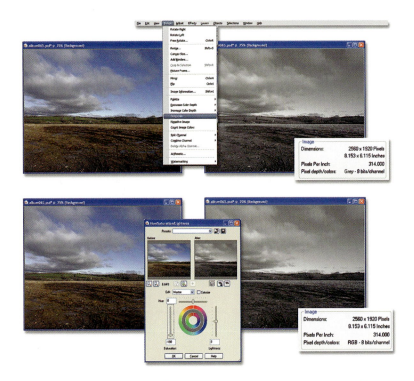

FIG 4.11 Top: Converting a photo to greyscale using Image > Greyscale removes the color data, which results in a smaller file size, but is irreversible. Use Hue/Saturation/Lightness to convert to black and white, but retain the color data should you want to reintroduce color to the image later.

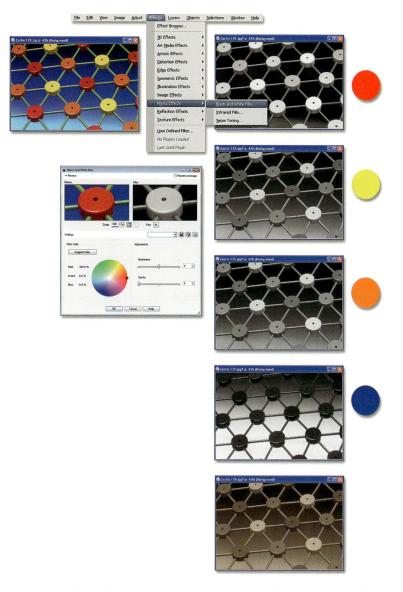

FIG 4.12 You can simulate the action of colored filters on black and white film using Black and White Film photo effects. Colored filters used in this way lighten the tone of same-colored objects and darken those with complementary colors. On this image, red lightens the red disks and darkens the blue background. Because of its proximity to yellow and orange, red also lightens the yellow and orange disks to a degree, but yellow and orange have a greater effect on their respective colors in the image. Blue has the reverse effect, lightening the blue background and darkening the disks. You can save commonly used filters like yellow, orange, and red as presets. Bottom: You can also use the Photo Effects Sepia filter to apply a quick sepia tone to an image, but the Colorize option on the Hue/Saturation/Lightness dialog box provides more scope for color-tinting of black and white photos.

Tip

The Channel mixer produces the same effect as yellow, red, or other colored filters on the camera with black and white film; use it to create dramatic skies and other effects.

PaintShop Photo Pro X3 provides several methods of converting color images to black and white ones. These are:

- Image > Grayscale. This converts the image to an 8-bit single-channel grayscale image and discards the color information. Once the image is saved in this mode there's no getting the color data back, so if you want to keep the color image, make sure to keep a backup copy and choose File > Save As so you do not overwrite your original.
- Adjust > Hue and Saturation > Hue/Saturation/Lightness. By dragging the Saturation slider all the way to zero in the Hue/Saturation/Lightness dialog box, you can completely desaturate the image. The difference between doing this and converting to grayscale is that, although you can no longer see it, the color information is still there. You can go back to Hue/Saturation/Lightness at any time and put the color back by dragging the slider in the opposite direction. You can also introduce new color in ways we'll look at shortly.
- Effects > Photo Effect > Black and White Film. This filter can convert your photos to black and white and at the same time simulate colored filters placed over the lens to help differentiate color with similar gray tonal values. For example, when shooting black and white landscapes a yellow filter is commonly used to darken blue skies and help pick out cloud detail. Like Hue/Saturation/Lightness, using the Black and White Film effect retains the color channels in the file so you can add new color effects, but the effect isn't reversible – you can't get the original colors back once the file is saved.
- Adjust > Color > Channel mixer. The Channel mixer works in a similar way to the Black and White Film effect, only it provides a lot more control. Whereas the Black and White Film effects are confined to a limited number of filters – Red, Green, Yellow, Orange, and Blue – using the Channel mixer to combine the data from the red, green, and blue channels you can produce a widely varied range of tonal effects.

Tinting Black and White Photos

In the last section we described ways to use PaintShop Photo Pro to convert a color picture to black and white. Now we'll take a look at how to color-tint a black and white photo. Why color-tint? Most black and white pictures reproduce only a limited tonal range: 256 tones to be exact. The addition of color, albeit in subtle amounts, produces a print apparently much richer in tonal scale.

This process is sometimes called a 'duotone'. Adding three colors to a black and white photo in the same fashion is called a 'tritone'. Adding a fourth color makes this a 'quadtone'. Aside from increasing tonal depth, making a duotone can be a cheaper way of introducing color to commercially printed jobs (because adding a second color is cheaper than producing the full four-color print process).

How It's Done

Aside from using Effects > Photo Effects > Sepia Toning, which, as we've seen, limits you to fairly crude applications of a single color, the simplest way to tone a black and white photo is using Color Balance. Remember, you can only produce color effects like this (or in fact carry out any color editing, such as adding colored text) on an image that, though it may appear black and white, is an RGB color file. So, if you're starting with a full color image, desaturate it, as explained previously. If it's a grayscale image convert it to an RGB one by selecting Image > Increase Color Depth > RGB – 8 bits/channel. Now open the Color Balance dialog box by selecting Adjust > Color Balance and uncheck the Advanced Options box to turn off the advanced controls if they are displayed. Now all you have to do is drag the slider to the right or left to make the image warmer or cooler. Warmer adds red and yellow to the image and Cooler adds blue. The further you drag the slider the more color is added. To add other colors to the image, check the Advanced Options box and use the More Purple/More Green slider.

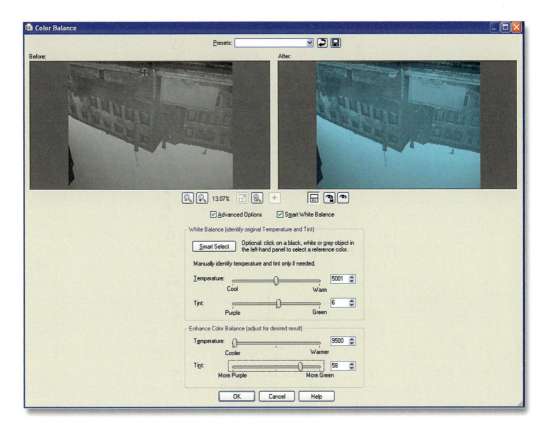

FIG 4.13 Use the Color Balance dialog box to add a tint to previously desaturated images. Stick to the sliders in the Enhance Color Balance panel, which work more intuitively than the others.

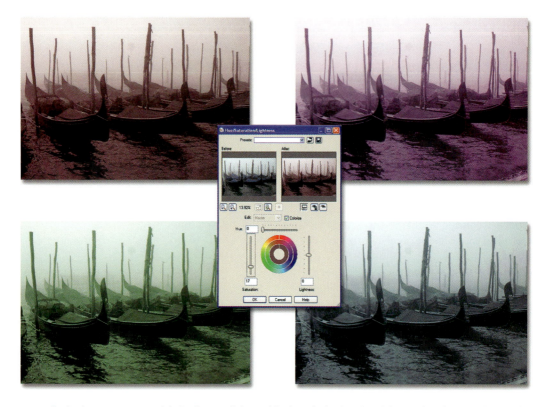

FIG 4.14 For the ultimate in tinting control the Hue/Saturation/Lightness dialog box is hard to beat. Control the tint color with the Hue slider and the strength using the Saturation slider. You can also adjust image brightness using the Lightness slider, though adjustments of this kind are usually best left to Levels.

Tip

Color Balance and Hue/Saturation/Lightness are best applied as Adjustment layers, so that changes remain editable and can be removed later if required (see Chapter 6).

It's easy to get confused when using the Color Balance dialog box in Advanced mode. It helps if you stick to using the sliders at the bottom of the dialog box in the Enhance Color Balance (adjust for desired result) panel as these work intuitively. The sliders at the top are for manual identification of an existing color cast in the image that you want to remove and so can appear to work counter-intuitively. For example, if you drag the Tint slider towards purple, this is telling PaintShop Pro that the image has a purple cast that you want to remove – so it adds green.

You can add a wider range of tints to a photo using Adjust > Hue and Saturation > Colorize. This is actually pretty simple to use. First select a color using the Hue box on the left – the colors won't mean much to you so click the down arrow to display a Color picker. Next, adjust the strength of the tint using the Saturation slider.

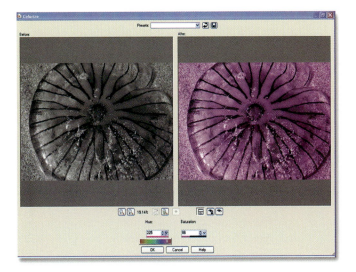

FIG 4.15 The Colorize command provides the best balance between control and ease of use. Just select your tint color using the Hue color picker, then adjust the strength using the Saturation slider.

Again, if you click the down arrow you can work with a visual tint gradient rather than a number.

You can also use the Hue/Saturation/Lightness dialog box with the Colorize box checked to tint a monochrome photo. This works in pretty much the same way as the colorize method, using the Hue and Saturation sliders to set the tint color and strength. The Hue/Saturation/Lightness dialog box (as its name implies) also provides a Lightness slider.

Whenever you're tinting images in this way its a good idea to use an Adjustment layer, rather than applying color changes directly to the image. Using an Adjustment layer will allow you to easily make changes to the tint at a later stage in the editing process – for example, if you add some text and decide that a different colored tint would work better. You can even remove the tint altogether if you decide against it.

Adjustment layers also provide additional control over the effect. You can reduce the strength of the effect and blend it with the original using layer opacity and blend modes. See Chapter 6 for more about how you can use Adjustment layers to edit images non-destructively.

> **Tip**
>
> For an interesting effect use a Hue/Saturation/ Lightness Adjustment layer in Colorize mode to apply a tint, then reduce the layer opacity to blend it with the original color.

Creating Color Overlay Effects

In an earlier edition of this book we devoted these pages to a technique that involved using the Color Balance tool to apply a multi-tone effect, using different colors for the image shadows, highlights, and midtones. While PaintShop Photo Pro's Color Balance tool is easier to use, it no longer lets you apply color changes individually to the highlight, midtone, and shadow regions of a photo. But we're not going to let that get in the way of a good technique! Here's how to achieve the same effect using a layer property called 'Blend Range', which masks parts of a layer that fall within a tonal range that you specify.

Open the image you want to tint and duplicate the Background layer twice by selecting it in the Layers palette, right-clicking it, and selecting Duplicate from the context menu. Rename the new layers after the color you intend to use for the tints; here I've called them red and blue. Tint the layers using the colorize technique described on page 118.

Double-click the top 'blue' layer in the Layers palette to open the Layer Properties dialog box and click the Blend Ranges tab. If it isn't already selected, choose Gray Channel from the Blend Channel pull-down menu and take a look at the two graduated bars underneath it. You can use these bars to control how pixels in the two layers are displayed. The top bar, labeled 'This layer', can be used to hide pixels on the upper (blue) layer using the four triangular-shaped buttons. Drag the buttons on the left to hide pixels in the shadows and those on the right to hide highlight pixels. By dragging the top and bottom triangles to different positions you can create a smooth transition between the layers, rather than have the color change abruptly.

The bottom slider essentially does the same thing in a different way. Think of it as forcing pixels on the layer below (in this case the blue layer) to show through the top (red) one. I find it keeps things simpler to ignore the Underlying Layer controls and just use the controls for the upper layer to choose which parts of the tonal range I want to appear in that color.

Tip

Like Adjustment layers, the changes you make using Blend Ranges aren't permanent and you can go back and edit them at any stage. Try combining Blend Ranges with blend modes to produce interesting graphic effects.

Using the Warp Tools

PaintShop Photo Pro has several powerful brush tools that can be used to radically bend and distort the pixels in a photo. These are the Warp Brushes.

Why Use a Warp Brush?

- To create zany, surreal pictorial effects
- To increase eye size in a portrait (i.e. to enlarge a model's pupils for that wide-eyed look; it can also be used for reducing the size of other unsightly body parts like noses, if it's important)
- Straighten facial detail (i.e. a broken nose)
- To entertain your kids.

The Warp Brush works just like any other brush in PaintShop Pro in so far that you can run it over the picture and it applies a direct change. In this situation

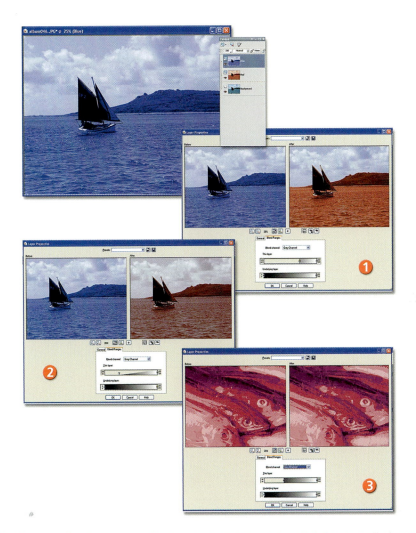

FIG 4.16 Use Blend Ranges to confine color tints to parts of the image like the highlights or shadows. (1) Confining the top blue layer to the highlights creates a hard-edged transition between red sea/land and blue sky. (2) Soften the transition by creating a 'ramp', allowing the red to bleed into the sky and vice versa. (3) You can use this technique on high-contrast images to produce two-color posterization effects.

you have massive influence over how the pixels bend and warp under the brush. Some computing power is needed to make this work swiftly.

There are eight warp modes that can be combined or used individually. Brush effects are: 'Push', 'Expand', 'Contract', 'Right Twirl', 'Left Twirl', 'Noise', 'Iron Out', and 'Unwarp'.

If you don't like what this brush does, click the Cancel tab. Other options include 'Brush Size', 'Hardness', 'Strength', 'Step', and 'Noise'. When you have finished the warping process, click the OK check mark to render the warping

121

action. The neat thing about this tool is that you can preview everything in four different 'Draft' quality modes depending on how much of a hurry you might be in, and then finish the job in two final 'Render' Quality modes.

If you are in a hurry, use the Coarse Draft mode but render in the Best mode. For best-quality results, use the Finest Quality settings in both modes.

FIG 4.17 Like many things digital, it is quite easy to use the Warp tools but hard to get a result that is useful, flattering, funny (or all three).

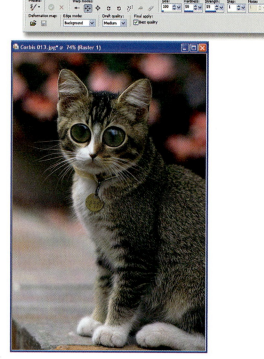

Scripting

Scripting is a powerful PaintShop Photo Pro feature introduced in version 8. It allows you to automatically combine several editing steps and apply them to another image. Say, for example, you have a whole folder of images and you want to do the same thing to each of them – open them, resize them, unsharp mask them, add a frame, and save them. That's the kind of repetitive work that scripting was designed for (PaintShop Photo Pro's One Step Photo Fix is a script).

Scripts are easy to create. The Scripting toolbar works a little like a VCR, with a Record button that when pressed keeps track of everything you do and produces a script so that the same process can be applied with a single click to any other image. There's also a selection of pre-supplied scripts, including 'Border with drop shadow', 'Black and white sketch', 'EXIF captioning', 'Photo edges', 'Sepia frame', 'Simple caption', 'Vignette', and 'Watercolor'.

You can add scripts as buttons to toolbars, which makes them even easier to apply. Right-click on the toolbar and select Customize from the contextual menu, click the Scripts tab in the Customize dialog box and select the script you want to add from the pull-down menu. Choose an icon, click the Bind button and the Script button will appear in the Bound Scripts pane. Now drag this icon from the Bound Scripts pane on to the toolbar. Now all you have to do to apply the script to any image is click the button.

Pre-written scripts are all very well, but what if you want a script to handle a repetitive task that doesn't appear on the Scripts toolbar drop-down list? Well, you can record your own, but you can also edit the existing scripts. PaintShop Photo Pro's scripts are written in a scripting language called 'Python'. You don't need any special scripting knowledge to edit existing scripts, but if you're interested in finding out more about Python take a look at http://wiki.python.org/moin/BeginnersGuide.

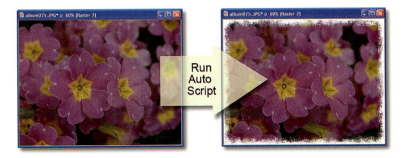

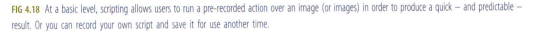

FIG 4.18 At a basic level, scripting allows users to run a pre-recorded action over an image (or images) in order to produce a quick – and predictable – result. Or you can record your own script and save it for use another time.

To edit a script, click the Edit Script button on the Script toolbar. Some of the PaintShop Pro scripts provide editing tips. For example, the Thumbnail 150 script begins:

if you want thumbnails generated at a different size just change this to the desired value.

MaxThumbnailSize = 150

The # symbol at the beginning of the first line denotes a comment – what follows is ignored by the script interpreter – but its meaning is clear enough to anyone else.

PaintShop Photo Pro X3 has an even easier way of creating scripts – called 'Quickscripts' – using the History palette. The History palette automatically records everything you do in PaintShop Photo Pro. You can use the History palette as a super-undo feature. While selecting Undo from the Edit menu (or pressing Ctrl + Z) will take you back through recent editing in linear steps, the History palette can be used to selectively undo. You can, for example, undo the Lens Distortion filter effect you applied 10 minutes ago, but keep the cropping, Red-Eye Removal, and Automatic Color Balance subsequently applied.

To create a Quickscript, select the steps you want to use by Shift-clicking (Ctrl-click to select non-contiguous steps) them in the History palette and click the Save Quickscript button. To apply the Quickscript to the current image, click the Run Quickscript button. What could be simpler? Well, it would be nice if you could save more than one Quickscript. As it is, when you save a new Quickscript it overwrites the old one.

Clearly, scripts can save you a lot of legwork if you need to apply the same editing sequence to a large number of images. But you still have to open the image and click the button. It may not sound like hard work, but if you have to do it 300 times, or every time you download a batch of pictures from your digital camera, you'd be forgiven for considering it quite a chore. This is where Batch Process comes in. The Batch Process feature can automatically apply editing commands to an entire folder of images. Combine batch processing with scripting and you have some real image-editing power at your fingertips.

PaintShop Photo Pro's Batch Process feature grew out of a Batch Convert feature designed to allow you to convert a bunch of files from one format to another. It was extended in version 8 to allow you to apply scripts and there's also a useful Batch Rename feature, which you can use to change the anonymous names of digital camera images to something more meaningful.

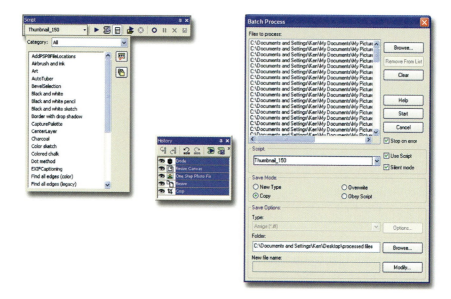

FIG 4.19 Use the Script toolbar (left) to select and apply scripts to the current image. You can create Quickscripts from the History palette (center). Combining scripts with the Batch Process feature (right) is the route to major effort-saving automation.

To open the Batch Process dialog box select File > Batch Process. Click the Browse button, navigate to the folder of images you want to process, and click the Select All button. Before you do this make sure to back up the originals somewhere safe and work on a copy of the images so that, if something unexpected happens, you still have the originals to fall back on.

Check the Use Script box, select a script from the pull-down menu, and check the Copy Radio button. This will save a copy of the processed image into the folder you specify in the Save Options pane. Click the Browse button and create a new folder called something like 'processed files' on your hard disk. The Save Mode pane provides other saving options. If you haven't included a Save As command in your script, check the Script Save Radio button. If you check the Silent Mode box, Batch Process will run the selected script and apply the settings you used when you recorded it. If you leave the Silent Mode box unchecked, a dialog box will open at relevant points in the script for each processed image, requiring you to enter values.

When you're sure everything is correctly set, click the Start button, sit back and watch while PaintShop Photo Pro does the hard work for you.

Step-by-Step Projects

Technique: Restoring Badly Damaged Photos

Tip

A pressure-sensitive stylus and tablet (see Chapter 1) makes retouching much easier. Use the Brush Variance palette to determine how the brush responds to stylus pressure. When you press harder, the brush can get bigger, or change opacity or thickness.

Once you've mastered the retouching techniques demonstrated in this chapter, and elsewhere in the book, you'll be able to make improvements to digital photos that aren't quite 'right' as well as scanned pictures in need of restoration. With skilled use of the Clone Brush, in combination with the other retouching tools, there's little you won't be able to fix. This step-by-step project shows how to restore an old photo that's suffered quite bad damage, in this case more due to lack of care than the aging process. Don't be put off attempting to restore old photos because they look past saving. Even very severe damage, such as tears, staining, fading, and folds, can be reduced or eliminated altogether with the repeated application of the simple techniques shown here. And if your first efforts don't meet with much success, keep trying; retouching is one of those things that improves with practice.

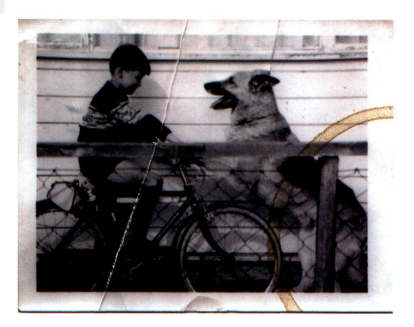

STEP 1 This photo is about 40 years old. It hasn't aged too badly, but it has a couple of serious fold marks, one running upwards from the dog's ear and another running vertically through the middle, as well as a nasty stain from a coffee cup. Overall the picture has accumulated some dirt and grubbiness, most noticeably in the white border area.

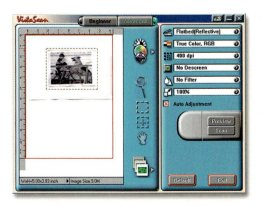

STEP 2 Even if the original is black and white, scan it as an RGB color image. The additional channels in an RGB image can bring out (or cover up) detail, which will help in the retouching process. Scan at a high resolution so you can zoom in and work on small details; you can always downsample the photo later for printing or web use.

STEP 3 Crop the picture to get rid of that grubby border. Depending on the shot, you can save yourself a great deal of work by cropping close and removing a lot of material that you might otherwise have to retouch, but here we want to keep everything other than the border.

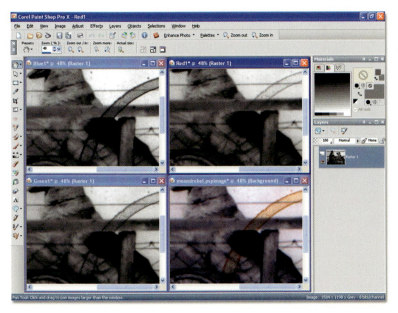

STEP 4 From the Image menu select Split Channel > Split to RGB to separate the photo into its constituent red, green, and blue channels. Select Tile Horizontally from the Window menu to compare the channels. Notice how the coffee stain isn't nearly so obvious on the red channel. This is the one we'll use for our retouching. Close the original scan and the green and blue channels, and resave the red channel.

127

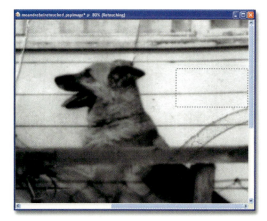

STEP 5 Click the New Raster layer button at the top of the Layers palette to create a new layer – call it 'retouching'. First we'll deal with the coffee stain. Sometimes it's easier to deal with big problems like this using copy and paste rather than the Clone Brush. Use the rectangular marquee with a feather setting of 1 and select an area just above the stain. It's a lucky coincidence that this selection is exactly the same, bar the stain, as the area below it, but you'd be surprised how often this happens.

STEP 6 Select Copy Merged from the Edit > Copy Special menu followed by Paste As New Selection and position the pasted selection over the coffee stain, taking care to match the horizonal line of the wood cladding. Press Ctrl + Shift + F to defloat the selection. Repeat the process with different selections to cover as much of the stain as possible. Press Ctrl + D or choose Select None from the Selections menu.

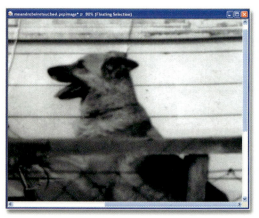

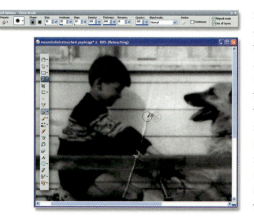

STEP 7 Select the Clone Brush and set the size big enough to cover the width of the fold in one hit. Set the hardness to around 50 and make sure that Aligned mode and 'Use all layers' are both checked. Right-click with the brush just to one side of the fold to set the sampling point, then move on to the fold and left-click to clone. If your cloning isn't seamless try again from a slightly different start point. You'll need to experiment with the brush size, opacity, and blend mode; you'll get better results using many short strokes, rather than one long one, and you'll also need to frequently reset the source point.

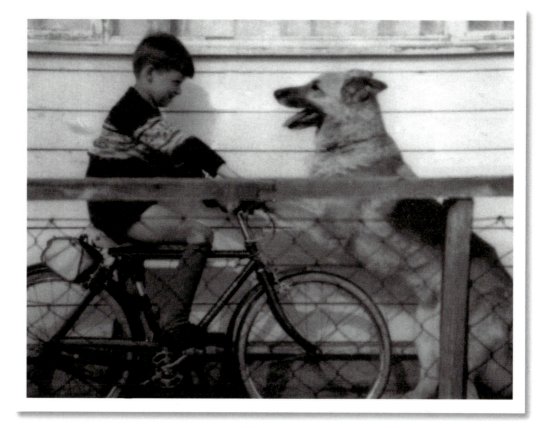

STEP 8 Continue with the Clone Brush down the length of the fold. Usually, best results are achieved by sampling close to the area to be cloned as you will get a better match. Sometimes this will be to the left of the damaged area, sometimes to the right. Occasionally you may find there is no suitable material close by and you'll need to sample from a more remote location with similar detail. After cloning out the two fold lines I've gone back and removed the traces of the coffee stain from the area below the fence using the Clone tool. Picking the green channel, where the mark was least visible, meant that very little work was needed to remove the remaining traces. Finally, I've added a nice clean white border.

Technique: Hand-Coloring Black and White Photos

In the days before color photography, a commonly used technique was to add color to black and white prints using inks and a small retouching brush. The aim of this process wasn't to create an exact facsimile of a scene in full color, but rather to add a little color detail to heighten the realism and add a little life to what otherwise may have appeared a little drab and austere.

If you've ever seen a hand-colored black and white print you'll know just how charming they can be. Using PaintShop Photo Pro you can recreate this effect either to add a new dimension to archive family photos, or to produce an interesting new take on more recent digital images.

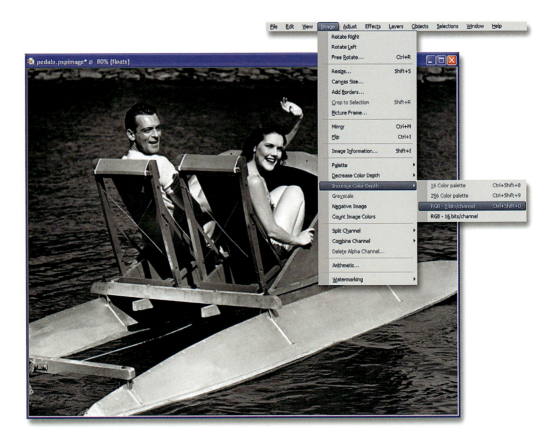

STEP 1 If you're starting off with a scanned black and white photo in Grayscale mode you'll need to convert it to RGB by selecting Image > Increase Color Depth > RGB – 8 bits/channel. If it's a color image, desaturate it using Hue/Saturation/Lightness as described earlier in the chapter.

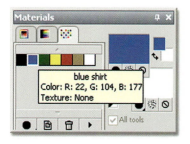

STEP 2 You'll get a more realistic result using a limited color palette. Using the Materials palette in Swatch mode, create up to six colors. Depending on the image, you might, for example, choose a skin color, red to add color to lips and cheeks, one or two colors for items of clothing, and another one or two swatches for other detail such as sky, a car or, as in this case, a pedalo. You might also find it helpful to name the swatches appropriately, e.g. 'skin tones'.

STEP 3 Select the Paint Brush and choose one of your color swatches. Use the Tool Options palette to set the brush size, shape, hardness, and other parameters. To a degree these will depend on the detail you are coloring, but generally you'll find that soft-edged brushes with reduced opacity give good results. You might also try the Airbrush.

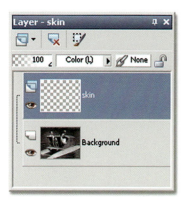

STEP 4 Create a new raster layer on which to add the color. There are two reasons for doing this. Firstly, it's always a good idea to keep any retouching on a separate layer as it leaves the original untouched on the Background layer and, if things go drastically wrong, you can always delete the retouching layer and start again. Secondly, it gives you a lot more control over your editing. You can change the opacity to fade the retouching and make it less obvious, and use PaintShop Photo Pro's blend modes to produce a more natural look.

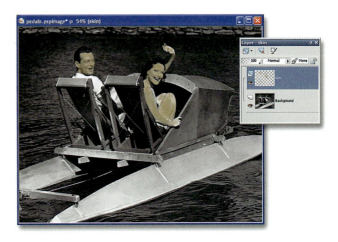

When you change the Layer blend mode to Color (Legacy), the paint that you've applied with the Brush tool adopts the tonal characteristics of the underlying (gray) pixels. Dark pixels pick up darker color and vice versa. It pays to be realistic in your choice of colors. If your subject is wearing a dark shirt, you won't be able to paint it light blue. If colors don't come out as expected, try using the Hue/Saturation/Lightness controls to change the color of the paint layer – another good reason for keeping each color tint on a separate layer.

STEP 5 Making sure the new layer is selected, start to paint over the background image. At this stage the paint will go on thickly and may even completely obliterate the detail below, producing a crude and ugly result. Don't worry! Once you've applied a few strokes to a small area of the picture, stop painting.

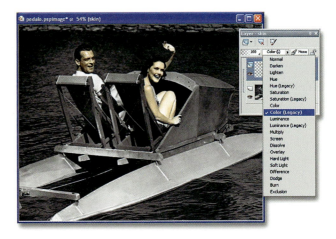

STEP 6 In the Layers palette change the blend mode from Normal to Color (Legacy). Now, your brush strokes apply color to the image but maintain the original tone, producing a more natural effect. As well as retaining the underlying detail, you'll notice that the color varies from your original swatch, depending on how light or dark the underlying pixels are.

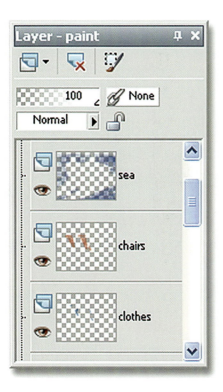

STEP 7 When you've finished painting all of the image detail in one of your palette colors, for example all the skin tones, create another new layer and continue painting in the next color. You could put all your colors on to one layer, but using a different layer for each color gives you more control over the finished result. Suppose, when you are nearing completion, everything looks OK, but the skin tones look a bit over the top, like everyone's had a bit too much sun. By reducing the opacity of the skin tones layer you can correct this problem without affecting the other colors.

STEP 8 The great thing about hand-coloring is you don't have to be a great artist or even incredibly accurate, as this screenshot of all the paint layers at 100% opacity in Normal mode shows!

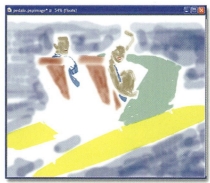

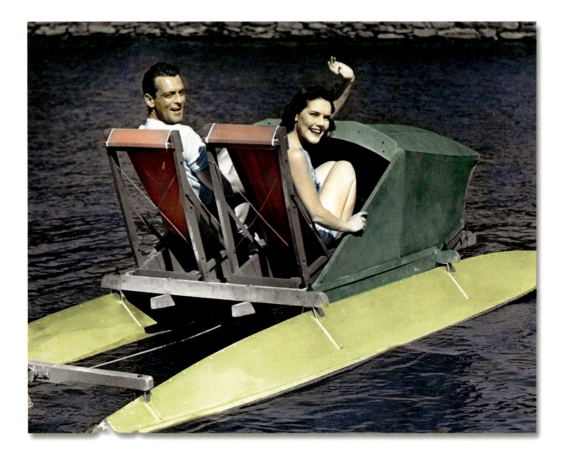

The final result

CHAPTER 5

Using Selections – Controlling Change

What's Covered in this Chapter

- This is a short chapter, but it covers crucial techniques that will take your photo-editing skills way beyond what we've covered up to now. This chapter is all about selections and how to make them. Selections, and their close relatives mask layers and alpha channels, allow you to confine changes to a part of the image – a bit like using a stencil.

- PaintShop Photo Pro X3 has more than 20 selection tools, but the most commonly used are the Geometric selection tools, the Freehand selection tool, and the Magic Wand. One of the keys to successful selection is knowing which tool to use for particular selection tasks, how to set the tool options so that you get exactly what you want – nothing more and nothing less – and, if you don't get quite what you want, how to add to and subtract from existing selections.

- The selection tools can take you only so far. For one thing, they're not permanent so if you want to close your photo and come back to work on it later, you'll need to save your selection; this is where alpha channels and

PaintShop Photo Pro X3 for Photographers. DOI: 10.1016/B978-0-240-52165-7.10005-X mask layers come in. As well as allowing you to make selections permanent, alpha channels and mask layers can be worked on with PaintShop Photo Pro's brush tools. Masks produced in this way can show or hide anything in your photos, even things with indistinct edges, like fur, hair, clouds, and water. Once the mask is made you can use it as the basis for selectively applying filters, making tonal and color changes, or anything else. This chapter introduces alpha channels and mask layers. In Chapter 6, you'll learn some more advanced masking techniques using layers.

· The three step-by-step projects at the end of the chapter demonstrate how to use selections to achieve three different outcomes – blurring the background to produce artificial 'depth of field', fixing an overexposed sky, and cutting out an object from its background.

Tip

As with many other aspects of photo editing, making selections, particularly with the Freehand selection tool, is much easier with a graphics tablet and stylus than with a mouse.

There comes a point in the digital learning curve where it's vital to embrace the concept of selection. We have seen that PaintShop Photo Pro's filter effects, tonal adjustments, and various color controls work on the entire image. Each is said to function 'globally'. For a lot of pictures you'll find this works well enough, but there'll come a time when it's necessary to limit this effect to a smaller, more controlled section in the picture. The easiest and most accurate way to make this happen is to generate a specific selection that restricts the action of a tool to a certain physical area.

Understanding Selections: Adding Creative Power

PaintShop Photo Pro has several tools that allow the isolation of specific areas within the picture based on certain selection criteria such as color, tonality, contrast or simply by drawing around it. You have to distinguish the best selection tool, or tools, to use for the picture in question. For example, sometimes it's possible with one mouse-click to get a good, clean selection around an object. Sometimes it is not so easy because the photo might be multicolored or irregular in tone. In this case you'd use a combination of selection tools to successfully 'grab' the object cleanly. PaintShop Photo Pro also has a number of tools that you can use to clean up these selections once started. These are called 'Selection Modification' tools.

Selection tools are divided into three types:

· The Freehand selection tool, which has edge-seeking ('magnetic'), point-to-point (polygonal line), smart-edge (linear 'magnetic'), or just freehand characteristics.
· The Geometric Marquee selection tool, which comes in rectangular, square, circular, star, triangular, and 10 other preset shapes.
· The Magic Wand tool. This finds pixels either of a similar contrast, color, hue, brightness, or opacity within the picture.

That's a combination of 20 selection tools to choose from.

Bear in mind that the Options palette has more refining controls for most of the tools mentioned (some already mentioned are accessible through this palette only). Controls include a Tolerance level, Blend mode, Anti-aliasing, Smoothing, Feathering, and Match mode.

In addition to the selection tools, PaintShop Photo Pro X3 has a couple of ways to cut out and remove objects from photos. These aren't strictly speaking selection tools; they go beyond mere selection and actually remove parts of the image for you in one single operation.

The Object Extractor does exactly what it says: it cuts out part of an image – say a person, car, flower, or whatever your subject happens to be – removing the background. To use the Object Extractor, select Object Extractor from the Image menu. The Object Extractor opens in its own window, which displays a large image preview, below which are some tools and settings. To use it you select the Brush tool, set an appropriate brush size and paint an outline around the edge of the object you want to cut out. If you make a mistake you can erase with the eraser. When the outline is complete, click inside it with the Fill tool to fill the selected area with a red mask, then click the Process button.

PaintShop Photo Pro X3 now makes a first attempt at extracting the object from the background. If it doesn't get it right the first time, try experimenting with the Accuracy slider – each time you move it the image is reprocessed and you'll have to wait a few seconds. Subjects with more detailed edges will require a higher accuracy setting (and better skills with the brush), but as long as the subject that you're attempting to extract is reasonably well iso-lated from the background you should be able to get a good result. To get a better look check the Hide Mask checkbox and if you want to go back and edit the outline in an attempt to improve the result, click the Edit Mask button. When you're happy that you've got the best possible result, click the OK button to extract the object. What happens now is that the background is deleted, leaving your object cut out on its layer.

The Object Extractor, like the Background Eraser, which works in a similar fashion, works best on objects that are well isolated from their backgrounds, e.g. those shot against a plain background – like the sky in our example. To cut out objects with more complex backgrounds you'll get a better result using the selection tools already discussed and – even better – masking, which is explained towards the end of this chapter. You could also take a look at the step-by-step project at the end of this chapter that shows exactly how to deal with objects that have fussy background detail.

One other new feature of PaintShop Photo Pro X3 that I want to mention here is the Smart Carver, which combines retouching and cropping in one operation, allowing you to resize an image while preserving some details and removing others. Again, though it's not strictly speaking a selection tool, it uses simple selections as a basis for automating what would otherwise be a complex retouching task.

137

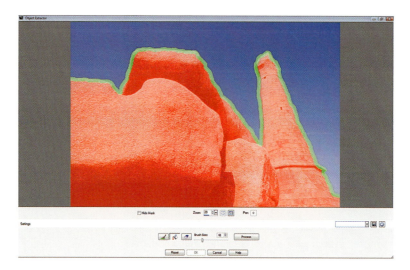

FIG 5.1 The Object Extractor makes light work of removing a subject from its background. It works best on subjects like this, which are clearly defined against a plain background like the sky. It's very simple to use: you just paint an outline around the subject, fill it, then click the Process button. PaintShop Photo Pro X3 then deletes the background detail.

The Smart Carver is on the Image menu just above the Object Extractor and opens in its own window. It has two brushes: one for preserving detail and the other for removing it. You simply paint over what's important with the green brush and daub what you want to lose with the red brush. I use the word daub advisedly. The great thing about the Smart Carver is that you don't need to be too careful about going over the edges. As long as what you want to keep or lose is covered in paint it works just fine.

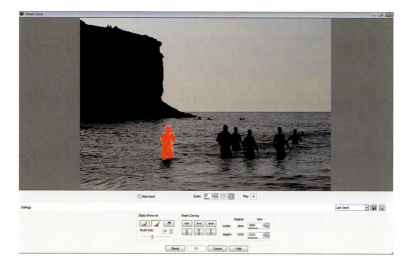

FIG 5.2 Smart Carver resizes photos, removing unwanted detail in the process. Unlike cropping, the bits you want to get rid of don't have to be near the edges. You can seamlessly remove detail from anywhere in the frame.

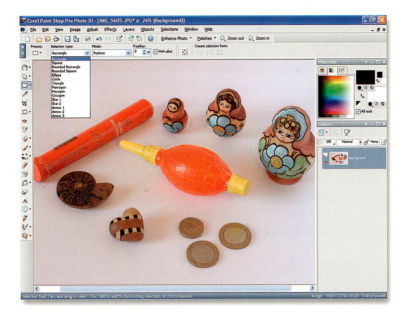

FIG 5.3 PaintShop Photo Pro has a wide range of special selection tools, but for cutting irregular objects out from a background the best options are the Freehand selection tool or the Magic Wand tool. Few objects are perfect geometric shapes and these selection tools are really intended for producing graphics by making a selection and filling it. If you are taking a photo of objects you intend to cut out, shoot them on a white or plain-colored background to make the task of selecting them easier.

Having done your painting there are buttons for resizing the image both vertically and horizontally. The most useful of these are the Auto-contract buttons on the right, which resize the image sufficiently to remove all unwanted detail.

What Else Can You Do With Selections?

- All selections can be saved and stored for later use in an alpha channel, or to a designated area on your hard drive like any other file.
- Selections can be used like a painter's drop sheet – to inhibit brush actions along straight edges, and to stop paint from getting into areas that you don't want to get paint into.
- All selection tools have an 'Add To' and a 'Subtract From' function. Hold the Shift key when making a second selection and it's added to the first. Keep holding the Shift key to add further selections. In this way you can build, or reduce, extremely accurate selections.
- To further refine the process, selection tools are interchangeable. Make an initial selection using the Magic Wand tool, for example, and add to that using a Marquee tool. Finish off using the Freehand selection tool. Use the Shift and Ctrl keys to apply additions and subtractions, or set the same parameters in the Tool Options palette.

> **Tip**
>
> Instead of trying to select an object, it's often easier to select the background, then invert the selection (press Ctrl + Shift + I). You can also try using a Levels adjustment to make a light background completely white and much easier to 'grab' using the Magic Wand tool.

- Use the Options palette to make custom selections using numerical values in the fields provided ('Customize Selection' in the Options palette).
- PaintShop Photo Pro also has an Edit Selection mode (Selections > Edit Selection). In this mode, all the raster painting/drawing tools and many filter effects can be used to modify the selection marquee. In this mode the selection is rendered in a red opaque color so it's easy to see. This is a powerful and fast way to make an average-looking selection into something that has professional accuracy.
- Perfect the selection using the Selection Modify tools. These will allow you to produce surprising accuracy from even the roughest of initial selections.

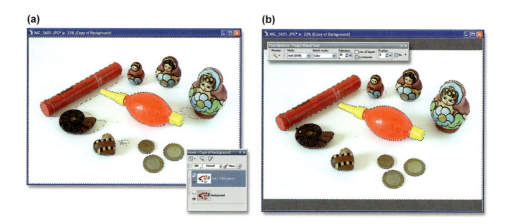

FIG 5.4 (a) To select these objects using the Magic Wand tool, I first duplicated the Background layer and used a Layers adjustment to make the background as white as possible. (b) Refine the selection using the Magic Wand tool in Add mode (or hold down Shift). You should be able to select all of the background using this method.

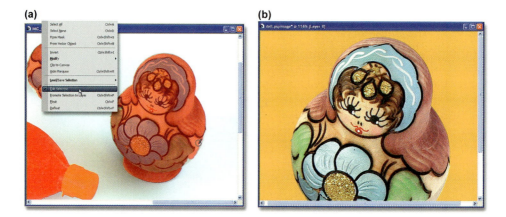

FIG 5.5 (a) Invert the selection (press Ctrl + Shift + I) and choose Edit Selection from the Selections menu to alter the selection using the brush tools. (b) Using the brush tools with Edit Selection enables you to make a very accurate, soft-edged selection that won't 'show the join' when you paste.

Using the Geometric Selection Tools

PaintShop Photo Pro's Geometric selection tools are the easiest to use because they are 'preset'. They don't rely entirely on the accuracy of the mouse action.

Open a picture and duplicate the Background layer (Layers > Duplicate) so that you can practice on a copy of the original rather than the original itself. Make sure that the top layer is active (click once on its title bar on the Layers palette to do this).

Choose the Rectangular Marquee selection tool from the Tools toolbar, left-click and drag the cursor across the picture about 20% from the edge of the image. The moving line that appears where the selection was drawn is called the 'selection marquee'. Any further editing on the picture applies to the area inside this selection only. Because we want to add an effect to the area outside this selection it must be reversed or 'inverted'.

Choose 'Selections > Invert' from the Selections drop-down menu and note how it selects the entire image up to the borders of the original area selected. Use the keyboard shortcut Ctrl + Shift + M to hide the marquee to make it easier to see any tone changes you make. Note that, though it is hidden, the selection is still active.

Open the Levels dialog window (Adjust > Brightness and Contrast > Levels) and drag the gray diamond slider (the middle one) to the right. This darkens the selected area. Push the slider far enough to make the edges significantly darker, but still keep them semi-transparent.

You can refine all selections using the Feather adjustment. This blurs the selection line across an adjustable pixel width so that you can soften those typical scalpel-sharp selection cut-lines.

Adding to the Selection

To add to a selection, hold the Shift key down and make several more geometric selections, adding one on top of the other to build up a complex irregular but still geometric selection with each new mouse drag. Change the shape of the selection (circular, square, octagonal, etc.) using the Options palette. Remember at all times to update the save to preserve the selection information in an alpha channel (Selections > Save to Alpha Channel).

The Magic Wand Tool

You may find that the Geometric selection tools are not accurate enough or simply not the right shape to capture the subject in the picture. In this case, the Magic Wand tool is what you need. This is the most versatile selection tool available to you and can capture just about any selection you ask of it. The key to success with the Magic Wand tool lies in correctly setting the options and this often involves some trial and error. With a little experience, however, it will become second nature to you and take very little time – certainly a lot less time than having to make the same selection manually.

Select the Magic Wand tool from the Selection tool fly-out on the toolbar and click inside an image on an area of fairly similar color and tone. The resulting selection marquee may cover a little of the image or a lot of it, and it may be one big selection or there could be smaller islands of selected image dotted about – it all depends on the image.

What the Magic Wand does is select pixels of similar values, within a range that you specify, throughout the image. As a starting point the Magic Wand tool uses the pixel that you click on. It then selects all the pixels with an RGB value within the range specified by the value in the Tolerance field of the Tool Options palette; the larger the tolerance, the more pixels will be selected. If what you're trying to select is a very specific color, a red door for example, you can use a low tolerance setting to select all of it. If it contains a wider range of colors, like a sky or the leaves on a tree, you might need to increase the tolerance to capture all of the hues.

Sometimes, increasing the tolerance means you capture pixels you don't want, which happen to have similar values to those you do. If this happens

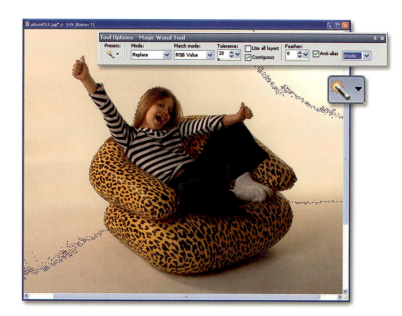

FIG 5.6 Successful use of the Magic Wand tool depends on making good tool options choices and adopting appropriate techniques. In this case it's easier to select the background and invert the selection to capture the subject. Rather than increasing the tolerance in an attempt to get everything in one bite, which will most likely just capture unwanted areas of the image, use a smaller tolerance setting and Shift-click to add to the original selection.

you need to try a different tack. One method is to Shift-click to add to the existing selection. If you get an unsatisfactory result press Ctrl + Z, rather than trying to subtract from the selection by Ctrl-clicking with the Magic Wand tool. Alternatively, it's often easier to select a background with the Magic Wand tool then invert the selection (Selections > Invert or press Ctrl + Shift + I) to capture the subject.

There are other options that can help you fine-tune a Magic Wand selection. Match modes enable you to make a selection on the basis of color, hue, brightness and opacity, as well as RGB values. Using the Brightness Match mode is one way to select shadow or highlight detail if you want to make selective tonal adjustment to an image.

Click the Sample Merged checkbox if you want the Magic Wand tool to base its selection on all pixels in the image, rather than just those in the active layer (if you get very unexpected results with the Magic Wand tool, e.g. everything selected wherever you click, it's probably because you're clicking in an empty layer with Sample Merged turned off). 'Contiguous' selects only pixels that are next to each other, so you get one selection marquee. Turn off Contiguous and the Magic Wand tool can jump over non-selected pixels to select in-range pixels anywhere within the image. In Non-Contiguous mode you'll get little pools of selection all over the image.

Finally, you can elect to anti-alias a Magic Wand selection's edge pixels. Use the pull-down menu to determine whether pixels outside or inside the selection border will be anti-aliased.

The Tool Options palette isn't the last word on modifying Magic Wand selections. On the Selections > Modify menu you'll find a host of additional fine-tuning adjustments that will allow you to, among other things, expand, contract, select similar, feather, smooth, and remove specks and holes from your selections. These can, of course, be used with any selections, not just those created with the Magic Wand tool.

Alpha Channels and Masks

When you make a selection, PaintShop Photo Pro stores it in an alpha channel. Channels are a bit like layers; an RGB image is composed of three channels, one each for the red, green, and blue image data. Alpha channels are grayscale – pixels in them are either black, white, or one of 254 shades of gray. In an alpha channel, pixels within a selected area are white, unselected pixels are black, and gray pixels are partially selected.

How can you have a partially selected pixel? Well, pixels in a feathered selection are partially selected. If you looked at the alpha channel for a circular feathered selection, there would be a white hole in the middle

> **Tip**
>
> The results of a Magic Wand tool selection depend on the precise pixel you click on. Even in what looks like an area of flat color, pixel values vary, so if your first attempt isn't successful, press Ctrl + Z to undo and click again on a neighboring pixel.

> **Tip**
>
> Using the Brush tools to paint directly on to a mask layer is often a much easier way to obtain a selection than using any of the selection tools.

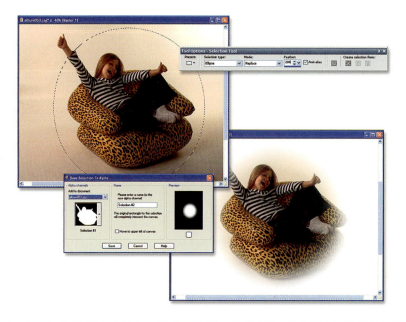

FIG 5.7 This selection was made using the Elliptical selection tool feathered by 200 pixels. The corresponding alpha channel shows the selected area in the center, gradually fading to black, and the bottom right image shows the actual selected pixels.

with a soft edge gradually fading to black. Any editing applied to image pixels selected using an alpha channel with gray pixels will have a partial effect, which is extremely useful for subtle image editing without 'hard' edges. It means you can apply filters and other effects with a gradually tapering effect.

At their simplest, alpha channels are simply a useful method for permanently storing selections. To do this, all you have to do is click Selections > Load/ Save Selection/Save Selection to Alpha Channel. Usually, you'll want to save a selection to the image you created it from, but you can also save and load selections into other documents.

Masks

Masks are a little like alpha channels in that they use a grayscale image to determine what happens to corresponding image pixels. Masks are in fact a special kind of layer. Grayscale mask pixels determine the opacity of image pixels in underlying layers. Masks provide a useful means of hiding image pixels without actually deleting them. By directly editing masks (and, for that matter, alpha channels) you can perform sophisticated image-editing techniques in a non-destructive way, without altering the pixel values in the affected layer.

To create a mask, first make a selection, then choose Layers > New Mask Layer > Show Selection to show the selected parts of an image layer and hide the rest. To mask (hide) the contents of the selection and show the unselected bits choose Layers > New Mask Layer > Hide Selection.

Selections, alpha channels, and masks are interchangeable. You can turn a selection into an alpha channel or a mask, create an alpha channel from a mask, load a mask from an alpha channel and, of course, load selections from masks and alpha channels. You can discover more about masks in the following chapter.

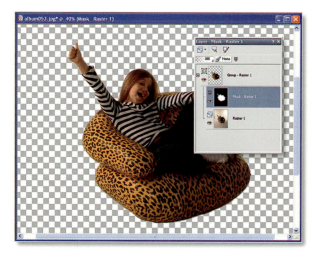

FIG 5.8 A Mask layer hides parts of underlying layers without actually deleting pixels.

Step-by-Step Projects

Technique: Creating an Artificial Point of Focus

Because life is never straightforward, PaintShop Photo Pro has a Freehand selection tool. This is used to manually draw around an object for the purpose of isolating it from the rest of the picture. While this can be the most accurate of all the selection tools, it can also be the most tricky because you have to rely on the accuracy of the mouse, which is a bit like drawing with a bar of soap at the best of times.

This project shows you how to achieve an artificially narrow depth-of-field effect using freehand selections and the Gaussian Blur filter. PaintShop Photo Pro X3 has a depth-of-field effect that can achieve something similar quickly and with much less effort. Doing it this way takes longer and it's trickier, but the accurate selections you make will produce a more realistic effect – one that looks like it was produced in the camera, rather than with software.

As with all tools, the Freehand selection tool comes with a wide range of control options available through its Tool Options palette.

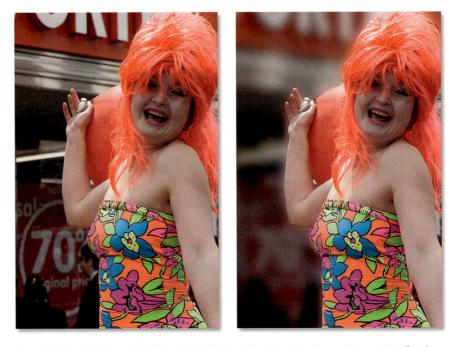

You can blur distracting background detail in a photo by shooting with a wide aperture. You can achieve a similar effect after the event by using carefully made selections and the Gaussian Blur filter.

STEP 1 Open the photo and copy (duplicate) the Background layer by right-clicking it in the Layers palette and selecting Duplicate. Rename the new layer 'Focus'.

STEP 2 Choose the Freehand selection tool and decide its selection parameters: 'Freehand' works simply by dragging the mouse over the canvas. Its 'Edge Seeker' option works as if it has slightly magnetic properties. Use the Smoothing option to make the selection line, well, smoother. 'Point to point' draws a straight line from point to point, creating points with each mouse-click, and is ideal for selecting regular objects such as products. The Smart Edge mode drops a wide line over the desired edges and locates the contrast or color differences underneath that line. Draw your selection around the object or person in the picture you have opened.

STEP 3 Right-click the 'Focus' layer in the Layers palette and select New Mask Layer > Show Selection. This creates a mask layer that covers up the background detail in your 'Focus' layer and allows the Background layer to show through.

STEP 4 Press Ctrl + D to select None and click on the Background layer in the Layers palette. Choose Blur > Gaussian Blur from the Adjust menu and set the Radius to around 20. Click the Preview on Image box to see the results. Don't overdo it – too much blur will look unnatural.

STEP 5 In the example on the previous page the background is all the same distance from the camera. Where the background stretches away into the distance a more natural result can be produced by making several feathered selections radiating out from the subject (three is usually enough) and blurring each one by a progressively greater amount. This simulates objects becoming more out of focus the further away from the camera they are.

Technique: Fixing an Overexposed Sky

All cameras have a habit of making exposure 'mistakes'. Very often this produces a picture with a correctly exposed land section and a poorly exposed sky section. This is usually because the sensor in the digital camera cannot cope with the contrast differences between the land and the sky. Even with many film types, a wide contrast range is hard to record accurately.

The problem can be fixed, but it requires a little ingenuity. If you make an overall Levels adjustment to darken the sky, you'll darken the subject as well, so in this project we'll use a mask layer so that the Levels adjustment applies only to the sky and the correctly exposed subject is untouched. The advantage of this approach is that if the sky is beyond saving with a Levels adjustment you can simply replace it.

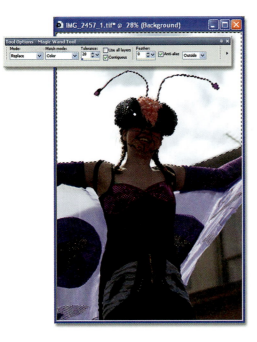

STEP 1 Duplicate the Background layer by right-clicking it in the Layers palette and selecting Duplicate, and call the new layer 'sky'. Select the 'sky' layer and use the Magic Wand to select the sky. You might need to Shift-click the sky several times to grab all the tones. Use Tool Options to vary the Tolerance value to make this more accurate. Consider using the range of Selection Modifiers (Selections > Modify) to make the sky 'grab' more accurate. Here I was lucky and managed to get it all in one hit with a Tolerance setting of 20. You can also apply a small feather to this selection to soften the line where the sky and the land join (i.e. set the selection feather to a value of 1 or 2 pixels only). Alternatively, try using the Background Eraser Brush to cut out the sky (i.e. to make a matte).

STEP 2 Check the accuracy of the selection up close using Selections > Edit Selection to display the mask. If there are any missing bits, I'd suggest using the Remove Specks and Holes Selection Modifier (Selections > Modify > Remove Specks and Holes) to clean it up. When you're happy with it, right-click the 'sky' layer and select New Mask Layer > Show Selection. This masks everything but the sky on the 'sky' layer. With the mask in place you no longer need the selection, so press Ctrl + D to select None.

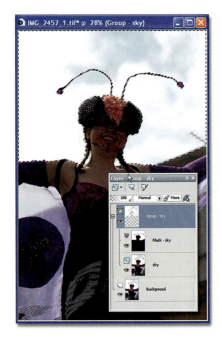

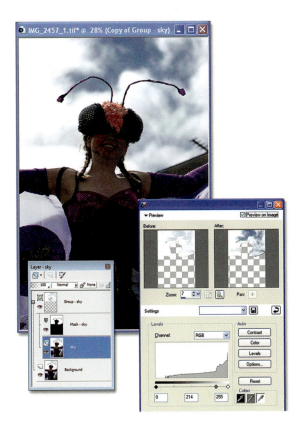

STEP 3 Select the 'sky' layer and choose Brightness and Contrast > Levels from the Adjust menu. Drag the center diamond under the histogram to the right to darken the sky.

STEP 4 If there's no tone in the original (unlikely, unless the sky is drastically overexposed), you'll have to copy another sky from a different picture. Here's where the advantage of using a Mask layer becomes apparent. Just paste the sky detail as a new layer within the mask group.

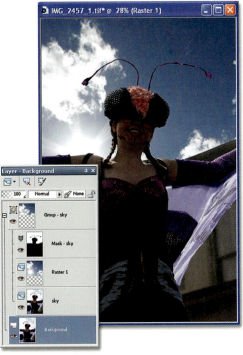

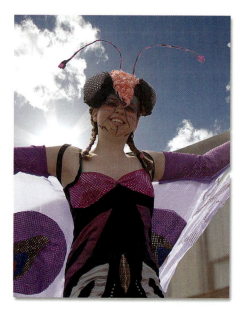

STEP 5 Another advantage of using Mask layers to either make tonal adjustments to the sky or paste in a new one is that you can make adjustments to the rest of the image without affecting what you've already fixed. Here a Levels adjustment has been used on the Background layer to brighten the subject detail.

Technique: HDR Photo Merge

This project has been included here not because it involves making selections, but because it uses a feature introduced in PaintShop Photo Pro X2 that helps to overcome burnt out skies and similar exposure problems. The previous project showed you one way of solving the problem. HDR Photo Merge is a new way to deal with subjects where the range of brightness is too great for your camera to cope with.

To be able to use HDR Photo Merge, you need to take several pictures of a scene, and you also need to be able to manually adjust the exposure controls on your camera. Even compact digital cameras that automatically calculate the exposure for you usually have some form of manual override and some cameras will automatically take several bracketed exposures for you. Check your camera documentation to see if this is possible. If you know all about your camera's aperture and shutter speed settings then you're ready to take advantage of a new and exciting development in digital photography.

Throughout this book you'll see references to exposure problems where the range of light in a scene is too great to be adequately recorded by your digital camera's sensor. Either the shadows are dense and filled in, or the highlights are 'blown' – registering as pure white. HDR Photo Merge allows you to take several different exposures of the same scene and merge them to produce one 'High Dynamic Range' image with much more detail than it's possible to record in a single exposure. In this example we've used three photos; you can use between two and nine, but best results are achieved with three to seven exposures.

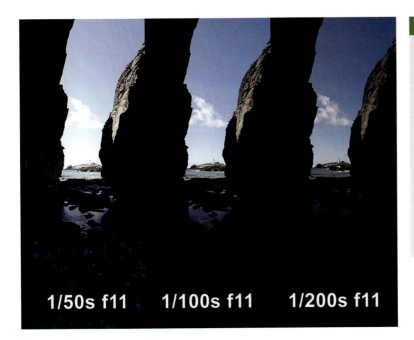

1/50s f11   1/100s f11   1/200s f11

Tip

When shooting, use a tripod if you have one, or rest the camera on something – a wall, the car roof, anything that will keep it steady from shot to shot. Try to ensure there is nothing moving in the frame – wait for people, cars, cyclists, or other moving objects to get out of the way.

STEP 1 Take at least three shots using different exposure settings. Make the first exposure using the correct setting as determined by your camera's metering system, then take additional shots over- and underexposing in one-stop increments. Here, I've made three exposures, one at the indicated setting of 1/100th of a second at f11, another at 1/50th of a second at f11 (one stop overexposed), and a third at 1/200th of a second at f11 (one stop underexposed). It's better to vary the shutter speed, rather than the aperture, so as to maintain the same depth of field in all three exposures.

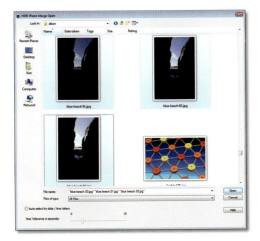

STEP 2 Select HDR Photo Merge from the File menu, click the Browse button, and locate the photos on your hard drive. Hold down the Shift key and click to select adjacent photos in the list or hold down the Ctrl key to select non-adjacent photos. When you've selected all the photos click OK.

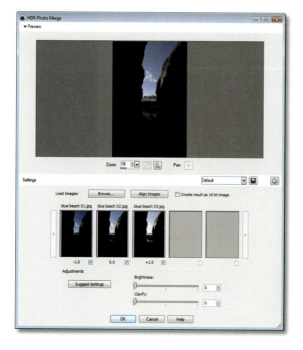

STEP 3 The three images appear in the strip below the preview. The figures below each thumbnail are exposure values – the middle image is correctly exposed and those to the left (−1.0) and right (+1.0) are under- and overexposed by one stop. Detail from all three images is combined and displayed in the preview above. If you used a tripod in Step 1, which I'd strongly recommend if at all possible, all your images will align. If you shot hand-held, click the Align Images button.

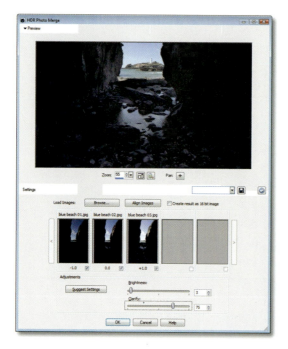

STEP 4 Use the Brightness slider to adjust overall brightness and the Clarify slider to bring out the shadow and highlight detail. Use the Zoom slider to increase the size of the preview so you can see the effect moving the sliders has on the shadow and highlight detail. You can click the Suggest Settings button to automatically adjust the Brightness and Clarify sliders for you, but the results can be erratic. Best results are usually obtained with very small Brightness adjustments and Clarify settings in the range 20–100, but look at the preview and let your eyes be your guide.

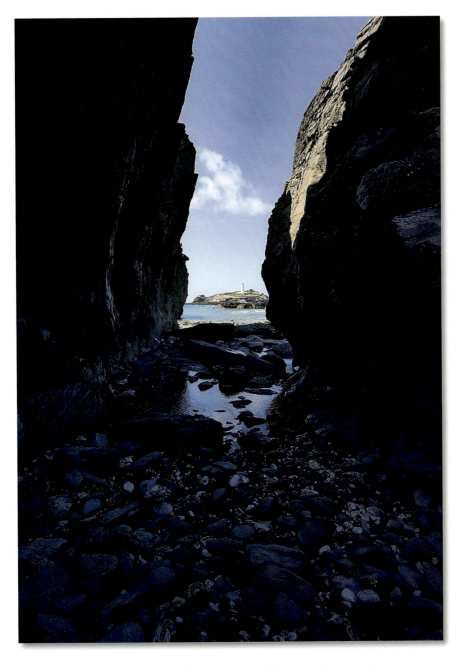

STEP 5 Check the Create result as 16 bit image checkbox to retain as much detail as possible in the final result and click OK to merge the images. The file size will be larger than for an 8-bit image and some filters and adjustments won't work on 16-bit images. You can convert the image to 8 bits per pixel later by selecting Image > Decrease Color Depth > RGB – 8 bits/channel.

Technique: Object Cut-Out

Creating a cut-out, either to replace the background in a photo or to move an object from one photo into another without its background, requires a high degree of selection accuracy. If your cut-out isn't pixel accurate, tell-tale messy edges will give the game away. But with a little care and a technique designed to make the work of the selection tools easier, you can achieve seamless cut-outs.

STEP 1 Open the image to be cut out and rename the Background layer 'Original'. Duplicate it twice and rename the two new layers 'Cut-out' and 'Selection', so that the layers are ordered from top to bottom 'Selection', Cut-out', 'Original'.

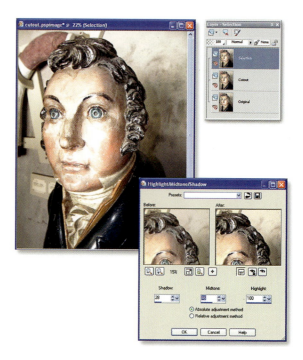

STEP 2 Click the Selection layer in the Layers palette and select Adjust > Brightness and Contrast > Highlight/Midtone/Shadow and increase the Highlight value to 100. This creates greater edge contrast between the figurehead and the background, making it easier for the selection tools to differentiate between the two.

STEP 3 Make sure the Use all layers box in the Tool Options palette is unchecked and use the Magic Wand tool, with a fairly low Tolerance setting, to select portions of the background by Shift-clicking. If you inadvertently select object pixels, press Ctrl + Z and try again, changing the Tolerance or Match mode if it helps. Don't worry if the selection isn't perfect at this stage.

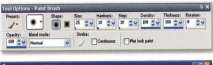

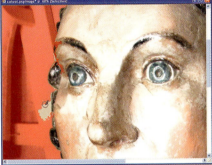

STEP 4 Choose Selection > Modify > Remove Specks and Holes, and save the selection to an alpha channel (Selections > Load/Save Selection > Save Selection to Alpha Channel). In Edit Selection mode (Selections > Edit Selection) paint out any remaining holes in the selection and tidy up the edges using a small, soft-edged brush.

STEP 5 Exit Edit Selection mode (Selections > Edit Selection) and resave the selection, overwriting the existing alpha channel. Press Ctrl + Shift + I to invert the selection, then – and this is very important – in the Layers palette click the eye to turn off the 'Selection' layer and click the 'Cut-out' layer to make it active.

STEP 6 Press Ctrl + C to copy the selection and open the image you want to paste it into. Press Ctrl + E to paste the selection and position it. Press Ctrl + Shift + M to hide the selection marquee.

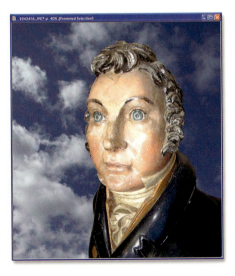

STEP 7 Finally, press Ctrl + Shift + F to defloat the selection and add it to the current layer, or Ctrl + Shift + P to promote it to its own layer and save the new image.

Combining Images – Layers and Masks

- This chapter is all about layers. We've already come across layers in earlier chapters and in some of the step-by-step projects, and we've seen how you can use Adjustment layers to make editable changes to image tones and color.

- Layers are extremely useful as they allow you to combine different elements – photos, text, and graphics – all in the same document. Layers are a little like sheets of tracing paper in a pad – you can see through the topmost layers to those below. PaintShop Photo Pro X3's Layers palette allows you to organize layers into groups, shuffle them around so that some things appear on top of others, change their opacity to make them semi-transparent, even change the way that upper layers interact with what lies beneath.

- As well as learning how to use the Layers palette, this chapter shows you how to combine several photos into one image using layers, how to use PaintShop Photo Pro X3's rulers, grids, and guides to position and align layers, what you can do with Adjustment layers, and how to combine layers.

PaintShop Photo Pro X3 for Photographers. DOI: 10.1016/B978-0-240-52165-7.10006-1

- We'll also take a detailed look at Mask layers, briefly introduced in the last chapter. In the step-by-step projects section at the end of the chapter, I'll show you how to put together everything you've learned to create a photomontage from a bunch of holiday photos, how to use layer deformations to create realistic shadows, and how to mask an Adjustment layer to produce a graduated color effect.

Layers allow you to combine several images – each stacked one above the other – in a single document. The biggest advantage of layers is that they allow you to put elements on top of one another without destroying what's underneath. But, as we shall see, the advantages of using layers go far beyond that.

Understanding Layers

What is a layer? A layer is simply one picture sitting directly on top of another. Layers can contain whole photos, text, vector drawings, scanned art or anything else that can be digitized. You can add as many layers as you want in one document, depending on your requirements. The reason for building up these layers is to maintain the picture's editability. While a picture retains its layers, it can always be edited. Flatten (or squash) those layers, so that it can be emailed, for example, and you lose the power to edit it.

PaintShop Photo Pro has quite sophisticated layering capabilities. What I mean by that is, not only does it allow you to create montages from multi-layered documents, but it also has a range of features like Adjustment Layers that open up even more editing possibilities. So much so that every stage in the image-building process can be deconstructed, changed, altered, improved, and returned to its place, over and over again, with incredible accuracy and remarkable ease.

Who Uses Layers?

Layers are used by anyone who adds text to a document, whether a single character or a page of copy for a brochure. Layers are used to make multi-image montages where several pictures blend seamlessly into one. Layers are used extensively by designers, illustrators, and web designers – anyone, in fact, who uses images that have more than one picture element in them.

What Can You Do With Layers?

A layer is like a clear sheet of acetate. Layers can be opaque or transparent, and they can contain pixels (bitmap) or vector data (text and shapes).

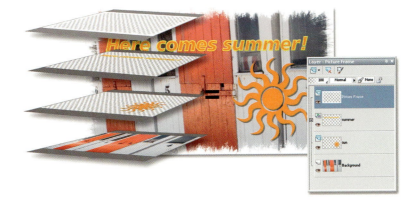

FIG 6.1 The illustration here shows how a layered image works. Viewed from above (i.e. in the work area) the picture looks perfectly normal, but exploring the Layer palette shows that it is in fact composed of four separate layers – all of which can be moved or can have their color/tones changed independently. Layers files must be saved as either '.pspimage' files or, for more cross-computer compatibility, in the '.psd' (Adobe Photoshop) file format. Using either of these file formats preserves the layer integrity.

You can cut, copy, and paste layers from one document to another. Layers can be flipped, rotated, resized, distorted, rearranged, or grouped in any number of combinations. You can apply color and tonal adjustments to single layers – and you can add a full range of filter effects, as if one layer were a single picture. Only while the layered document retains its original layers does it remain editable. For seasoned image-makers, this layer editability remains a powerful attraction. How many times have you finished creating a particular work of art only to spot something that you missed but that you now can't change? If you use layers, and have saved the layered version of the image (as mentioned previously), you can make that change!

Before you get too excited, layers have disadvantages:

· Multiple layers create a spaghetti-like complexity that can be hard to keep track of and results in latency (the program taking a moment or more to execute or finish a command).
· The more layers you add to a document, the harder it becomes for the computer to process changes. Each additional layer adds to the document file size.

Layers offer a tremendous potential for the creative image-maker. Simply adjusting the opacity of an individual layer allows you to see everything on the layer beneath. Each layer also has a range of blend modes. These can be adjusted in order to radically change the way the pixels in the layer react with the pixels in the layer directly below.

Once you understand that layers are similar in appearance to Disney-style punched animation cells or kids' cartoon flip-books, you can begin to appreciate the idea behind their function.

159

We already know that PaintShop Photo Pro has an almost limitless Undo feature (Ctrl + Z). This means that you can reverse the picture-building process by up to 1000 steps; however, in accepting an Undo command and then saving, those steps are lost forever. If you are working with layers, you can apply major editing stages to different layers and retain everything in the one document, regardless of whether you are using it or not. Each layer has a small eye icon called the 'Visibility toggle'. Click the Visibility toggle to switch the layer 'off', click again to switch it back 'on'.

Like the Disney animation process, layers sit perfectly aligned ('registered') over the layer beneath. If the top layer has an opacity of 100%, you won't be able to see through it to the layer underneath. Reduce its opacity (or change the blend mode) and you'll see the layer, or layers, beneath it. Reduce the size of the contents of the top layer and you'll be able to view the content of at least some of the layers below.

If you build up the number of layers in a document, the total file size increases. Image-makers need to be aware of this because if the computer has limited amounts of RAM or processing power, it might affect performance. To make this less of a hassle, PaintShop Photo Pro allows you to merge selected layers into each other. You'd do this to layers, or groups of layers, that are similar or are finished with (i.e. you are sure that they'll never need changing).

You might also do this to layers that, once merged, can be separated again if necessary using a selection. Though merging or flattening layers frees valuable computer resources, RAM is cheap enough, so I'd suggest buying more and keeping the layers for editing because you never know.

FIG 6.2 The Layers palette is the control center for layers and the things on them. It helps you organize and keep track of all the layers within an image. There are five layer types – Raster, Vector, Art Media, Adjustment, and Mask layers. Layers are arranged in order in the Layers palette. The topmost layer in the image appears at the top of the palette; you can rearrange the layers by dragging and dropping. This is the Layers palette showing the individual layers and thumbnail images of the content on each for the montage created in the step-by-step project at the end of the chapter. It is composed of several layers organized into groups. Each group consists of two layers – a Raster layer containing the image and a Mask layer. (a) New Raster layer (other layer types are available from the pull-down menu). (b) Delete layer. (c) Edit Selection. (d) Layer blend mode. (e) Layer link toggle. (f) Layer opacity. (g) Layer group. (h) Raster layer group. (i) Mask layer. (j) Raster layer. (k) Visibility toggle. (l) Click the plus sign to expand and see each object in a layer group and the minus sign to contract it. (m) Lock transparency.

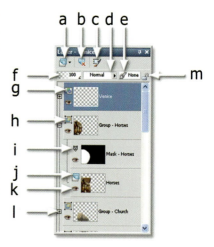

What Features Can Be Found in Layers?

- Move the picture elements on layers in any direction
- Change the tone, color, contrast, and alignment of any layer
- Mix Vector and Bitmap layers in one document
- Create new, blank Vector and Bitmap layers at the press of a button
- Collect selected layers into Layer Groups
- Copy single layers, or groups of layers, into the same or a new document
- Convert selections into layers
- Paste layers and selections from other documents into a new document
- Layers can be reordered by dragging them up or down in the Layers palette
- Layers can be switched 'on' and 'off' by clicking the Visibility toggle (the eye icon) in the Layers palette
- You can paste the contents of the clipboard into a new layer
- Duplicate a layer using the Duplicate command (Layers > Duplicate) or by pressing the Duplicate tab in the palette
- Use the Edit Selection button in the Layers palette to edit a selection (Selection Edit mode).

Combining Pictures

PaintShop Photo Pro permits the user to create and save every stage of the image-building process as a separate layer. These layers can be switched on or off according to their application. You can also store masks and selections as separate channels in layered documents. These too can be switched on and off. In PaintShop Photo Pro, any document that has layers, masks, or selections has to be saved in a special native PaintShop Photo Pro file format with a '.pspimage' file ending.

While '.pspimage' retains layers, this file format is for use only in PaintShop Pro; you cannot use '.pspimage' files for email and (some) other jobs. The file has to be converted first or copied to a more suitable file type, such as JPEG or TIFF. First you must flatten the file (Layers > Merge > Merge All (Flatten)). Doing this turns it into a single-layered document. This loses most of its editability, which is why you should only do this to a copy of the original '.pspimage' file. Save your layered documents as master files and then make copies from that master for use in other, non-layered file applications.

The simplest way to combine two pictures into one document is to copy one and paste it as a new layer into the other. While these multiple layers are totally separate from each other, it's important to note that they can be edited at any time as if they were two totally different picture elements. However, because they are in the same document, you also have to contend with their relationship. While copying and pasting one picture into another is by far the easiest way to add another picture to a document, there are a few points to consider first.

> **Tip**
>
> The base layer is called the 'Background' and is, in fact, not a layer at all. However, it can be 'promoted' (converted) into a layer if needed (right-click on the Background layer in the Layer palette and choose 'Promote Background Layer' from the contextual menu). If you don't want to promote the background, you can simply duplicate it.

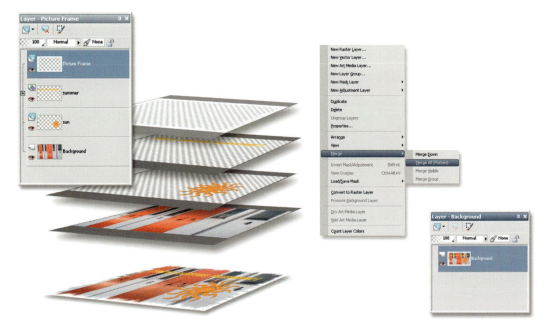

FIG 6.3 A layered (.pspimage) document is more editable than any other format. Because of this it's also too large for many applications, such as emailing or storage on a limited size disk. For this reason it is important to make a copy and to flatten or merge those layers so that the resulting single-layered document can be resaved in a smaller file format, like JPEG or TIFF.

The resolution of the pasted image, measured in pixel dimensions or dots per inch, is relevant. For example, if this is larger than the receiving image it will overspill (bleed off the edges) once pasted. However, even though it looks as if the edges of the pasted image have disappeared, the program does not discard them; they are still there but only become visible if dragged into view using the Move tool ('M').

Another factor to watch out for when combining pictures is their respective color mode and bit depth. Providing that the color mode of the master document is either 24-bit or grayscale, it will prevail over what is being pasted into it. If you copy an 8-bit picture into a 24-bit color picture, the Bit depth of the pasted picture will be increased to match that of the host document. On the other scale, if you try to paste a color picture into a black and white image, it will be converted into the mode of mono image.

PaintShop Photo Pro offers a number of ways to paste copied images into another document via the Edit menu, by right-clicking in the new document, or using keyboard shortcuts (see list at the back of the book). These are:

Tip

To maintain the aspect ratio of a layer while resizing it (in other words, to avoid stretching or squeezing it), use the right mouse button to drag a corner handle.

- Paste as New Image. This creates a new picture on its own background.
- Paste as New Layer. This adds the contents of the clipboard to the selected document background. PaintShop Photo Pro automatically creates a new layer for the pasted image. If the pasted image matches the physical dimensions of the target image, it will obscure the lower layer or background picture.
- Paste as New Selection. This pastes the newly selected picture into the target document, but it remains attached to the cursor so that it can be positioned somewhere other than directly on top of the background. Left-click to offload the layer and view the selection marquee. The pasted layer then becomes a floating selection until it is deselected. You can save this selection as an alpha channel (in case it is needed again: Selections > Save To Alpha Channel). If you already have a floating selection, it will be defloated and deselected before another picture can be pasted into the document (i.e. you can't have two floating selections in one document).
- Paste as Transparent Selection. This command does the same as the Paste as New Selection command, but enables you to import transparency from another image. Because of this transparency, the pasted layer is attached to the Move tool for easy repositioning. Click in the image to free it once it is in the right position.

What Can You Do With Layers?

- Change the individual tonal appearance of each layer
- Make and edit selections on individual layers
- Add blend modes to individual layers for special effects
- Save layer selection and mask information to an alpha channel and to disk
- Add Adjustment layers
- Apply any of PaintShop Photo Pro's filter effects to a layer
- Bend and transform the shape of any object on a layer
- Convert Vector layers to Bitmap layers.

Advanced Layout Tools

As we have seen, there are many ways to use PaintShop Photo Pro for combining multiple layers into a single document. In the following section we'll take a look at some of the features designed to make laying out and arranging multiple picture documents easier. You'll find these tools useful for positioning and aligning multiple photos as well as for adding annotation labels.

Tip

To remove all of the guides on a photo select Change Grid, Guide & Snap Properties from the view menu (or double-click one of the Rulers), click the Guides tab if it isn't already displayed, and check the Delete guides box. You can delete guides from the current image or from all open images.

Under PaintShop Photo Pro's View menu there are a number of highly useful productivity-enhancing features designed to make aligning and arranging multi-layer images faster and easier. These are:

- Rulers. The keyboard shortcut 'Ctrl + Alt + R' adds rulers along the X- and Y-axes of the picture window. You can change the units of measurement (pixels/inches/centimeters) through the program's General Preferences (File > Preferences > General Program Preferences, then click on Units in the Preference column on the left). Place the cursor anywhere in the image and you can read out the exact location in the corresponding margin. It's a handy tool, especially if you are working with extremely small picture elements on multiple layers.

- Grid. If you find the grid too heavy, double-click on the rulers in the margin and you'll see the Grid, Guide & Snap Properties dialog. Change the units used and the color to make it appear friendlier. You'll need to make adjustments every now and then for different-sized pictures. This is a useful feature for precise layer or picture element alignment.

- Guides. This is one of the neatest design assistants in PaintShop Photo Pro. It works only if 'Rulers' are switched 'on'. Guides are colored lines that can be pulled out of the margins (using the cursor regardless of the tool currently selected) and dragged over the picture to form, well, design or layout guides. There are no limits to the number of guides that can be used in one document. Guides can be repositioned by grabbing the guide

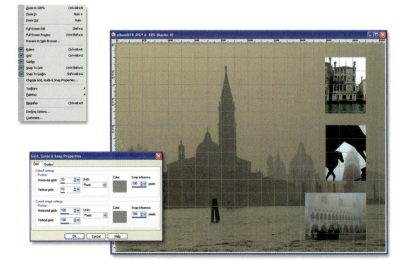

FIG 6.4 PaintShop Photo Pro's rulers, guides, and grid enable you to accurately position and align elements. Snap to Grid and Snap to Guides make the grid and guides behave as though magnetized – they attract and hold dragged objects that are in close proximity. Double-click the rulers (or select View > Change Grid, Guide & Snap Properties) to change grid spacing and other grid and guide properties.

handle (that's the thicker bit of guideline that appears inside the ruler margin as you move the cursor over it). If you want to change the guide properties, double-click the ruler to open its window or just click the guide handle in the margin to open the Grid, Guide & Snap Properties dialog. This allows you to change its color, position, or existence!

·   Snap to Guides. This function adds tremendous power to the task of aligning multiple layers along a common axis – by selecting this option and making sure that, in the Grid, Guide & Snap Properties dialog, the Snap Influence setting is set to more than 1. The effect of this is that if you grab an image layer using the Move tool and drag it towards the guide, it appears to be magnetically attracted to the line. In fact, it 'snaps' to the line. Increase this value to increase the magnetic power.

You can change any of these settings for the opened document only, or for the default settings. This feature is a real production enhancer. Under the Layers palette we have:

·   Layer Opacity. All layers have an opacity scale controlled from the Layers palette. The default setting is 100%. Reducing this allows you to see through the layer to whatever lies beneath. Do this to help align specific pictures or graphic elements with stuff that lies beneath.

Under the Layer menu we find:

·   Arrange. This feature allows you to swap the layer order, although you can also do this by using the cursor to grab a layer in the palette and dragging it to another position in the stack.
·   View. This controls which layers are visible and which are not. You may also switch a layer 'on' and 'off' by clicking on the eye icon in the palette itself.
·   Merge. Merge allows you to do just that: merge or blend selected layers. Merge Visible flattens only the layers with the eye icon switched 'on' (i.e. those that are visible on the desktop).

Using Adjustment Layers

Making tonal adjustments to a digital photo, for example brightening the midtones and shadows with a Levels adjustment, changing the color balance, or using the Fill Flash filter, changes the value of pixels within the image. Other than by pressing Ctrl + Z to undo, these changes are irreversible. Opening, say, the Levels dialog box and making an adjustment in the opposite direction will not get you back to where you started.

But what if you could apply such changes and, if you later changed your mind, remove them, as if they'd never been applied in the first place? Adjustment layers allow you to do exactly that. Adjustment layers are a safer, more versatile way of applying image adjustments because, as well as turning them 'on' and 'off' just like other layers, you can apply Adjustment layers to one or several layers within the image.

> **Tip**
>
> To change the ruler units, choose File > Preferences > General Program Preferences, and select Units from the list in the Preferences dialog box. You can choose between Pixels, Inches, and Centimeters.

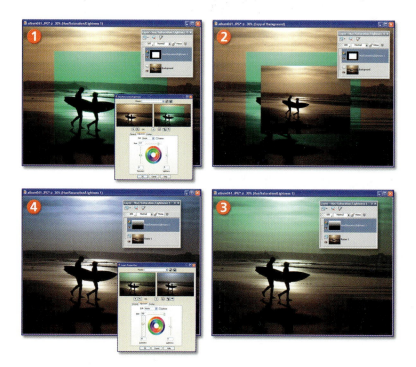

FIG 6.5 Clockwise from top left: (1) Here, I've made a rectangular selection and added a Hue/Saturation/Lightness Adjustment layer. The new Layers palette displays a thumbnail of the mask. (2) The Background layer has been duplicated, resized, and dragged to the top of the stack – the Adjustment layer affects only the original Background layer below it. (3) Filling an Adjustment layer with a linear gradient applies more correction at the top, gradually reducing towards the bottom. (4) An Adjustment layer is infinitely editable with no loss of image quality.

You can also go back to Adjustment layers and edit the settings at any time without causing any degradation in image quality. With Adjustment layers, doing the opposite to a previous adjustment does get you back exactly where you started. Earlier we spoke of layers as being like acetate sheets stacked on top of the background image.

Think of Adjustment layers in the same way – as a clear sheet to which you can apply adjustments and through which you view layers below. The appearance of the pixels in the underlying layers is affected by the Adjustment layer, but the pixels themselves are not altered.

Whereas an adjustment affects only the active layer, an Adjustment layer acts on all the layers beneath it, or all the layers within a Layer Group. By careful positioning of Adjustment layers you can change only one part of an image. Adjustment layers are frequently used when combining images to make the new image elements match in terms of color and lighting.

Another way of limiting Adjustment layers is by editing them in the same way as Mask layers. You'll remember from the previous chapter that Mask layers are grayscale and pixel values in the Mask layer affect the opacity of corresponding pixels in underlying layers. Adjustment layers are also gray-scale and their effect on underlying layers is likewise dependent on the pixels within the mask. Black pixels apply no correction, white pixels apply the full amount of correction, and gray pixels apply varying amounts of correction in between.

You can vary the overall effect of an Adjustment layer using its Opacity slider in the Layers palette. Alternatively, you can apply the Adjustment layer to a selection, or paint directly on to it to isolate the parts of the layer you want the adjustment to affect.

Layer Types

You can add the following types of Adjustment layer:

·   Color Balance
·   Hue/Saturation/Lightness
·   Channel mixer
·   Brightness/Contrast
·   Curves
·   Levels
·   Invert
·   Threshold
·   Posterize.

Advantages of Adjustment Layers

·   Add a range of tone and effects changes to a layer or layers without actually changing the original layer.
·   Useful for applying overall color or tone changes to multiple layers at a time.
·   Can be removed by deleting the Adjustment layer, or switching it 'off'.
·   Ideal for anyone working with panoramas.

Creating Layer Blend Mode Effects

Blend modes determine how pixels in a layer interact with corresponding pixels in underlying layers. The default blend mode is 'Normal' – the pixel in the top layer is superimposed on (and therefore hides) the pixel in the underlying layers (subject to transparency settings).

There are 20 other blend modes in addition to 'Normal' and each provides a slightly different result. 'Darken', for example, displays only pixels in the selected layer that are darker than corresponding pixels in underlying layers; lighter pixels in the selected layer disappear. The Lighten blend mode does the opposite. 'Color' applies the hue and saturation of pixels in the selected layer to underlying layers without affecting lightness and 'Difference' subtracts the selected layer's color from the color of underlying layers.

Some blend modes have practical applications. 'Darken' and 'Lighten' are useful for retouching and cloning. You can also use 'Darken' to get rid of a white background on a logo or other arwork. 'Multiply', which combines the colors in the selected layer with underlying layers to produce a darker color, is useful for producing realistic drop shadows.

Because the outcome depends on initial pixel values in the selected and underlying layers, the results of some blend modes can be hard to predict. If you are working with two layers, simply swapping the layer order can produce very different results. This makes blend modes an excellent tool for creating special effects with multiple images, and works especially well with text, but a certain amount of experimentation is often required to get a good result.

Blend modes can be selected for most of PaintShop Photo Pro's Brush tools as well as layers – the Blend mode pull-down menu in the Tool Options palette provides exactly the same options as are available in the Layers palette.

Using Mask Layers

A Mask layer works a bit like a stencil – holding back some parts of the image and revealing others. We briefly looked at Mask layers in the previous chapter on using selections. Mask layers, alpha channels, and selections are a bit difficult to pin down in terms of definitions because they all do pretty much the same thing – control which parts of the image are displayed or affected by an adjustment – in slightly different ways.

Earlier, we saw how Adjustment layers could be used as Mask layers to confine their corrections to one part of the image, but a Mask layer is more often used to hide parts of the image without actually deleting it. The advantage of this should be fairly obvious; you can subsequently edit the mask to reveal hidden parts of the underlying layers or, conversely, to hide more.

Usually, the best starting point for creating a mask is a selection. Make a selection using one or a combination of the selection tools and modifiers, and from the Layers menu choose New Mask Layer > Show Selection to create a mask that shows the selected parts of the layer and hides everything else. To create a mask that hides the selected area choose Layers > New Mask Layer > Hide Selection. If you are masking a Background layer, Paint-Shop Photo Pro will display an alert box notifying you that 'the target must be promoted to a full layer'; click OK.

PaintShop Photo Pro automatically creates a new Layer Group containing the selected layer and the new mask. This is so that the mask doesn't affect other layers in your image. If you want the mask to apply to all the layers beneath it, drag it in the Layers palette from the Layer Group to the top of the layer

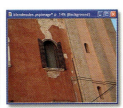

Top

Bottom

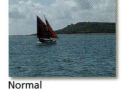

Normal

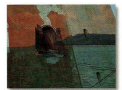

Darken

Lighten

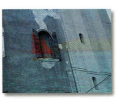

Hue

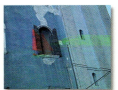

Hue (Legacy)

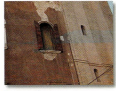

Saturation

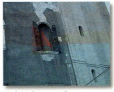

Saturation (Legacy)

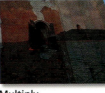

Color

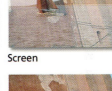

Color (Legacy)

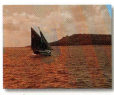

Luminance

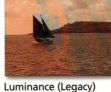

Luminance (Legacy)

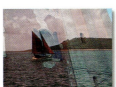

Multiply

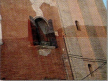

Screen

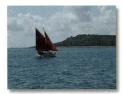

Dissolve

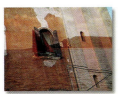

Overlay

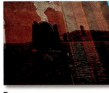

Hard Light

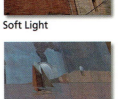

Soft Light

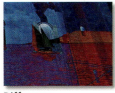

Difference

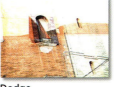

Dodge

Burn

Exclusion

FIG 6.6 PaintShop Photo Pro's 21 blend modes as applied to the two images 'Top' and 'Bottom'. Results depend on layer content and order. Layer modes can be particularly effective when used with Text layers. Legacy modes maintain compatibility with earlier versions, so if you want to replicate an effect you created in PaintShop Pro 9 you shouldn't have any difficulty. Generally, though, the newer versions produce better results.

stack. With the mask in place, you can press Ctrl + D or Selections > Select None. If you need it, you can recover the selection at any time with Ctrl + Shift + S or Selections > From Mask.

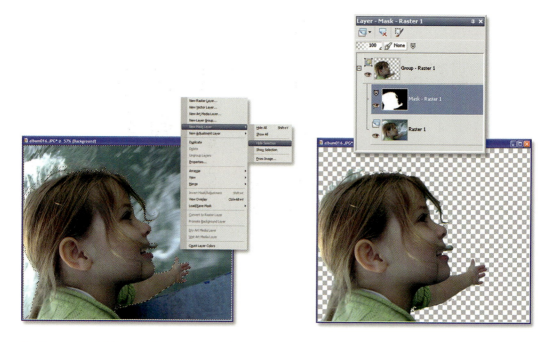

FIG 6.7 A selection is often the best starting point for a mask. The existence of two options – Show Selection and Hide Selection – negates the need to invert the selection if you want to hide the selected area, as here.

Modifying Masks

One of the best things about masks is that you can use PaintShop Photo Pro's Brush tools to edit them. Painting masks is often an easier and more accurate way to clean up selections than using the selection modifiers. You can, for example, use a soft-edged brush to clean up the edge detail of difficult subjects like fur, hair, or indeed anything that doesn't have a clearly defined edge.

To use the Brush tools to directly edit a Mask layer, select the Mask layer in the Layers palette and choose the Paint Brush tool. You may have noticed that the foreground and background swatches in the Materials palette change to grayscale when a Mask layer is selected; remember, mask layers are grayscale, so you can only paint on them using black, white, or one of 254 levels of gray. Painting on the mask with black will add to the mask and remove detail from the underlying layer. Painting with white will remove the

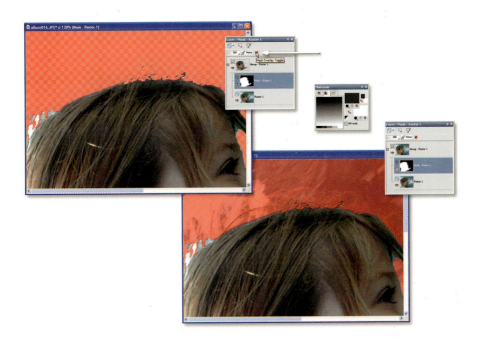

FIG 6.8 Painting on a Mask layer provides a simple, yet effective, method of cleaning up selections. Click the Mask Overlay button to display the mask as a red tint on the underlying layer; turning the Mask layer off allows you to view both masked and unmasked detail.

mask and reveal detail on the underlying layer. If you paint with gray, you'll make parts of the underlying layer semi-transparent. It's usually easiest to use just black and white and change the brush settings in the Tool Options palette to achieve the required effect. As we've said before, this kind of editing is made much easier using a tablet and stylus.

Adding to the mask – painting out detail on the underlying layer – is quite straightforward because you can see what you are doing. Painting detail back in by removing black areas from the mask is trickier because you can see neither the mask nor the detail. To display the mask, click the Mask Overlay button on the Layers palette. This overlays the Mask layer with black areas displayed as a 50% red tint over the target layer(s).

Combining Layers

Some digital image-makers work with multiple images and image masks. In this situation it is vital to remember exactly what you are doing and what the final planned result should look like. To this end, use sketches to keep your mind clear where each image is to be placed in the frame and try to label all the layers, Layer Groups, and masks. Doing this (by double-clicking each layer and entering the details in the dialog) will make the masking and blending process somewhat clearer, especially when there are 20 or more layers to contend with.

171

As we've seen, images with lots of layers create large file sizes and it's often difficult to discover which bits of the image are on what layer. You can simplify PaintShop Pro images and drastically reduce the file size by flattening them, or merging layers together. There are four merge options on the Layers > Merge menu – Merge Down, Merge All (Flatten), Merge Visible, and Merge Group. Masks that are associated with underlying layers as part of a Layer Group can easily be merged using Layers > Merge > Merge Group.

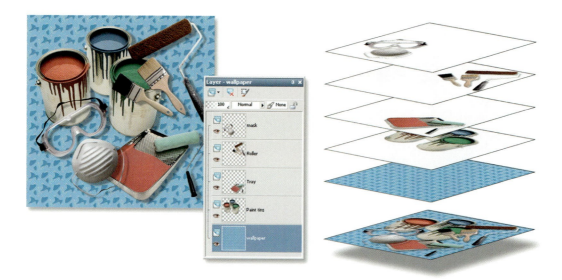

FIG 6.9 Combine Raster layers, Vector layers, Art Media layers, Adjustment layers, and Mask layers to simplify images and produce smaller files. Keep a backup copy with all the layers intact in case you need to re-edit the image.

Tip

Displaying the Mask Overlay, but turning off the Mask layer itself, shows the mask on top of the unmasked layer below, making it much easier to see what you're doing when painting on to the mask.

When you do this, the mask is applied to the image and masked areas are deleted. Simply deleting the mask has the same effect.

Merging layers means you no longer have the editing flexibility that they provided, so if you're likely to want to carry out further changes later, make a backup copy with all the layers intact using File > Save Copy As before you start merging.

Saving Masks

To save an image with masks, use the '.pspimage' format. You can save a Mask layer to its own file on disk – choose Layers > Load/Save Mask > Save Mask To Disk. The default location for saved masks is in the Masks folder in the My PSP Files folder, which is installed into your My Documents folder by default. This folder is where all your custom content (Tubes, Masks,

Selections, etc.) is saved. You will also find a selection of ready-made masks in the Masks folder in the PaintShop Photo Pro program folder. These can be used for framing and other effects.

Only two formats support images with masks and other types of layer: they are the '.pspimage' and '.psd' (Photoshop) formats. If you want to save your image with all layers intact use one of these two file formats. If you attempt to save your image in a file format that doesn't support layers, PaintShop Photo Pro warns you before flattening the image and saving it.

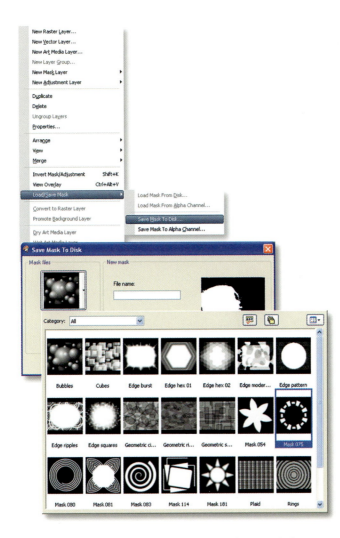

FIG 6.10 As well as saving your own masks to disk, PaintShop Photo Pro provides a selection of existing masks that you can use to frame layers and create special effects.

Step-by-Step Projects

Technique: Creating the Perfect Shadow

PaintShop Photo Pro's Drop Shadow Layer Style and filter are great for adding drop shadows to two-dimensional objects like photos and text, but if you want to add a realistic drop shadow to a 3D object you need to create additional layers and use the deformation tools to produce a realistic shadow shape. It's not a difficult technique, and once you've mastered it you'll be able to add realistic shadows to all manner of things from signposts, cars and coffee cups to people, even painters and decorators.

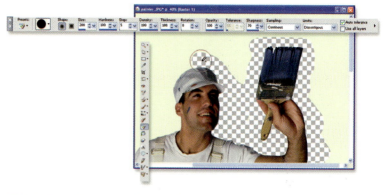

STEP 1 Right-click the Background layer in the Layers palette and select Promote Background Layer. Unless you're lucky, the object you want to create a shadow for won't be on a transparent background, so you'll have to cut it out. If it's on a complicated background you can use the object cut-out technique demonstrated on page 154. This one has a white backgound, which the Background Eraser makes light work of. While you're using the Background Eraser, hold down the space bar to temporarily access the Pan tool and move around the image.

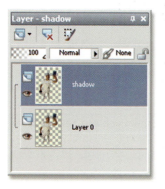

STEP 2 When all of the background is removed, duplicate the layer by right-clicking it and selecting Duplicate from the context menu. Rename the duplicated layer by clicking its name in the Layers palette (or by right-clicking the layer and selecting Rename) and overwriting it. Call it 'shadow'. The Layers palette should now look like this.

STEP 3 Open the Brightness and Contrast dialog box (Adjust > Brightness and Contrast > Brightness/ Contrast) and drag the Brightness slider all the way to the left until the Brightness field reads −255. You'll see the preview thumbnail turn black and the image window will mirror this change if you check the Preview on Image checkbox. Click OK to apply the adjustment.

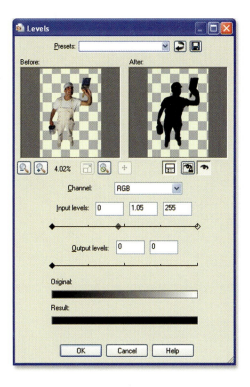

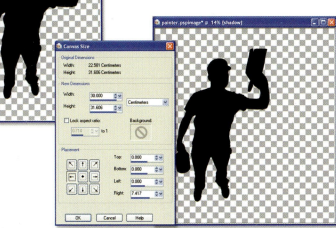

STEP 4 You may need to add more canvas to fit the shadow in. Select Image > Canvas Size and increase the width and height as necessary. To add canvas on the right, click the top left placement button, select Centimeters from the pull-down menu, and add around 4 cm to the existing width value, e.g if the original width is 16.5 cm make it 20.5 cm. If you add too much canvas either press Ctrl + Z to undo and try again or remove it using the Crop tool.

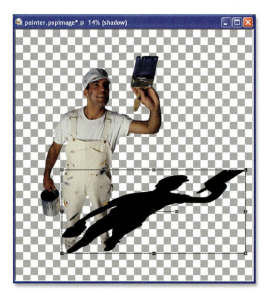

STEP 5 Select the Pick tool and click on the shadow object. Hold down the Shift key and drag the middle handle on the top edge sideways to the right to skew it. Let go, then drag the handle (this time without holding down Shift) downwards to shorten it. Make further skew and shortening adjustments until the shadow shape fits with the kind of lighting setup you are trying to create. The higher the light the shorter the shadow will be, and the further to the right the more skew you will need.

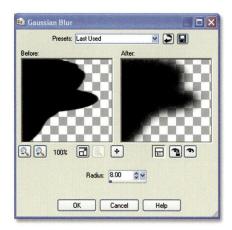

STEP 6 It's beginning to look more like a shadow, but we're not there yet. Select Adjust > Blur > Gaussian Blur and enter a value in the Radius field of around 8, just enough to soften the edges. Click the Preview on Image button to preview the effect in the image window. Pixel value settings like Radius are dependent on the size of the image, so if you're working on a smaller photo for the Web a lower Radius value of 2 or 3 would be enough.

STEP 7 The problem with adding computer-generated effects to photos is that they lack texture, and everything in a photo, even shadows, has texture. Use the Add Noise filter (Adjust > Add/ Remove Noise > Add Noise) to put some texture into the shadow. Check the Gaussian button and Monochrome box and use a noise setting of around 15%. Click OK to apply the noise.

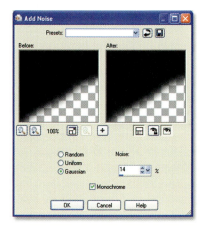

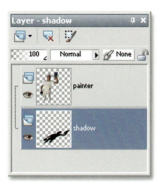

STEP 8 Shadows generally appear behind rather than in front of objects, so drag the shadow layer to the bottom in the Layers palette. You could also rename the other layer 'painter' or something else appropriate to your subject. Naming layers like this can help you keep track of things. It's not so important when there are only one or two layers, but in more complex images with multiple layers and Mask layers it helps to keep things organized.

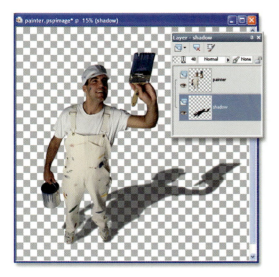

STEP 9 Shadows are rarely solid black. Reduce the shadow layer opacity by dragging the Opacity slider in the Layers palette to around 50%.

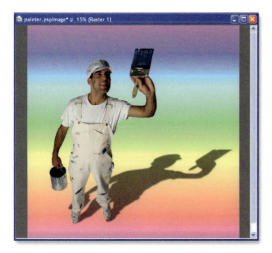

STEP 10 Add a Background layer. Select Layer > New Raster Layer and click OK to accept the default settings. Drag the layer to the bottom of the Layers palette, then use the Materials palette to select and apply a solid color, gradient, or pattern to the new layer.

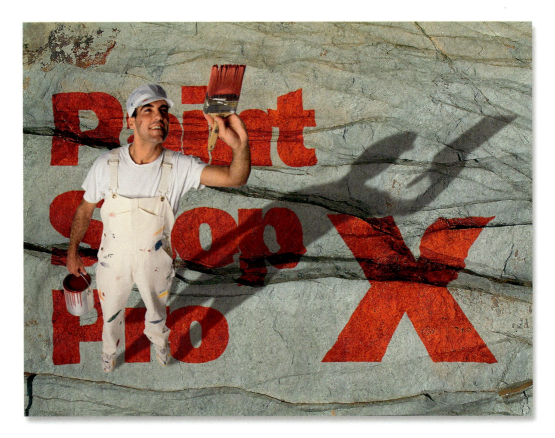

You can, of course, place your transparent object and shadow on any background, including other pictures. Here, the painter has been superimposed on the rock image from Chapter 7. His shadow has been deformed, like the type, to follow the contours of the rock face using the displacement map technique described on pages 234–238. The paint on the brush and in the tin has been changed from blue to red using the Hue Map.

Technique: Creating Graduated Effects with Masks

As we've seen in this chapter you can use masks to selectively apply adjustments, effects filters, and other changes that are usually global to specific parts of the image. We've seen how you can make a selection, save it as a mask, and then paint on the mask to restrict or spread the scope of changes at will.

All of this takes time and a little skill. In this project I'll show you how you can apply effects selectively using masks produced with a gradient fill. This is very simple and takes only a few seconds, but the results can look stunning. You can use these masks with adjustment layers, special effects filters or any other process you've applied to an image, so the possible applications are limited only by your imagination.

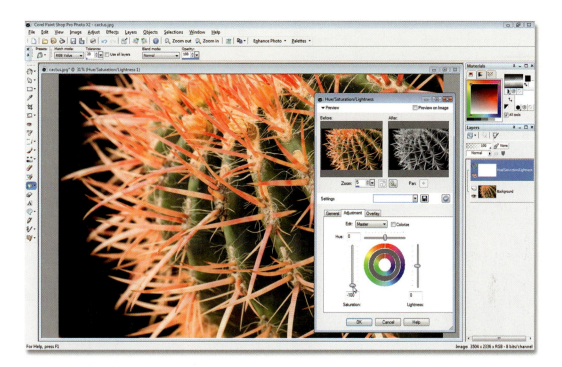

STEP 1 Open the photo you want to work on – you can use this one if you want, download it from www.gopaintshoppro.co.uk. From the Layers menu, select New Adjustment Layer > Hue/Saturation/Lightness and drag the Saturation slider (the one on the left of the dialog box) down as far as it will go to −100, then click OK.

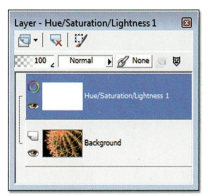

Tip

Click the Mask Overlay toggle button in the Layers palette to overlay and edit the Adjustment layer mask on the image.

STEP 2 The image is now desaturated – but the color is still there in the Background layer. Take a look at the Layers palette and you can see the untouched Background layer with the layer thumbnail showing the full color photo. Above it is the Hue/Saturation/Lightness Adjustment layer. Its thumbnail shows the layer mask; in this case it's completely white, indicating that the Adjustment layer works on the entire image area.

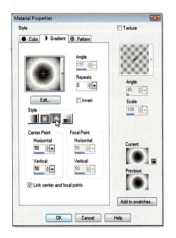

STEP 3 Now to choose a gradient that we'll apply to mask the Hue/Saturation/Lightness Adjustment layer. Click the Color button in the Materials palette and select the Gradient fly-out, then click the Foreground and Stroke properties swatch to open the Material Properties dialog box. Choose from one of the available gradients – this one is called Gray Accent; click the Sunburst Style button to make the gradient radiate out from the center to the edges, then click OK. When used as a mask the black areas will hide the Adjustment layer and the white areas will show it, so there will be color in the center and the image will fade to black and white towards the edges. For color at the edges, fading to black and white in the middle, click the Invert button.

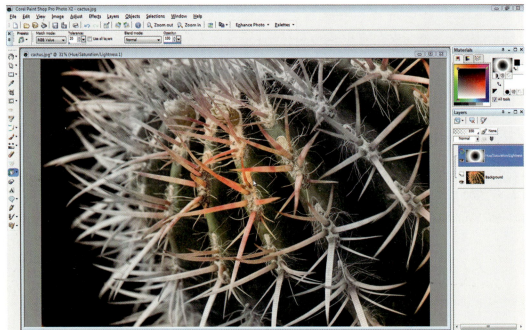

STEP 4 Select the Flood Fill tool from the Tools toolbox, make sure the Hue/Saturation/Lightness Adjustment Layer is still selected in the Layers palette, and click anywhere on the photo to apply the gradient. Two things will happen now. The color will reappear in the center of the photo as the gradient fill is applied to the Adjustment layer's mask. Take another look at the Hue/Saturation/Lightness Adjustment layer thumbnail in the Layers palette and you'll notice that it now shows the gradient fill that you just applied. Everywhere that appears black on the Adjustment layer thumbnail, the effect of the Adjustment layer is masked and the Background layer color shows through.

STEP 5 If you're not happy with the way things look just press the Delete key to remove the fill from the Adjustment layer mask, or press Ctrl + Z to undo. Then select a different gradient and try again. On the website at www. gopaintshoppro.co.uk, you'll find an extended version of this project that shows you how to use a similar technique to mask filter effects.

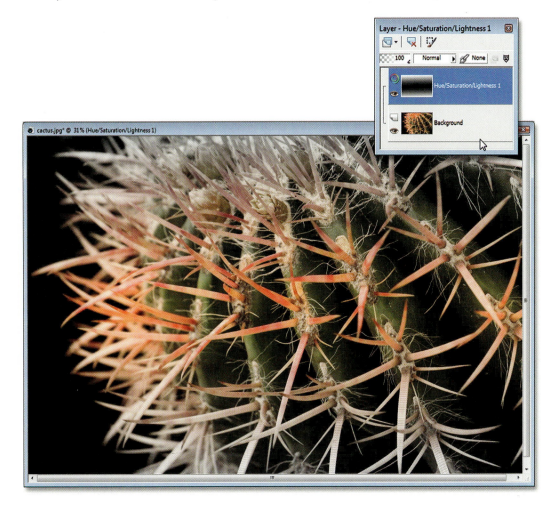

Here I've deleted the gradient fill used in Step 4 and applied a linear white/ black/white gradient, which I created by editing one of the gradient presets in the Material Properties dialog box. This is very easy to do: just select one of the presets, click the Edit button, and experiment with the color sliders on the gradient ramp. As layer masks are grayscale it's best to stick with black to white gradients, but you can apply the color presets – they're automatically converted to grayscale when applied to a mask.

CHAPTER 7

Text and Shapes – Understanding Vector Graphics

What's Covered in this Chapter

- It may seem over the top to devote an entire chapter to text in a book about photography; after all, PaintShop Photo Pro X3 isn't a word processor. But the fact is that there are all sorts of occasions when you need to add words to your pictures. Whether it's producing family calendars and Christmas cards, event posters, advertising, or just having a laugh with some speech balloons, PaintShop Photo Pro's text tools will help you get the job done.
- Text works in a fundamentally different way from photos – the shapes are described by mathematical formulae, rather than being just a bunch of pixels. Objects, including text, that are produced like this are called 'vector graphics' and this chapter starts out with an explanation of the difference between pixel-based things like photos (sometimes called 'bitmap' or 'raster' images) and vectors.

PaintShop Photo Pro X3 for Photographers. DOI: 10.1016/B978-0-240-52165-7.10007-3

- As well as the Text tool, PaintShop Photo Pro has a range of tools for creating geometric and irregular shapes. You'll learn how to use all of these, including the all-powerful Pen tool which can be used to draw any shape that you can imagine.
- As well as creating text, this chapter shows you how you can manipulate it. You can apply any of the filter effects to text providing you first convert it to a Raster layer. PaintShop Photo Pro X3's new Layer Effects have no such limitations and you'll find out how to use these to good effect to produce striking and impactful typography. You'll also discover how to make text follow any path – around a circle or along a wavy line, for example – and how to distort letter shapes to create your own type forms.
- At the end of the chapter you'll find two step-by-step projects that show you how to make a greetings card and use text selections to create special type effects.

In this chapter we take a look at PaintShop Photo Pro's text and vector drawing tools. These features expand PaintShop Photo Pro's capabilities and broaden its use beyond photo editing into the realms of illustration and graphics. In practical terms this means that as well as editing photos you can create illustrations from scratch and produce a range of photo-based projects like greetings cards, invitations, calendars, flyers, and even brochures.

How Text and Vectors Work

Up to now nearly everything we've done in PaintShop Photo Pro has involved manipulating pixels. Text and vector objects work in a different way to pixel-based images and this provides them with some advantages. Whereas a pixel-based bitmap is composed of many individual dots, each described in terms of its red, green, and blue component values, vector objects and text are mathematically defined shapes. The object's properties are defined and from these the computer constructs them. A circle, for example, might be described in terms of its radius, stroke weight and color, and fill. The user isn't necessarily aware of this and just uses the available Shape tools and the Materials palette to draw the required shape, or the Text tool to enter type.

Vectors have two distinct advantages over bitmaps. Because they need minimal data to describe them, they take up very little memory and disk space. And because they are generated by the computer they are resolution independent, which is another way of saying you can make them as big as you like with no loss in quality.

Vectors also have their limitations. They're a good way of producing regular shapes like letterforms, geometric shapes, and even irregular curvy shapes, but they're not great at representing real-world textured, detailed scenes, which is why we need the pixels for photographic images. For this reason vectors tend to be confined to type and 2D illustration with flat color or mathematically predictable gradations.

Adding Basic Text

PaintShop Photo Pro's Text tool is used to add text to any type of document, whether photo, vector illustration, or scan. Choose the Text tool from the Tools toolbar and double-click anywhere in the document. If you're using an earlier version of PaintShop Photo Pro, this will open the Text Entry dialog box. Type what you want in this box, click OK, and watch as the text appears somewhere in the document canvas.

PaintShop Photo Pro X3 treats text in a radically different way. When you click on an image with the Text tool and begin to type, text is added directly in the image workspace – there's no box to get in the way, so you can see exactly what you're doing.

The program automatically places the text data on to a Vector layer in the Layers palette. It remains in a vector format until you need to apply special effects to it. If this is the case, PaintShop Photo Pro asks you to convert the layer from Vector to Raster (more on this in the next section).

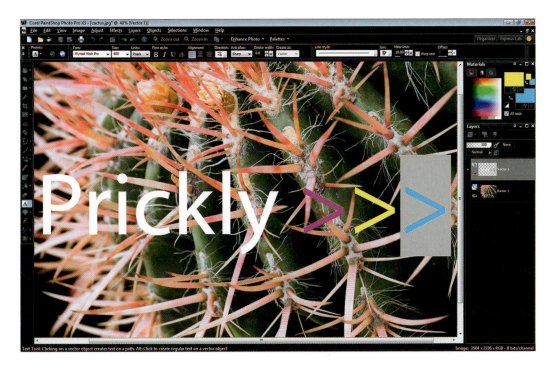

FIG 7.1 To create text select the Text tool, click anywhere in the image window, and start typing. Set the type size in either points or pixels and apply other text attributes, including alignment, direction, anti-aliasing, and stroke width, then click the Apply button on the Tool Options palette. Characters within a text block can be individually styled.

You can format text using the Tool Options palette to select the font, size, style, alignment, and other attributes. The text fill and stroke color are determined by the Foreground and Stroke properties and Background and Fill properties swatches in the Materials palette. To apply the formatting click the Apply Changes button (the green tick) on the left of the Tool Options palette or click the Cancel button next to it to exit from Text editing mode without saving your text. You won't be able to switch tools, make any menu selections, or make any other editing changes until you either apply or cancel your text edits.

Once you click the Apply button the text is added on its own Vector layer, but you can click on it with the Text tool and change the formatting at any time. And by selecting just a part of the text with the I-beam cursor you can apply individual formatting to sections of the text.

There are a couple of other formatting controls on the Tool Options palette that are worth a closer look. The Anti-alias menu has three settings – Off, Sharp, and Smooth – that determine the amount of smoothing applied to the edges of characters. When set to Off, type is not anti-aliased and you can see the stepped edges that result from the attempt at producing curved edges with square pixels; though text is defined by vectors it is displayed on screen and when you print using pixels. A smoother look is achieved using semi-transparent pixels to fill some of the gaps. As a general rule anti-aliased text looks much better so, other than for very small type, you'll usually want to set this to either Sharp or Smooth.

The next control along determines the stroke width of your text and can be used to produce a stroked outline effect if you set different foreground and background colors. For small text it's best to set the stroke width to zero, though you can use a narrow stroke of the same color as the fill to embolden text slightly. The stroke extends in both directions – inward and outward – so you need to take care not to overdo it and distort the shape of the type characters. Used moderately, however, applying a stroke to text is a great way to quickly produce a very classy-looking text effect.

There's one last thing on the Tool Options palette I want to look at before moving on to type effects. The 'Create As' drop-down menu on the Tool Options palette is set by default to Vector. This means that when you click the Apply button the text is added as a new Vector layer in the Layers palette. There are two other options that you might also want to consider using in some circumstances.

Selection creates a marquee selection from your text that you can then use to create text filled with images, text cut-outs, and other effects. Floating creates the text as a floating selection – it looks the same as your vector text but is added to the image as a floating selection, which you can move and trans-form. When you defloat raster text (Selections > Defloat or Ctrl + Shift + F), it's merged with the underlying Raster layer unless you promote it to a layer with Selections > Promote Selection to Layer or Ctrl + Shift + P.

Creating text as selections is fine for a quick and easy route to text effects but it's usually better to create the text as a Vector layer then make a selection from it. That way you can easily edit the text and reselect without having to start again from scratch. I'll look at the best way to do this a little later in this chapter.

Assuming you've created text as a Vector layer, once you click the Apply button the text appears with corner and edge handles, and can be moved and transformed in the usual way, by dragging the corner handles to resize, rotate, and skew. Transformed text remains editable at all times – just select the Text tool and click within the type area.

Special Text Effects

Now that you have had practice adding text to a picture, you'll want to try adding special effects to jazz up the results. In this section we run through some techniques for making your text look simply stunning.

Tip

Use the Presets button on the Tool Options palette to save frequently used text font, size alignment, and other attributes. You can then apply all the necessary text styling with a single click.

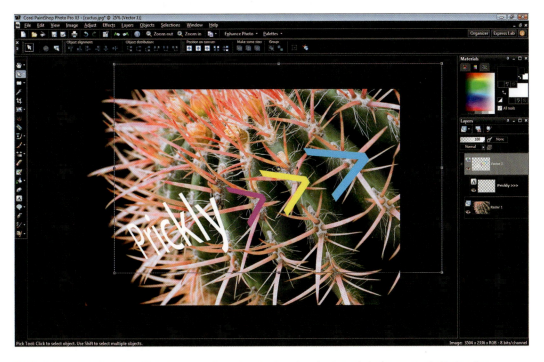

FIG 7.2 Having created the text as a Vector layer, it can be transformed – here sheared and rotated, the text remains editable throughout.

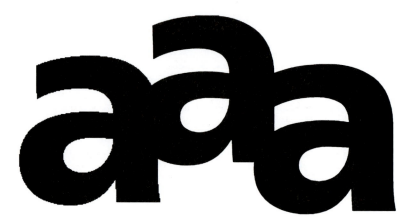

FIG 7.3 Anti-aliasing is the process of introducing semi-transparent pixels at the edges of an object, or text character, to smooth out jagged edges, or stepping, caused by square pixels. This is more noticeable at low resolutions, where fewer pixels are used to make up the characters. PaintShop Photo Pro has three anti-aliasing options: Off (left), Sharp (middle), and Smooth (right).

Layer Styles

Layer Styles make it much easier to create, edit, and apply certain special effects. You can apply Layer Styles to both Raster and Vector layers, and they work particularly well with type. When you apply a filter effect such as the drop shadow from the Effects > 3D Effects menu the effect is added as pixels to the layer, which makes it difficult to edit. If you decide your drop shadow is too dark or not in the right place, you have to undo it and start over. And if you want to apply effects filters to text you must first rasterize the layer, i.e. convert it from a Vector to a Bitmap or Raster layer. This makes it uneditable so if you later discover a spelling mistake, you're in big trouble.

The great thing about Layer Styles is that they are 'live' editable effects. If, at any stage in the editing process, you decide you want to change the size, opacity, position, or color of your drop shadow or any other layer style, you can. What's more, you don't have to convert Type layers to Raster layers to apply layer styles to them, so you can also edit the text with the Text tool and the layer style will automatically update.

To apply a Layer Style to some text, double-click the Vector layer in the Layers palette to open the Layer Properties dialog box and click the Layer Styles tab; click the Fit Image to Window button if you can't see the text in the preview. To apply a Layer Style and access its controls, click the checkbox next to it in the list. The layer itself is also included in the Layer Styles list so you apply a Layer Style but make the layer itself invisible.

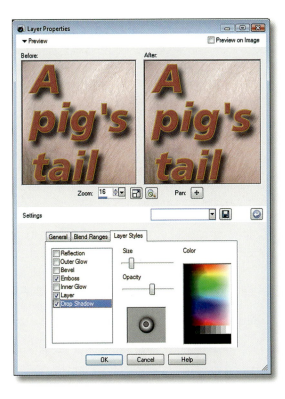

FIG 7.4 To access Layer Styles, double-click the layer thumbnail in the Layers palette and select the Layer Styles tab in the Layer Properties dialog box. You can apply any combination of the six styles available.

There are six Layer Styles to choose from:

- Reflection
- Outer Glow
- Bevel
- Emboss
- Inner Glow
- Drop Shadow.

You can apply more than one Layer Style at once – for example, you might want to emboss your text and add a drop shadow, but be careful not to go overboard. Once you've selected a Layer Style use the controls to change its size, opacity, position, color, and any other available attributes. As with most of PaintShop Photo Pro X3's effects, once you've found settings that work well you can save them as presets so you don't have to rediscover them every time you want to apply them in similar situations.

Tip

Preview on image can slow things down to a crawl with Layer Styles. Use the before and after previews to get the job done more quickly.

Special Effects Filters

With PaintShop Photo Pro you can add a wide range of effects to your Text layers. For most actions, with the notable exception of Layer Styles, the Vector Text layer must first be converted to a Raster layer – a warning dialog appears and PaintShop Photo Pro asks you if this is OK (if you don't want to be asked every time, click the 'Don't remind me' checkbox from the dialog that pops up on screen).

Select Chisel from the Effects > 3D Effects menu. The opening dialog offers a range of control options. The chisel effect extrudes the text shape outwards. Use the Size slider to determine the extent of the extruded effect and select one of the radio buttons to choose either a solid or transparent color fill. To select a color for the effect you can click the color swatch and use the Color Properties dialog box. Better still, move the cursor over the photo and it will change to an Eyedropper tool, which you can use to sample a color from the photo itself.

Other 3D effects for adding impact to text include: Drop Shadow, Cut-out, and Inner Bevel. Most of the 3D effects are available as Layer Styles and, as a general rule, where you have the option it's better to use a Layer Style than a filter effect. If you need to add something slightly more esoteric, then try some of the filters from the Artistic, Art Media, Distortion, or Texture filter drop-downs. Any of these filters will work on the Text layer as long as it has been converted into a Bitmap (Raster) layer first.

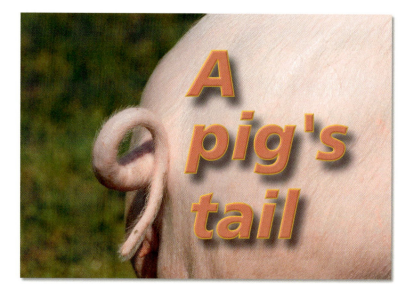

FIG 7.5 Layer Styles work well with Text layers. Here I've combined the Emboss and Drop Shadow styles to make the type stand out from the pig's, er, rear end.

Using Filter Effects: A Warning

Though almost all the filters under the Effects menu will have an effect on Raster Text layers, not all work well and some may not appear to do anything at all. The reason for this is that the filter action works across the entire frame and not just on the text on its own. If the filter has a global effect then it is more than likely to be seen on the Text layer, but if it is of a more random nature, it might or it might not. To make it work correctly you must first select the text and then apply the filter action. Do this by choosing Selections > From Vector Object or use the keyboard shortcut Ctrl + Shift + B and then apply the filter.

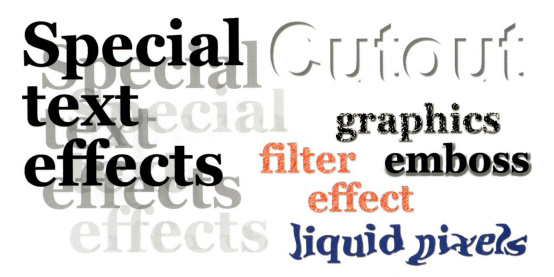

FIG 7.6 Over and above regular text effects, added via the Materials palette, it's possible to add tremendous three-dimensional power using any of PaintShop Photo Pro's filter effects. To do this you might have to convert the layer from Vector to Bitmap but still, the resulting effects, as seen here, are very impressive.

Adding Text to a Path

Adding text to a path can make for a dynamic and interesting design and is especially useful for creating company logos, web buttons, badges, CD and DVD labels, and the like. You can add type to shapes created with any of PaintShop Photo Pro's Shape tools (see the Vectors: Learning the Basics section later in this chapter), but it works best on gently sloping curves. Anything with sharp angles and lots of turns is unlikely to look good, or even readable.

To add text to a shape all you need to do is first draw the shape, then select the Text tool, and position the cursor on the edge of the shape. You'll see the cursor change from the normal cross-hairs with a capital A in the bottom right quadrant to cross-hairs with an A at 45 degrees and a curved line below it. When this happens, click on the shape and the Text Entry box will appear as usual, but any text you type will follow the outline of the shape.

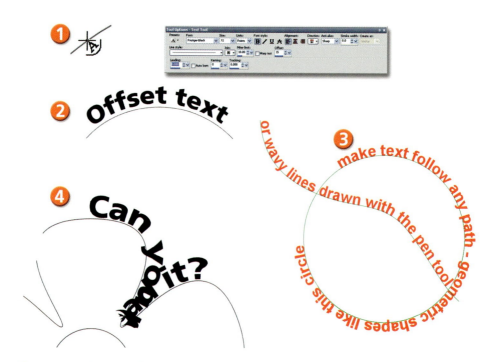

FIG 7.7 To align text to a path, position the Text tool over the object's edge – click to enter the text when the tool changes (1). To move the text above or below the line enter an offset in the Text Tool Options palette (2). You can run text along any vector path (3), but avoid sharp curves and sudden direction changes, which will render it unreadable (4).

- To move the text along the path, choose the Pick tool and click-drag the text. The small circle icon indicates the new start position of the text.
- To raise or lower the text on the path, enter a value in the Offset field of the Text Tool Options palette. A positive value raises the text above the path, a negative value lowers it.
- If you don't want the path to show, either select a transparent stroke and fill, or click the layer visibility icon in the Layers palette to turn it off.
- To detach text from the path, select either the text or its path using the Pick tool and choose Detach Object from Path from the Objects menu.
- To attach existing text to an object, select the text with the Pick tool, Shift-select the object, and choose Fit Text to Path from the Objects menu.

Editing Text Shapes

By converting text to a vector object you can use PaintShop Photo Pro's Vector Editing tools to alter the shape of individual characters by adjusting individual nodes. To convert text to a vector object, select it with the Pick tool and choose Objects > Convert Text to Curves. There are two options – you can convert the entire text block into one vector object by choosing Objects > Convert Text to Curves > As Single Shape. Alternatively, Objects > Convert Text to Curves > As Character Shapes converts each letter of the text into a separate vector object. Once the text is converted, select the Pen tool and click the Edit mode button in the Tool Options palette to edit the character shapes.

Bear in mind that once the text has been converted to Curves it can no longer be edited in the usual way, so now is not the time to discover you've made

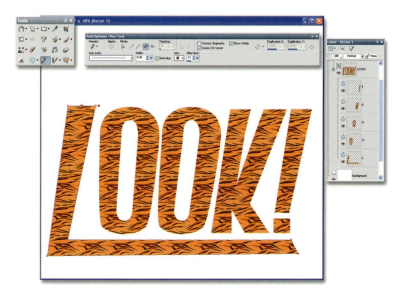

FIG 7.8 Once text is converted to paths, you can edit individual character shapes using the Pen tool.

a spelling error! You can cover yourself by duplicating the layer before converting it, so you have the original text to go back to if necessary. Once the text is converted to Curves, especially as individual character shapes, you will need to pay special attention to how the individual elements stack up in the Layers palette.

Making Selections From Text

Text selections form the basis for all kinds of effects using photos. You can paste photos inside a text selection, a particularly effective technique when combined with layers. Typically, an image layer is copied, pasted inside a selection, and overlaid on top of the original with the opacity reduced, the color desaturated, or some other effect applied.

You can make a text selection directly by selecting the Text tool and choosing Selection from the Create As pull-down menu in the Tool Options palette. This is useful for a quick text selection, but once the selection is made it can't easily be edited. A better method is to create the text as a vector, then choose Selections > From Vector Object. That way, if you decide to edit the text, even if it's only to open up the tracking a little, or reduce the leading, you can easily make a new selection.

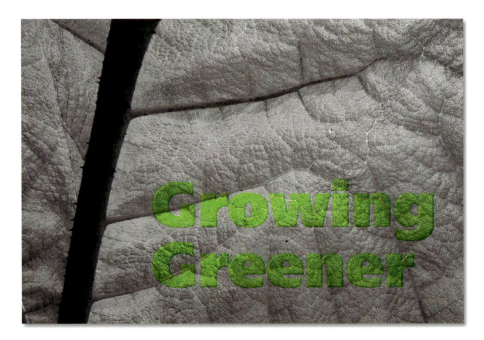

FIG 7.9 To create this text I made a selection from it using Selections > From Vector Object, then turned the text layer's visibility off. I pasted the background image into the selection (Edit > Paste Into Selection), then promoted the selection to a layer and applied the Emboss Layer Style. Finally, I made the Background layer black and white using the Black and White Film effects.

Vectors: Learning the Basics

Vector images are different to bitmap (raster) images. Whereas a bitmap image is made entirely of pixels, a vector image is made from a set of mathematical instructions or coordinates. Advantages of vectors are:

- They are quick to work with.
- Vector file sizes can be small and still display a large dimension.
- Vector graphics are highly editable with absolutely no loss of quality.
- They create perfectly clean, anti-aliased lines and curves.

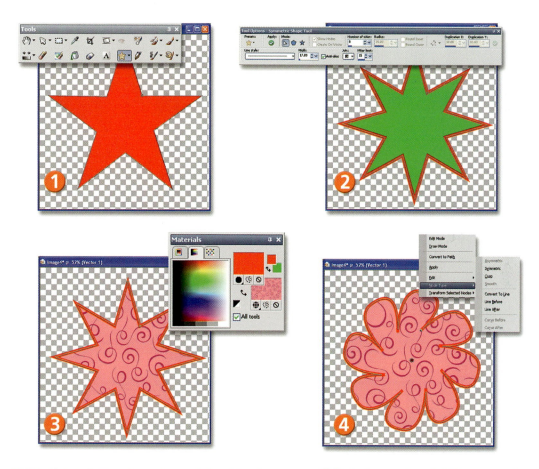

FIG 7.10 (1) Use the Symmetric Shape tool to create highly editable polygons and stars. (2) Edit the line style using the Tool Options palette and choose Stroke and Fill colors from the Materials palette (3). You can edit all of the nodes on a symmetric shape at once (4), so it's easy to quickly create variations on a basic shape theme.

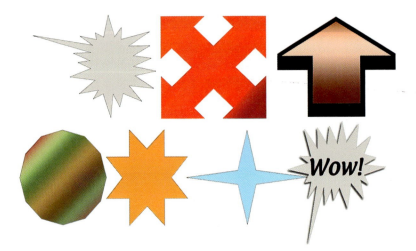

FIG 7.11 The Preset Shape tool is a powerful and quick way to make almost any size or shape of object for illustration.

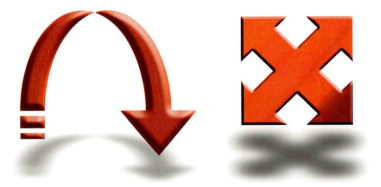

FIG 7.12 Take this one step further, adding drop shadows, bevels, and a range of other specialist (filter) effects to make those flat, unexciting shapes something special.

Vectors, therefore, are ideal for illustrations where scalable drawing, text, and shapes are required. PaintShop Photo Pro's Preset Vector Shape tool has a wide range of fully editable subjects in its library. If, for example, you like the shape in one of the presets, but not the color or edge detail, you can edit it using its Edit palette. If you need to create your own vector illustrations from the ground up, use the Pen tool.

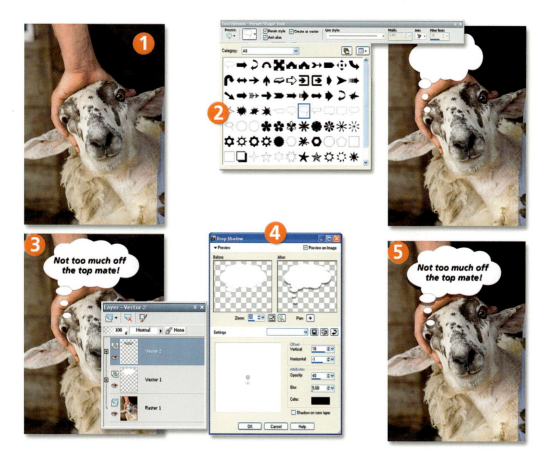

FIG 7.13 Adding a vector shape and text to a photo. (1) Open the photo. (2) Choose a preset shape from the drop-down Preset Shape Tool menu. (3) Use the handles to reposition and rescale the shape if necessary. (4) Reposition, rotate, or flip the vector shape using the Pick tool, then choose the Text tool and enter appropriate text in the Text box (do not click directly on the shape with the Text tool, or the text will follow the path as illustrated on page 192) and press 'Apply'. Once happy with the size and positioning of the new text, use PaintShop Photo Pro's Drop Shadow filter to add an effect to the speech bubble and save as a '.pspimage' file.

Working with the Pen Tool

The Pen tool is the ultimate vector shape creation tool. With it, illustrators and graphic designers can create any type of shape, line, or layer object they'd care to imagine. The Pen tool gives you scope to design any shape you can imagine; and, because the shapes it creates are formed using vectors, whatever is created remains infinitely editable at all times.

Drawing tools rely on manual actions for their accuracy and we all know how silly it is to try and draw with a mouse! It's like sketching with a house brick, only less accurate. The Pen tool allows you to ignore many of the physical limitations of the mouse and to apply extreme linear accuracy to the most delicate of shapes.

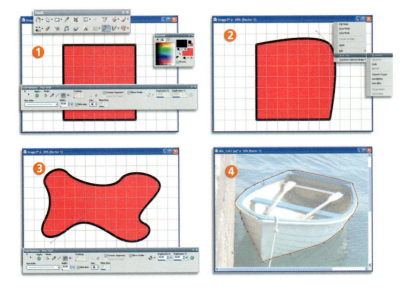

FIG 7.14 (1) Creating geometric shapes with the Pen tool is easy – but you can use the Symmetric Shape tool for that. (2) Change node properties by right-clicking or (3) create curves of any shape by click-dragging. (4) Use the Pen tool to trace shapes from photo layers.

The principal driving force behind this is the ability to draw using Bezier curves. These are editable lines that can be used to describe mathematically perfect shapes such as curves and circles. The curves were invented by Frenchman Pierre Bezier, who worked for the car manufacturer Renault. If you are not into vector illustration then this might not be a tool that you are likely to need but, for the designers among us, it's essential. Check out the stack of controls provided in the Options palette and you'll get an idea of how powerful this tool is. Here are some of its most important features:

· Draw lines and shapes of any size freehand.
· Draw a range of shapes using point-to-point techniques.
· Fill objects with color, texture, and transparency using the Materials palette.

The Pen tool works by dropping editable nodes into the picture, whether blank canvas or existing picture. Each mouse-click adds another node that's automatically joined to the previous one with a straight or curved line, depending on the type of drawing implement chosen. Clicking a node back on to the original starting point completes the shape. You can add as many, or as few, nodes as needed, though the fewer nodes you use, the smoother your shapes will look.

The Pen tool can be used to create new vector shapes and edit existing pictures in a wide range of styles. You can change any aspect of the Pen tool at any time – for example, thickness of line, color fill, texture, linear aspect, curve aspect, and more. Right-clicking displays its principal attributes, which include: Edit, Node Type, and Transform Selected Nodes. Using these allows you to perform more than 30 different edit functions.

Uses for the Pen Tool

- Creating accurate masks
- Creating complex vector shapes and illustrative elements using rectilinear or Bezier-controlled lines
- Creating perfectly curved lines around irregular objects.

Here's how to make a vector illustration:

STEP 1 Create a new document with a white background and a resolution of your choice (File > New).

STEP 2 Click the Pen tool icon on the Tools toolbar and select a line style and width from the Tool Options palette.

STEP 3 Select a line application – Lines and Polylines, Point to Point (Bezier Curves) or Freehand – from the Mode section of the Tool Options. You'll need to experiment to discover which suits the task in hand (see the notes below for the differences between these methods).

STEP 4 When you've drawn your path, select it with the Pick tool to display its bounding box. The handles on the box allow you to rotate, stretch, and deform the vector shape without losing detail. To change the appearance of the line, open the Layers palette, select the Vector layer, and click the '+' tab. This opens the Vector layer to display the individual elements. Double-click an element to open the Vector Properties box.

Note the following:

- 'Draw Lines and Polylines' draws straight lines between two points.
- 'Draw Point to Point – Bezier Curve' is an infinitely editable freeform line controlled by Bezier technology – grab a controlling handle to bend the line any which way. Bezier curves are ideal for creating seamless freehand shapes.
- 'Draw Freehand' is the same as drawing on a piece of paper.

Step-by-Step Projects

Technique: Creating a Greetings Card

To make a greetings card you'll need one large picture and possibly another smaller snap for the back, an inkjet printer, and a few sheets of A4 inkjet paper (preferably photo quality). Bear in mind that most photo-quality inkjet paper is single-sided and you can't print on the reverse. Look out for double-sided photo-quality inkjet paper or card.

STEP 1 First create a new document (File > New). Make it 300 pixels/inch at the size of the unfolded card, i.e. 297 mm × 210 mm for A4, or chose one of the presets if you have that size paper available or are going to cut it to size. Select a background color. Most greetings cards have a white base color but that does not need to apply to you! Choose a resolution that's suitable for your printer. Most produce pretty good results at a setting of 200–250 dpi. Set the document in a landscape format (i.e. wider than it is high for a portrait card, taller than it is wide for a landscape card).

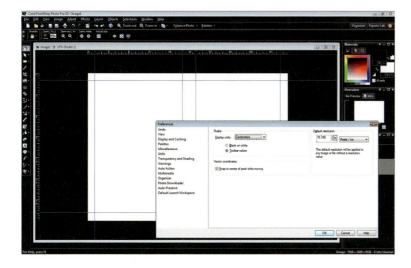

STEP 2 To make the layout easier, you can use PaintShop Photo Pro's Grid or its Guides. Do this by choosing Grid from the View menu. To get the guides displayed, first bring up the Rulers (View > Rulers or Ctrl + Alt + R) and then, clicking in the ruler margin, drag the guides one at a time on to the canvas. To change the color and the pattern of either, double-click the ruler margin to bring up the Properties dialog. You'll find it easier to position the guides if you change the ruler units to centimeters or inches. Select File > Preferences > General Program Preferences, click on Units, and select your preference from the pull-down menu.

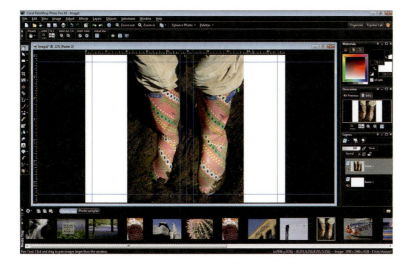

STEP 3 Now open the main photo from a media tray or the Organizer. Choose Selections > Select All, Edit > Copy and then close the image. Back in your card document choose Edit > Paste as New Layer.

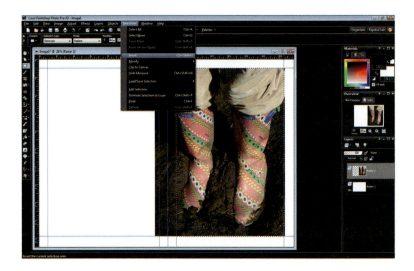

STEP 4 In all likelihood, the photo will be too big and you'll need to resize it. Select the Pick tool from the toolbar and drag one of the corner handles to resize the photo. Drag and position it with the Pick tool so that it fits within the guides on the front page of the card – which is the right side of your document. If the photo doesn't fit within the guides, i.e. it's either to long or too wide, make a selection within the guides using the rectangular marquee (this is easier if you turn on Snap to Guides on the View menu). Now choose Selections > Invert and hit Delete to remove the unwanted bits of the photo.

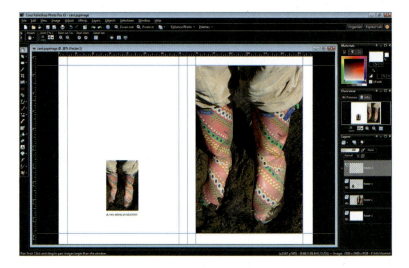

STEP 5 Now for the reverse. It's up to you what you put on here. We've copied the cover photo, pasted, resized, and positioned it on the back, then created an 'imprint' message using the Text tool. If you haven't done so already, now's a good time to save your work. Use the '.pspimage' file format to retain all the layers.

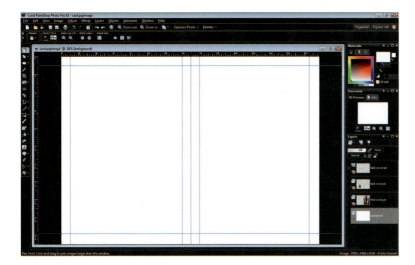

STEP 6 Now that the two pictures are in position we are ready to add the inside text. When you use the Text tool it creates its own new Vector layer. We're going to turn off the other layers before creating the text for the inside of the card so that we can see what we're doing. Turning off the other layers will also allow printing of the text only inside on the reverse of the paper. Turn off all of the layers apart from the bottom one by clicking the layer visibility icon (the eye) in the Layers palette. Select the bottom layer so that the Vector layer for the type you are about to create will appear above it. While we're here in the Layers palette it's a good idea to rename the layers with something more helpful than Raster 1, Raster 2, etc. Click on the layer labels to overwrite them; we've called them 'front cover pic', 'back cover pic', and 'back cover text'.

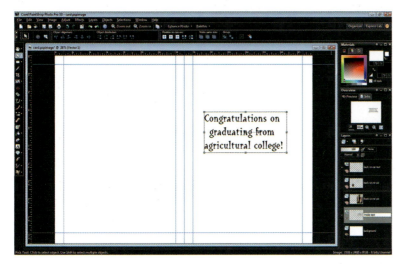

STEP 7 Select the Text tool, click on the right side of the page, and enter and format your message. Use the Tool Options palette to chose a font, size and style, then select the Pick tool and move the type into position. When the card is folded this text will appear on the inside right page. Click the Vector 1 label in the Layers palette and rename it 'inside text'.

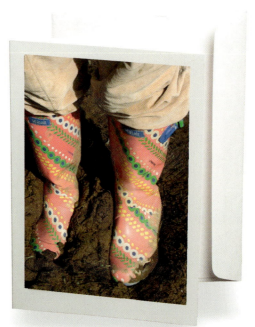

STEP 8 To print your card, first print the inside text with all the other layers switched off as it is now. Then reverse the paper. Turn the inside Text layer off and turn all the other layers on to print the outside. You'll need to work out how paper travels through your printer to make sure that the two sides appear the right way up – it's easy to get one side upside-down if you don't put the paper in the correct way around. Do a trial run in draft mode with some cheap photocopier paper.

Now all you have to do is find an envelope that fits!

Technique: Creating a Type Effect Using Text Selections

As we saw earlier in this chapter, Effects filters don't work with Vector layers, which must first be rasterized. The same thing goes for text, which by default is rendered as a Vector layer. One of the easiest ways to create stunning type effects, however, is to make a selection from your type and then apply the effect to an image using that selection. Here we're going to produce a beveled glass-type effect in four steps.

The success of type effects like this depends very much on choosing the right typeface. The Inner Bevel filter works well on big bold type. So avoid script fonts or anything with fine detail and keep the word count to a minimum – make a bold one-word statement.

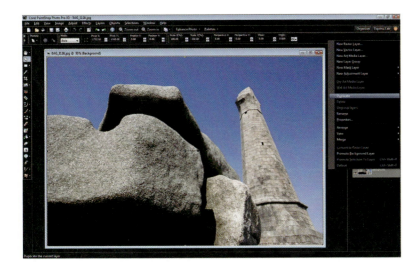

STEP 1 Open your image and create a copy of the Background layer by right-clicking it in the Layers palette and selecting Duplicate.

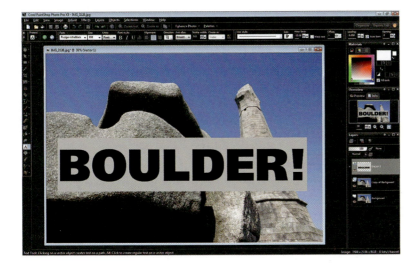

STEP 2 Select the Text tool, click on the image, and enter the type. For maximum effect keep it short – one or two words at most – and use a bold typeface; use capital letters for improved readability and make the type as large as you can. Click the Apply button in the Tool Options palette when you are happy with how it looks, then position the type where you want it on the background with the Move tool.

205

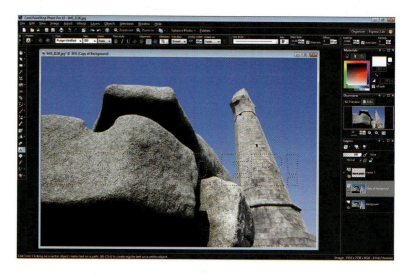

STEP 3 Choose Selections > From Vector Object (keyboard shortcut Ctrl + Shift + B), then turn off the Type layer by clicking its Layer visibility toggle (the eye) in the Layers palette. Click the Copy of Background layer in the Layers palette to make it active.

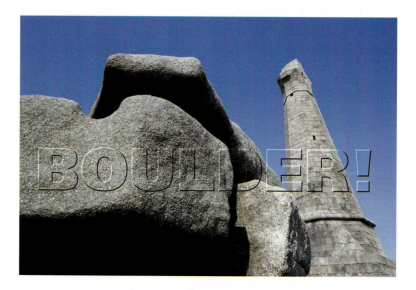

STEP 4 Choose Effects > 3D Effects > Inner Bevel and apply the filter using the default settings. Click the preview icon to see the result in the main image window. You can experiment with angle, smoothness, depth, and other settings, or try one of the available presets, but the default setting gives a pretty good result.

CHAPTER 8

Special Effects – Advanced Editing Techniques

What's Covered in this Chapter

- This chapter really covers two things: the first half is all about PaintShop Photo Pro X3's painting and drawing tools, the remainder explains how to create special effects.

- If you want to create illustrations from scratch you'll need to familiarize yourself with the workings of the Materials palette and PaintShop Photo Pro's Brush tools. All of this is explained in detail in the next few pages. Creating illustrations from a blank canvas can be a demanding task, even if you're a competent illustrator, but by using a photo as a source image and painting over it using layers you can achieve professional-looking results. PaintShop Photo Pro's Art Media tools mimic real-world materials like oils and pastels, and you'll learn how to use these to turn photos into paintings.

- Later in the chapter you'll find a comprehensive run-down of PaintShop Pro's filter effects, where to find them and how to use them. You'll discover how to use the Deformation tools to distort photos as well as how to correct distortion caused by ultra-wide-angle lenses using the distortion correction filters.

PaintShop Photo Pro X3 for Photographers. DOI: 10.1016/B978-0-240-52165-7.10008-5

- Special effect filters and distortion tools are often knocked for not being very 'useful'. That's not a criticism you could apply to PaintShop Photo Pro X3's lighting effects, which allow you to add lighting to a photo after you've taken it. Lighting effects are great for adding spotlights or colored lighting to a scene, or simply to shine some illumination and add depth to a picture that suffers from flat, featureless light. Turn to page 227 to find out how.
- There are lots of step-by-step projects at the end of this chapter. We kick off with a look at how to stitch multiple photos together to create a panorama and move on to creating realistic depth effects – making type follow the contours of a surface as if it's been painted on. Following these two advanced projects we'll tackle something a bit simpler – having a bit of fun with PaintShop Photo Pro's Picture Tube and adding edges and frames to your photos. The final step-by-step project in this chapter shows you how to respray your car using the Color Changer tool.

In this chapter you'll learn how to add special effects to your digital photos. Applying a special effects filter may be all that's needed to turn a so-so image into something special. But with a little more effort you can create jaw-dropping effects that defy reality – or what passes for reality in a photo.

Using the Materials Palette

One of the most used palettes in PaintShop Photo Pro is the Materials palette. This is where you go to change the colors used in any of the program's paint or drawing tools. In this section we look at how the Materials palette can be used in the creation of special effects and how it's used for mixing colors.

Choose the Materials palette from the View > Palettes menu (keyboard shortcut F6). There are three modes in which to work with this tool: Frame, Rainbow, and Swatch modes.

The Frame mode provides a quick and fairly intuitive method of picking colors. First left-click to select a foreground hue from the outer hue rectangle (right-click to select a background color), then click in the inner saturation rectangle to alter the saturation and brightness for the selected hue. If you hold down the mouse button and drag within the Saturation rectangle the value updates and a tooltip window tells you the RGB values at the cursor position. Alternatively, you can fine-tune the saturation and brightness by adjusting the triangular sliders at the bottom and side of the Saturation rectangle.

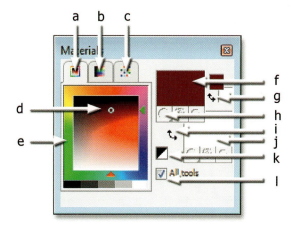

FIG 8.1 (a) Frame tab. (b) Rainbow tab. (c) Swatches tab. (d) Inner saturation rectangle. (e) Outer hue rectangle. (f) Foreground and Stroke properties. (g) Swap foreground and background colors. (h) Click the left button to change the color/gradient and pattern selected, click the middle button to change the texture, and the right button for transparency. (i) Swap foreground and background materials. (j) Background and fill color. (k) Select default (black and white) foreground and background colors. (l) Apply Materials palette settings to all tools.

On the Rainbow tab, position the cursor over the central colors panel; it changes to an eyedropper and a tool tip window displays the RGB values of the color beneath. Left-click to select the foreground color and right-click to select the background color. The Rainbow tab only needs one click to select a color, but provides less accuracy than the Frame tab.

If you're working with a limited palette, you may find Swatch mode simpler to use because you can make your own swatches. In many ways it's faster and more accurate to work with.

The two large colored boxes on the right of the palette influence the Foreground and Stroke Properties (upper left), and the Background and Fill Properties (lower right). Underneath the Foreground and Background Properties boxes a Style button provides three options: Color, Gradient, and Pattern. To these three modes can be added texture or transparency using the appropriate buttons. Two smaller colored boxes to the upper right are used to set the foreground and background colors.

Double-click either the Foreground or Background Color box to open the Color picker. Use this to choose more colors. To modify the gradient or texture, double-click the Foreground and Stroke or Background and Fill Properties box to open the Material Properties dialog box.

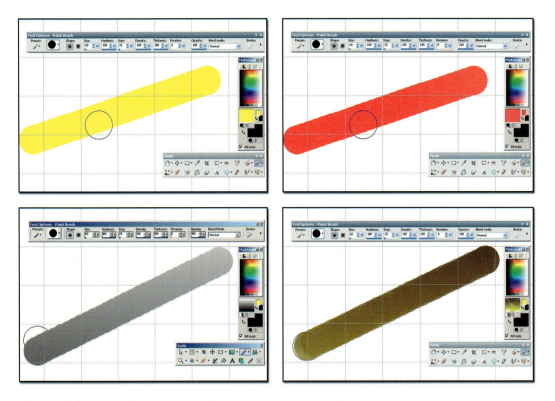

FIG 8.2 Top left: Click once in the Color picker to set the foreground color and paint. Top right: Click again elsewhere in the picker to change the color in the brush. Bottom left: Clicking the Gradient button at the base of the Foreground and Stroke Properties box accesses the gradients, all of which can be edited. Bottom right: Use the Texture button to choose a texture for the brush.

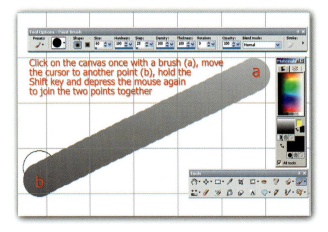

FIG 8.3 To draw a line between two points, mouse-click once, move the cursor to the end point and, holding the Shift key, mouse-click again.

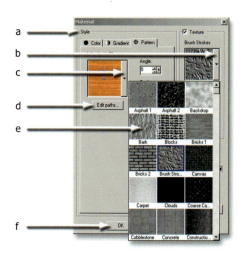

FIG 8.4 (a) The integrated Style palette. (b) Click this menu to view the texture choices displayed (e). (c) Click this tab to choose new patterns. (d) This allows you to define the path to the pattern files. (e) Textures available. (f) Once happy with choice and edit status, click OK.

a
b
c
d
e
f

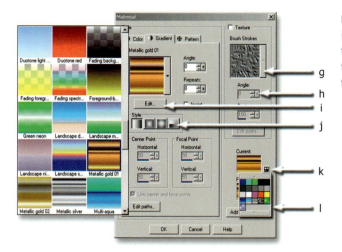

FIG 8.5 (g) Clicking here displays the textures on offer. (h, i) These give great edit power if the selected pattern/texture is not right for the drawing involved. (j) Change the gradient style here. (k) Click this small tab to bring up the Color palette (l).

g
h
i
j
k
l

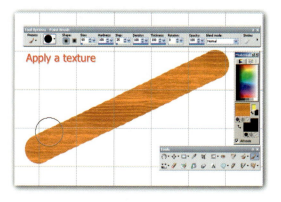

FIG 8.6 This is what a brush stroke looks like with a wood grain texture applied.

Apply a texture

FIG 8.7 Color gradients are easy to add and draw.

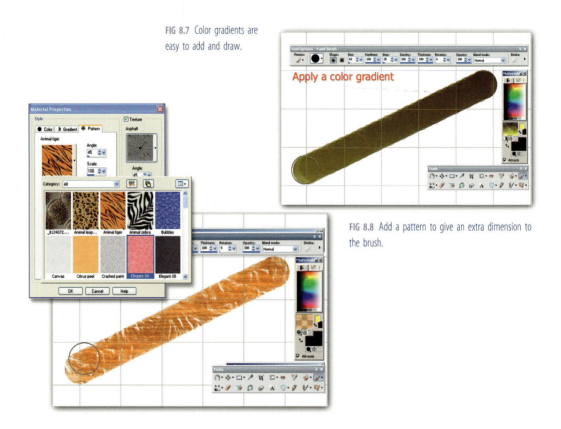

FIG 8.8 Add a pattern to give an extra dimension to the brush.

- Use the Swap buttons (double-headed arrows) to swap foreground and background colors and materials.
- Click the Style button at the base of the Foreground/Background Properties boxes to choose any of the three styles you wish to work with: Color, Gradient, or Pattern.
- Click the Texture button to add texture to the paint strokes.
- Click the Transparent button to add transparency to the brush.
- If you are happy with a particular combination in the palette, click the All tools checkbox to lock it and to apply the settings to all the tools.

Working with Brush Tools

PaintShop Photo Pro comes with a staggering array of brushes and brush tips, enabling the user to create a range of simple, or incredibly sophisticated, painting tasks. Brush tools introduce the photographer to the concept of original creativity – you can literally make something from nothing using one of PaintShop Photo Pro's brushes (in the same way that you might with a crayon and a blank sheet of paper).

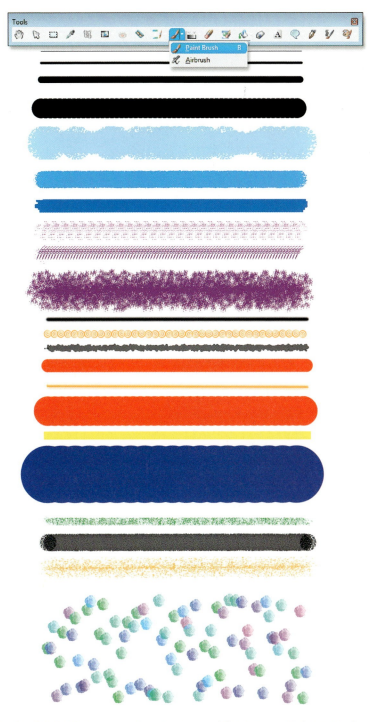

FIG 8.9 With PaintShop Photo Pro's Paint Brush you can produce a staggering array of effects, textures, and 'looks' simply by changing its tool set in the Options and Materials palettes. There are over 20 preset stock tips that vary greatly in each brush.

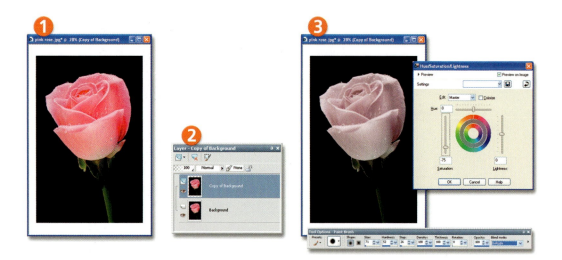

FIG 8.10 This is a very ordinary snap of a very pretty rose. There are a number of preset filter effects that I could apply to the entire photo or even to a selection. However, it is also possible to make quite radical changes merely by using a brush on the canvas. (1) Open the photo and enlarge the canvas to add a white border all round the edges. (2) Duplicate the layer. (3) Desaturate the color. Reduce it almost to black and white.

Use the Tool Options palette to change the physical nature of all brushes. Use the Materials palette to choose different brush colors as well as textures and gradients in the brush action. Simply paint over the image to add texture and additional color.

An advantage of this process is that brushes can be used to add a non-photographic influence to a picture in order to create the illusion that it's something other than a plain old photo.

Brush tools are infinitely variable in terms of size, density, opacity, and hardness. Naturally, the best results will only be attainable using a graphics tablet rather than a standard mouse. A graphics tablet allows you to draw, select, erase, and paint with the accuracy and delicacy of a real paintbrush, pencil or crayon. OK, it's not exactly the same, but it is 100% better than a mouse.

The Paint Brush can be used to add solid or translucent colors, gradients and textures all selected directly off the Materials palette.

Use the Brush tools for retouching photos or for combining freehand artwork with a photo. Besides the Paint Brush and Airbrush tools, PaintShop Photo Pro has a number of other brush-based tools designed specifically for working on a photographic image for the purposes of adding impact. These are:

·   Dodge tool. Lightens pixels under the brush – good for extracting detail in dark areas.
·   Burn tool. Darkens the pixels under the brush. Ideal for increasing density in overexposed pictures.

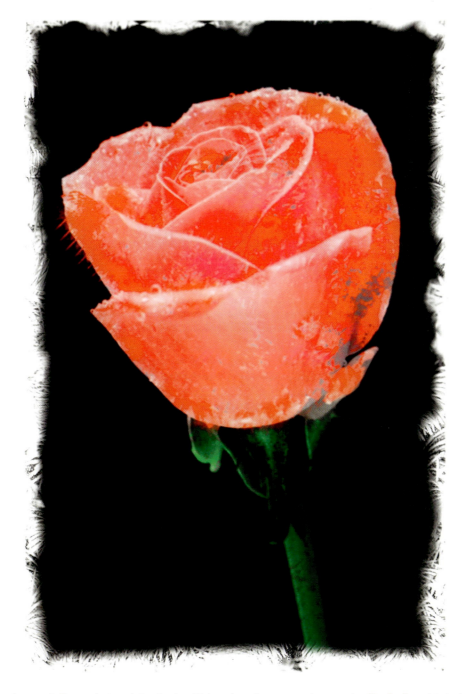

FIG 8.11 The textured effect can also be applied to the edges. Work at a lowered opacity to produce a seamless effect. Too fast and the brush marks become heavy and tell-tale, which is not usually desirable.

Original picture: John Shepherd, iStockphoto 1012211

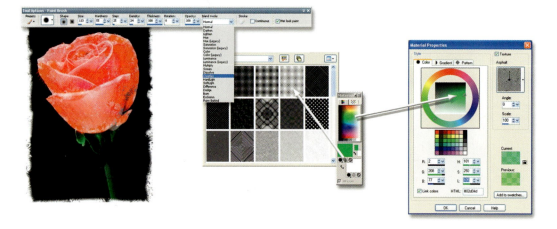

FIG 8.12 Use the Brush Options palette to change the physical nature of all brushes. Use the Materials palette to choose different brush colors as well as textures and gradients in the brush action. Simply paint over the image to add texture and additional color.

- Smudge Brush. Blurs and smudges the pixels under the brush action.
- Push. Makes all the pixels behave just like wet oil paint so that they can literally be pushed about the frame.
- Soften. Applies a localized soft focus effect.
- Sharpen. Increases the contrast, and therefore the apparent sharpness in the pixels.

Like the Paint Brush, PaintShop Photo Pro's Airbrush also has potential for terrific creativity. Once you hit on one combination, record it as a preset for use on other images.

FIG 8.13 PaintShop Photo Pro's Mixer palette works like the real thing, allowing you to partially mix colors and apply a smeared combination with the Oil Brush or Marker tool. (a) Mixer Tube. (b) Mixer Knife. (c) Mixer Dropper. (d) Tool size. (e) Mixer area. (f) Load Mixer Page button. (g) Open Page button. (h) Navigate button. (i, j) Unmix and remix buttons. (k) Mixer Palette Menu button.

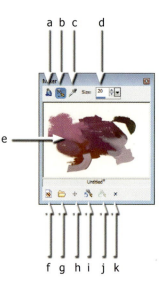

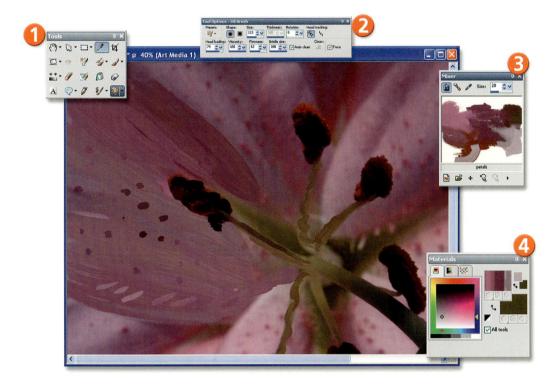

FIG 8.14 Select the Oil Brush from the Art Media tools fly-out (1) and use the Tool Options palette (2) to set brush parameters. Head loading determines how much paint is on the brush and how quickly it will run out. Click the Trace checkbox to automatically sample the color from underlying layers. Add color to the Mixer palette (4) using the Mixer Tube and mix the hues together with the Mixer Knife. Sampling an area of the Mixer palette with the Mixer Dropper adds the mix to the Foreground/Stroke swatch in the Materials palette — now you're ready to paint.

Using the Art Media Brushes

PaintShop Photo Pro X3 has a range of Brush tools called the Art Media tools. These tools are a radical departure from the usual kind of digital brush tool in that they mimic the behavior of real-world materials like oil paint and pastels.

Altogether there are nine Art Media tools: Oil, Chalk, Pastel, Crayon, Colored Pencil, Marker, Palette Knife, Smear, and Art Erasure. These tools can only be used on special Art Media layers; a new Art Media layer is automatically created for you when you start to paint with one of the Art Media tools.

Two of the Art Media brushes — Oil and Marker — are 'wet'; they simulate the wetness of their real-world counterparts. With a 'normal' PaintShop Photo Pro brush, if you paint by holding down the mouse button, or maintain pressure on the stylus tip, the paint just keeps on coming, but with a wet Art Media brush it runs out, just like the real thing. You have to finish the stroke and start a new one with a reloaded brush. Oil and Marker strokes stay wet, so if you paint over them with a new color the paint smears on the canvas.

Another aspect of real media that these wet brushes emulate is the ability to paint with multiple colors. A real brush might have mostly blue paint on it with a little bit of yellow, producing a smeared blue/green color, and you can simulate this effect with the Oil Brush and Marker tools. There's also a Mixer palette on which you can smear colors around and produce a messy mix of several colors to load on to your brush.

When using the Oil Brush or the Palette Knife, the size of the area sampled from the Mixer palette is determined by the brush size setting in the Tool Options palette, so the bigger your brush, the more paint variation you can have. For other Art Media tools, set the sample size using the Mixer palette's Size slider, up and down arrows, or enter in a value with your keyboard.

When using the wet painting tools, painting over existing strokes causes them to smear. You can 'dry' an Art Media layer, or make it wet again at any time by choosing Layers > Dry Art Media Layer or Layers > Wet Art Media Layer.

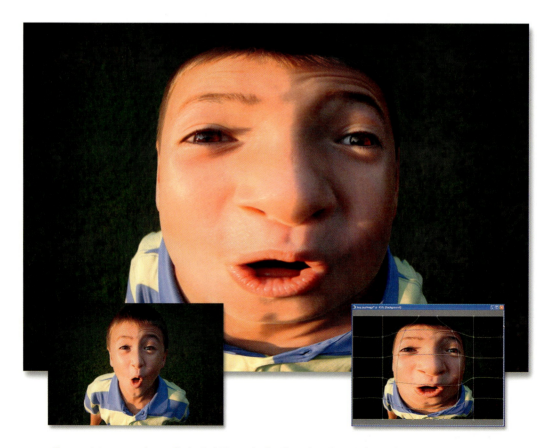

FIG 8.15 The most obvious or immediate use for the Mesh Warp tool is fun. Choose the tool, stretch the wire frame that appears over the picture, and watch PaintShop Photo Pro treat those pixels like so many rubberized elements!
Picture: MadJack Photography, iStockphoto 2126391

You can save and load Mixer palette pages and switch between them by choosing Save Page and Load Page from the Mixer Palette menu.

About Deformation Tools

Altering the shape or alignment of a layer is easy using PaintShop Photo Pro's Deformation tools. Why use the Deformation tools?

- To change the alignment of a layer
- To modify the size of the layer
- To modify the perspective and skew of a layer
- To significantly change the appearance of a picture.

There are four to choose from:

- Pick tool – used for relatively simple layer changes.
- Straighten tool – especially handy for straightening horizons in scans.
- Perspective Correction tool – for adding exaggerated (or corrective) perspective to objects.
- Mesh Warp – the 'big daddy' of the subset. Mesh Warp gives you the freedom to bend, distort, warp, and buckle 25 sections within a layer.

The procedure is simple enough: open the document and select the layer that needs deforming. Choose the Pick tool from the Tools toolbar. Note the bounding box and 'handles' that appear at the corners of the layer. If you hold the cursor over any of these handles, the normal four-pointed arrow Move symbol changes to a rectangle, indicating that you can scale the layer while maintaining its original proportions. If you don't want to maintain the original proportions, in other words to stretch or squeeze the layer, drag one of the handles located on an edge midway between the corners.

You can further change the type of the deforming action by holding down the Shift key for a shear action or by holding the Ctrl key to change it to Perspective Deform. The handle in the center, which resembles a stroked circle, moves all the contents in the bounding box. The Rotation Handle to the right of this (pre-rotation) rotates the layer. Use similar mouse actions to directly change the perspective (Perspective Correction tool) and to align the horizon (Straighten tool). Advanced users can use the Deformation tools to manipulate selected layers to create super-real perspective effects or to add extra realism, such as shadows to product photos.

Lens Correction Filters

PaintShop Photo Pro also has a range of filter effects specifically designed for correcting the detrimental effects caused by poor-quality lenses. These are: Barrel, Pincushion, and Fisheye distortion correction filters.

Tip

Many criteria come into play to influence the success or failure of a filter effect. Factors include the quality, focus, color, and contrast in the original snap. Don't use a filter to mask the fact that a snap is no good – because the filter effect will invariably be no good either!

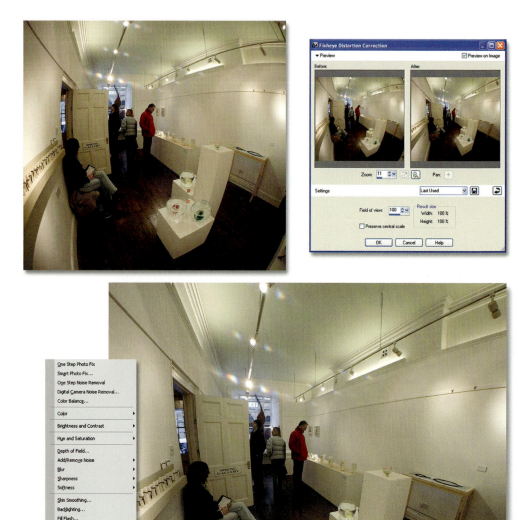

FIG 8.16 PaintShop Photo Pro X3 has three distortion correction filters – Barrel, Pincushion, and Fisheye – designed to correct for lens distortions. These distortions are often found in less expensive lenses, but they are usually quite minor and difficult to spot. Ultra-wide-angle lenses though, and in particular 'fisheye' lenses with a 180-degree field of view, suffer from severe barrel distortion. The orginal (top left) was shot with an ultra-wide-angle lens – notice how the straight lines, e.g. the lighting rail and skirting board, curve towards the edges of the image. The Fisheye distortion correction filter does an excellent job of straightening everything out.

Applying Filter Effects

Photo-editing applications are used to improve the look of digital pictures. Most contain filter sets. These are pre-recorded visual effects that can be applied to a picture at the press of a button (OK, at the press of two buttons).

PaintShop Photo Pro has many filters, designed not only to improve the quality of your work but also, in some examples, to radically change the nature of the picture. For example, you can increase or decrease color, contrast, hue, sharpness, and even black and white tone in a photo at the press of a button. These filters are regarded as 'standard issue' for most photo-editing products. PaintShop Photo Pro also has a range of creative and esoteric filter effects that are used to change the nature of a picture from a photo into something different, like a drawing, painting or even a sketch. In fact, with a bit of patience, you can create almost any type of special effect you care to think of, such is the power of the software filter set.

PaintShop Photo Pro has dozens of filters. The program is also compliant to a range of plug-in type filters. These are manufactured by third parties, like Flaming Pear and Auto F/X. These are loaded into the Effects menu just as if they were original integral products.

Tip

Effects filters usually work best when applied to one part of an image, e.g. to text, or a specific area. You can use the selection tools and masks to achieve this and there's a step-by-step project that shows how to apply filter effects using masks at www.gopaintshoppro.co.uk

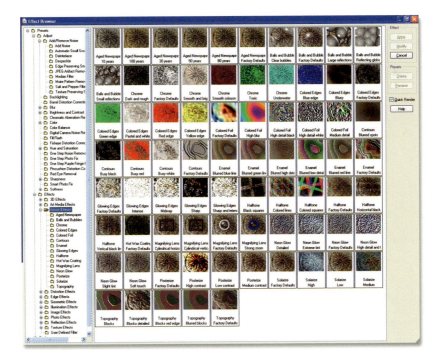

FIG 8.17 This is what the filter Effect Browser looks like. You can make it display a thumbnail of every filter in PaintShop Photo Pro, or you can be a bit more specific by choosing filters from individual subsets. Double-click the window that you like the look of to apply that filter to the picture open on the desktop.

Most of PaintShop Photo Pro's filters are subdivided into types under the Effects menu. These include:

- 3D Effects (6)
- Art Media Effects (6)
- Artistic Effects (15)
- Geometric Effects (8)
- Distortion Effects (13)
- Texture Effects (15)
- User Defined.

You'll also find more filters under the Adjust menu. These include:

- Add/Remove Noise (10)
- Blur (6)
- Sharpness (4)
- Softness (3)
- Red-Eye Removal.

There's also a powerful filter Effect Browser. This previews all the filter effects as thumbnails so that if you've no idea what to use, you can make an educated, illustrated guess.

Tip

If you hit on a filter effect that works really well, save it as a preset that you can later apply to other images with a single click. Click the Save Preset button (the disk icon) at the top of the Filter dialog box.

Each filter subfolder contains effects that can be applied to any picture globally, to a layer in that document, or to a specific selection. For example, Art Media filter effects include: 'Black Pencil', 'Brush Strokes', 'Charcoal', 'Colored Chalk', 'Colored Pencil', and 'Pencil'. Select any of these and the dialog that appears offers further refinements to the filter action. Some are quite basic while others have a range of controls.

There's no 'correct' use of a filter. Try to go for the subtle use although, in some cases, blatant can also work quite well, especially if you need to change the nature of the entire picture.

Filters to Try

- Time Machine
- Film and Filters
- Balls and Bubbles
- Brush Strokes
- Charcoal
- Halftone
- Trace Contour
- Soft Focus
- Digital Camera Noise Removal
- Fill Flash
- Backlighting
- Displacement map
- Radial Blur
- Object Remover
- High Pass Sharpen.

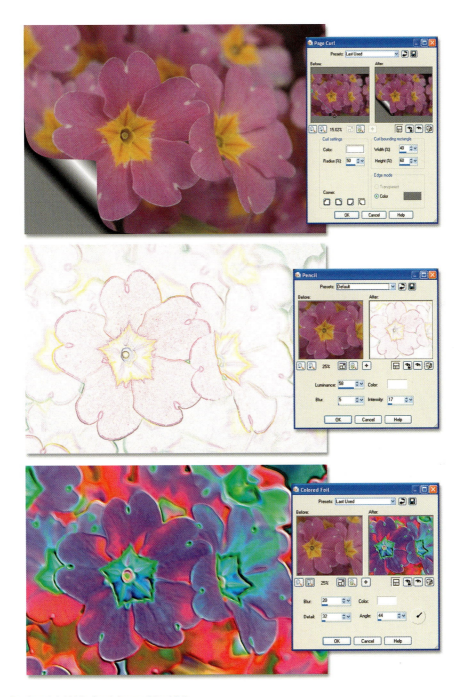

FIG 8.18 Top: Page Curl. Middle: Pencil. Bottom: Colored Foil.

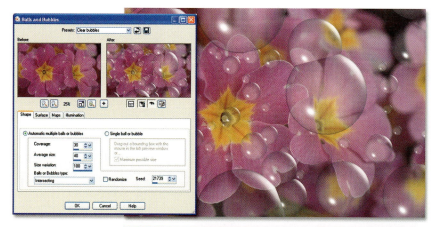

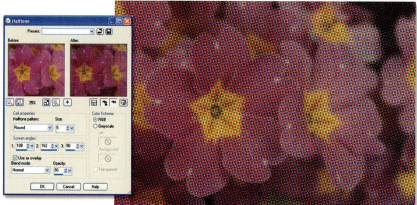

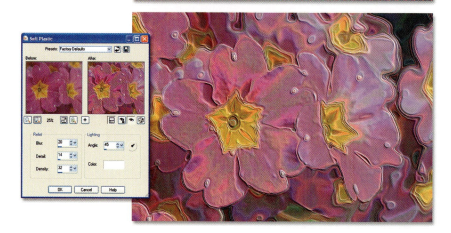

FIG 8.19 Top: Balls and Bubbles. Middle: Halftone. Bottom: Soft Plastic.

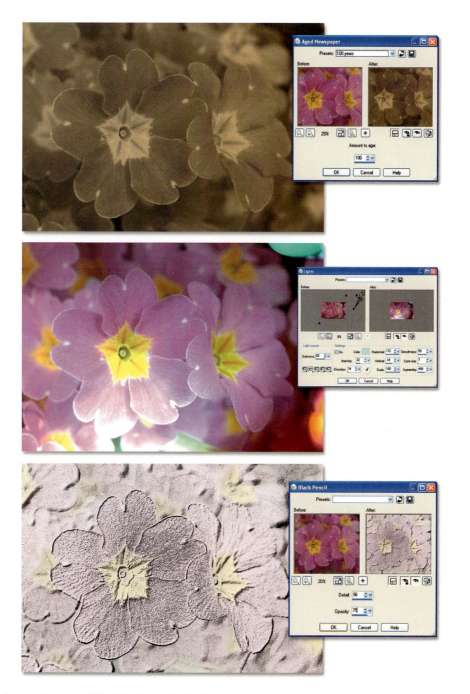

FIG 8.20 Top: Aged Newspaper. Middle: Lights. Bottom: Black Pencil.

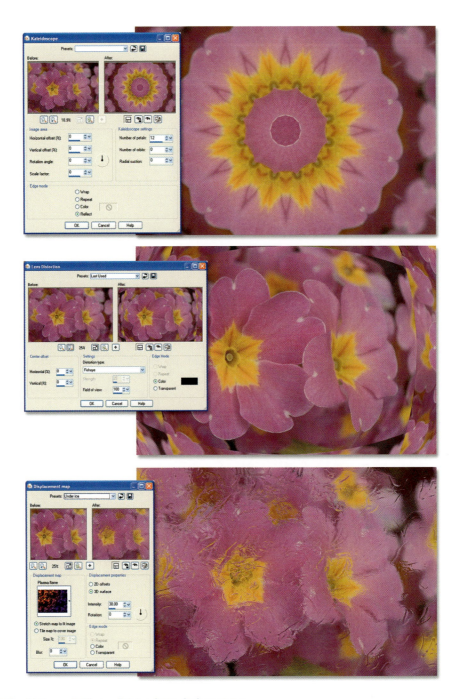

FIG 8.21 Top: Kaleidoscope. Middle: Lens Distortion. Bottom: Displacement map.

Adding Lighting Effects

PaintShop Photo Pro has a very powerful feature that allows you to add real studio lighting-type effects after the shot has been taken. It's a pretty cool filter-type effect that, when used with care, can add depth to an otherwise flat or lackluster picture.

PaintShop Photo Pro offers several light sources, exactly as you'd have in a real photo studio. Click on one and you'll be able to edit its behavior – widening or narrowing the spread of light has the effect of increasing or spreading the flood of light on to the picture. A narrow beam intensifies

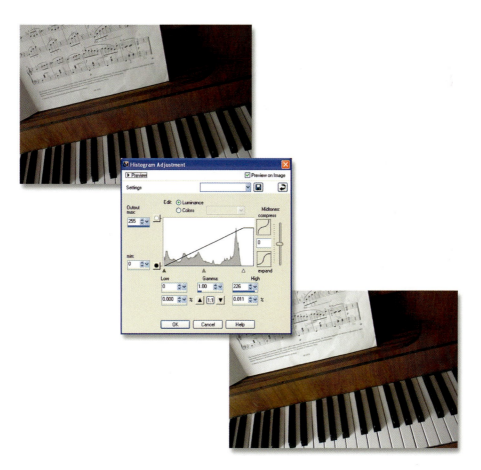

FIG 8.22 Lighting effects allow the image-maker to add lighting effects to the shot after it has been captured. This is done via a clever combination of directional contrast and brightness enhancements, simulating the effect of a floodlight or a spotlight. Though you should never use this as a substitute for shooting a frame properly, the addition of a lighting effect like the ones seen here can make or break a picture that is not as strong as it possibly could be. The first step is to use the Histogram Adjustment dialog to improve the tones and contrast in the photo.

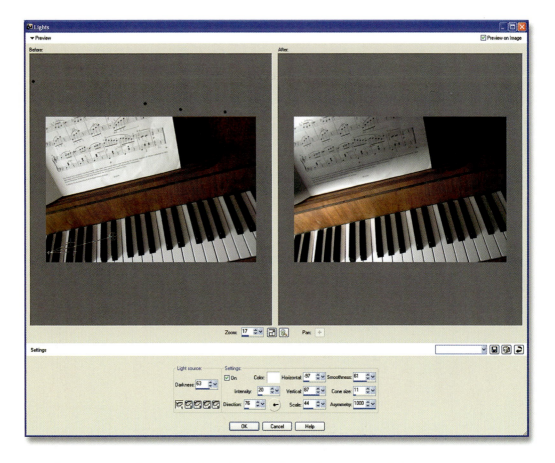

FIG 8.23 The Lights dialog box displays a 'before' and 'after' preview. Drag the lights in the 'before' thumbnail to position them and alter their 'cone size' – narrower angles produce a spotlight effect, broader angles a more diffuse style of light. There are five lights in all, but two, or at most three, will be adequate; uncheck the 'on' box to turn unwanted lights off. Here, I've used a spotlight (cone size 11) to illuminate the keyboard from a low angle and a more diffuse light above for the sheet music. You need to be careful not to overdo the intensity and create 'blown' highlights with no detail. Often, the best way to avoid this and produce creative lighting setups is to position the lights outside the image shining on to it.

the concentration of added light so take care not to 'overdo' this, otherwise you'll end up adding overblown highlights that take away from the subject matter. A little, in this case, will always produce a better result. The great thing about this tool is that its five light sources are infinitely adjustable. If you only need one or two lights, switch the others off by lowering their intensities to a zero value. Take care though, because you might end up spending a lot of time moving the 'lights' around the studio floor (i.e. the canvas). Keeping it simple will produce realistic and genuine improvements to any picture.

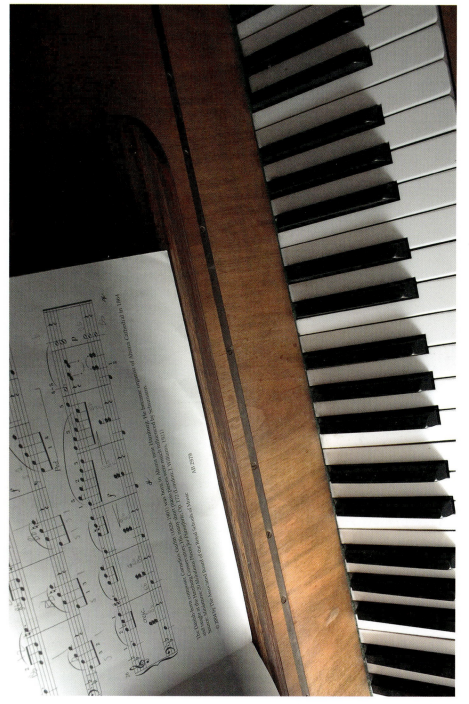

FIG 8.24 This is the final result – a snapshot with all the flair of a professional photo studio!

Step-by-Step Projects

Technique: Creating a Panorama

Panoramas are a great way to stretch your creativity, both through composition and all-over picture potential. So, what exactly is a panorama and what special gear is needed to make it?

A panorama is essentially nothing more than a group of pictures joined together, seamlessly, into one wide (or high) picture. Panoramas generally begin with more than two frames but can be constructed from up to 10 or more individual photo elements. How many you use for the panorama is dependent on how much detail is required in the frame. Once the components have been shot, they are stitched together using PaintShop Photo Pro and then the tone is adjusted for maximum picture impact.

Tips on Shooting Panorama Components

- Use a tripod or other stabilizing device for shooting your panoramas. It's important to keep the camera absolutely level at all times, otherwise the panorama segments won't stitch together correctly.
- Lock off the camera exposure meter (using its AE Lock feature) so that every component is exposed at exactly the same value.
- Lock off the focus (using the AF Lock function) so that each frame is focused to the same distance point.
- If your camera has a zoom lens, set it to the widest angle setting and leave it there for all the photos in the panorama.
- Overlap each panorama frame by about 20–30%. This will make it easier to align them when it comes to stitching them together.
- Remember that a panorama need not be horizontal – you can also make neat vertical panoramas.
- Because of their wide, all-encompassing nature, panoramas need to be composed very carefully to include sufficient foreground interest. But try to avoid fences, walls, and other detail in the very near foreground, which can cause stitching difficulties.
- It is possible to hand-hold the camera when snapping panorama components but extra care must be taken to get the level right.
- If you are hand-holding, rotate around the camera body rather than around yourself and you'll find your overlapping image edges match up more easily.
- Ensure that the camera rotation is around the nodal point of the lens, where possible. (Check the Internet for further information on estimating the nodal point for your camera model.)

Tip

It's not always possible, but try to avoid including moving subjects near the edge of your panorama images. If they move between two overlapping shots it can make stitching them together difficult.

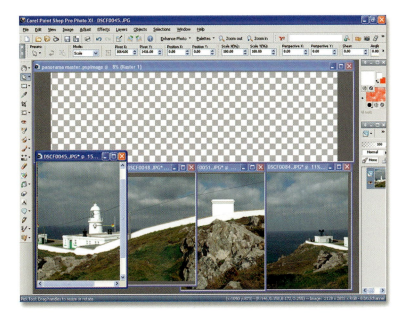

STEP 1 Once you've made all your exposures, import the lot into the computer, open PaintShop Photo Pro and create a new, blank canvas using the Panorama preset from the Presets pull-down menu in the New Image dialog box (File > New). It doesn't matter if it is too large – it can be cropped at a later stage.

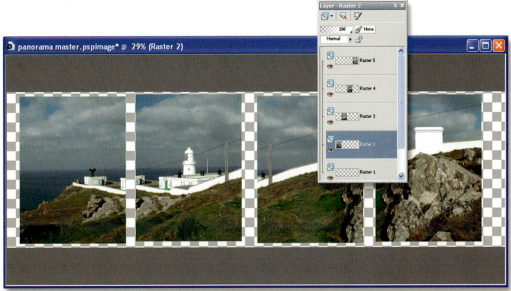

STEP 2 Find and open the panorama components. Copy each one and paste it into the new document as a new layer (press Ctrl + L). Try to keep the order of pasting the same as the order in which the elements were shot (i.e. left to right or right to left). If your photos are bigger than the canvas they will fill it and you'll only see the top layer. Either resize them before copying and pasting or use the Pick tool to resize them.

231

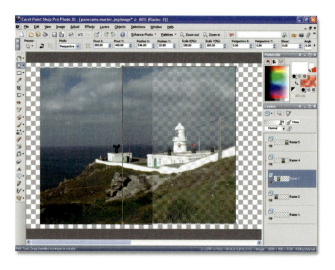

STEP 3 Choose the layer on which the left-hand panorama segment sits and, using the Move tool, drag it over to the left-hand side of the frame. Choose the second-to-left layer and, after reducing its opacity (in the Layers palette), move its left edge slightly over the right-hand edge of the first frame to get an exact fit. Jiggle the Opacity slider so that you can see through one layer to the layer beneath to make this process easier and then, once it's in position, return the opacity to 100%. Repeat this process for all remaining panorama components. You may find that some have been shot on a tilt, especially if the panorama camera was hand-held and not mounted on a tripod. If this is the case, use the Pick tool to straighten out the uneven horizon on that particular layer.

STEP 4 Once the entire set of images (components) has been overlapped successfully and all opacities are the same, save the file as a copy by choosing Save Copy As from the File menu or press Ctrl + F12. In Step 6, you will flatten the layers and the individual images will not be independently editable. If you later discover the images are not properly aligned you can go back to the original master and start from there.

STEP 5 Check that the density and the color values for all layers are the same, otherwise you might find that, even though the exposure was 'locked off' at the shooting stage, some frames are still darker or lighter than others. Use the Color Balance and Histogram Adjustment tools to make these tone corrections if necessary. Choose the Crop tool to cut off the extreme edges of the frame if there's a noticeable mismatch with the component segments.

Tip

If you haven't got a tripod and are hand-holding the camera, when you take the first image make a note of a reference point (a lamppost, for example) a quarter of the way in from the right-hand side of the viewfinder. For the second image, turn to the right until the reference point is on the left of the viewfinder.

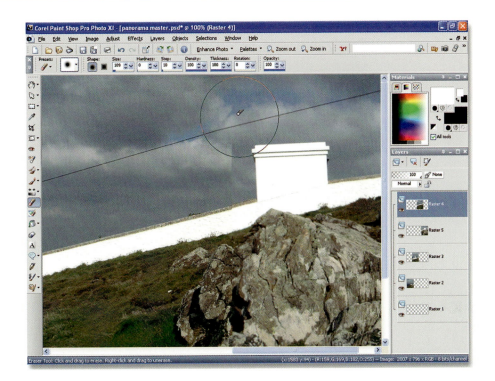

STEP 6 Visible seams can be retouched using the Clone Brush or, as here, simply by using the Eraser tool with a soft-edged brush to take the hard edge off the overlapping portion of the upper image layer. Flatten the layers in the copy (Layers > Merge > Merge All {Flatten}). Now you can adjust the global color and contrast values in the panorama to get the entire photo the way you really want it to look. Consider, at this stage, using one of PSP's darkroom tools to increase (or decrease) the density/color in selected parts of the scene using a brush.

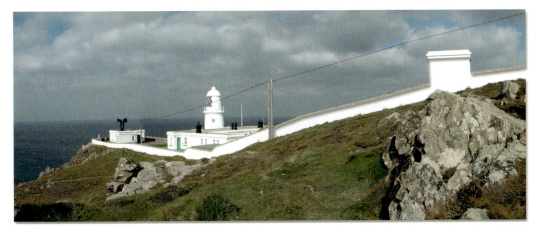

STEP 7 Save the panorama. This is the final, cropped, and color-balanced panorama.

Technique: Creating Realistic Depth Effects Using Displacement Maps

The displacement map effect was introduced in PaintShop Pro 9. Displacement maps have been a feature of that other professional image-editing application (OK, Photoshop!) for some time, but even professionals are often at a loss to know what to do with this effect. This is a shame, because you can use displacement maps to create amazingly realistic 3D overlay effects.

Let's say, for example, you want to overlay some type on a heavily textured background – a brick wall or a rocky cliff face – but you want it to look like it's been painted on, following the contours of the surface below, rather than floating on top the way a normal Text layer would. Displacement maps allow you to do just that.

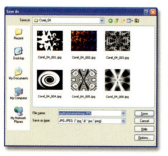

STEP 1 Open the base image (the rock face, or your own textured backdrop) in PaintShop Photo Pro and resave it as a copy (File > Save Copy As) into the folder containing PaintShop Pro's displacement maps. If you did a standard installation on your C drive for PaintShop Photo Pro X3 you'll find this at C:\Program Files\Corel\Corel PaintShop Photo Pro\X3\PSPClassic\Corel_04; for version X2 look in C:\Program Files\Corel\Corel PaintShop Photo Pro X2\Corel_04.

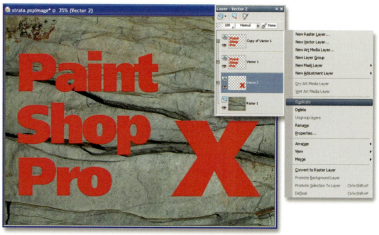

STEP 2 Add the type; the bigger and bolder the better. Here I've added two layers so that the number 'X' can be sized and positioned independently. Right-click the Type layer in the Layers palette and select Duplicate from the contextual menu.

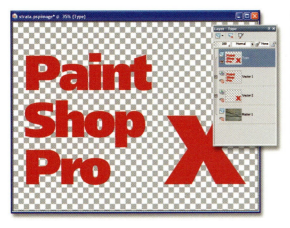

STEP 3 Select the duplicated Type layer in the Layer palette and choose Convert to Raster Layer from the Layers menu. If you used more than one Type layer, turn all the other layers off by clicking their Layer Visibility button (eye icon) in the Layers palette and choose Layers > Merge > Merge Visible to combine them. Double-click the merged layer and rename it 'Type' in the Layer Properties dialog box.

STEP 4 Turn the Background layer back on, make sure the Type layer is selected, and choose Effects > Distortion Effects > Displacement Map. Click the Displacement Map button underneath the 'before' thumbnail, make sure All is selected from the category pull-down menu and locate the copy image you saved in Step 1.

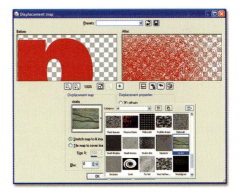

STEP 5 You should now see the type deform in the preview window. The displacement map moves pixels in the target image depending on the value of corresponding pixels in the map. There are two buttons in the Displacement Map pane that allow you to stretch or tile the map, but our map is the same image and, therefore, the same size as the target, so we don't need to bother with these.

Tip

You can use the background from the current image as a displacement map if you turn off visibility for all the other layers. But make sure you have the (invisible) Type layer selected before you apply the displacement effect.

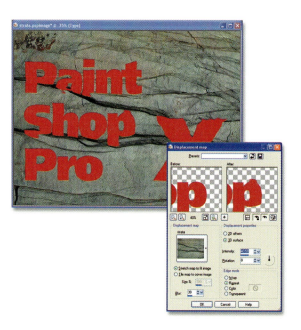

Sometimes you can get a more realistic overlay effect by switching the layers around and placing the Background layer on top of the Type layer and choosing an appropriate blend mode. You'll need to promote the background layer to a full layer to do this.

STEP 6 In all likelihood, the default settings won't produce a satisfactory distortion; there will either be too little or too much. There are two ways to control this. First, click the 3D Surface radio button in the Displacement Properties pane and change the Intensity. The Displacement Map dialog box only shows the Type layer. If you want to see the effect overlaid on your background image click the Proof button (the eye icon). Clicking the Auto Proof button will update the proof each time you make a change, but this can be quite time-consuming, especially with larger images.

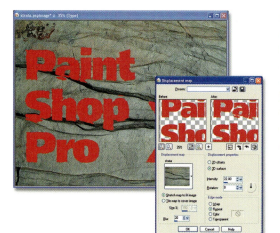

STEP 7 Generally, it's sufficient for the type to deform along the larger cracks and fissures in our background image, but ordinarily every little detail would produce unwanted distortions. The effect of the finer detail can be reduced by blurring the image. Drag the Blur slider until only the edges of the type are deformed and appear to be following the contours of the background image. Using trial and error, find the best combination of Blur and Intensity and, when you're happy with the result, click OK.

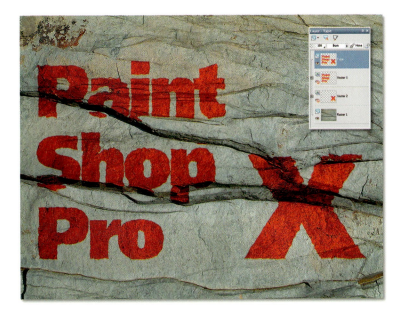

STEP 8 The type is now following the contours of the rock, but it doesn't look painted on and has an unnaturally flat look. Real paint would show through some of the rock texture and detail. You can create this effect using a Layer blend mode; here I've set the blend mode for the Type layer to Burn. Hard Light, Color, and Multiply are also worth trying – different images require different approaches. Sometimes, reducing the layer opacity helps heighten the realism of the effect.

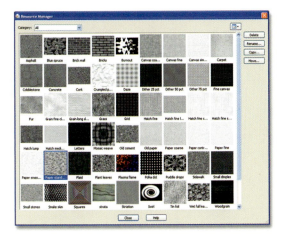

STEP 9 PaintShop Photo Pro X3 has an assortment of ready-made displacement maps, including geometric patterns and texture photos, which you can use to distort images. You can also make your own – save them in

the Displacement Map folder or use the File Locations button on the Displacement Map dialog box to add a folder of displacement maps. Grayscale images work best. Mid-gray pixels produce least distortion; black and white pixels distort pixels in the target image the most.

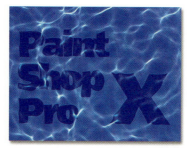
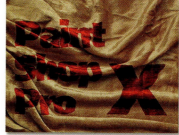
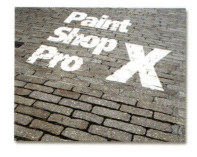
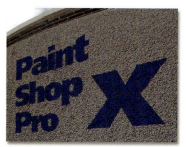

STEP 10 This technique can be used to apply all kinds of images to all kinds of surfaces. You can use it for lighting effects: to make a laser beam deform as it passes over objects; to produce realistic shadow effects; and to superimpose designs on to all kinds of backgrounds from crumpled material to water.

Technique: Having Fun with the Picture Tube

PaintShop Photo Pro's Picture Tube tool is one of the weirdest around. What does it do? The Picture Tube literally 'pours' pictures out of a tube on to the canvas.

Using graphics and photos as 'liquid paint' rather than flat color is an interesting concept, but it's one of those esoteric type tools that's almost impossible to find a proper use for. Unless, of course, you create your own specific Picture Tube files.

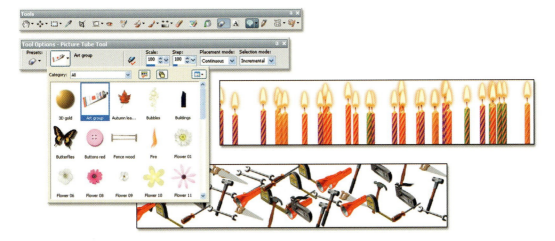

FIGURE 8.25 Use the Picture Tube to have fun, create borders, and even to decorate artwork destined for the inkjet printer.

Picture Tube Applications

- Creating fun effects
- Cool edges and borders for pictures
- Making unusual picture frame effects
- Entertaining your kids (and yourself)
- Creating textured backgrounds
- Adding specific, custom views to a picture (such as image grain, noise, and even textures).

How to Create a Picture Tube File

STEP 1 Open the pictures chosen to be in the set, ensuring that they are dust-free and clear from JPEG artifacts (use PaintShop Photo Pro's JPEG Artifact Removal filter to do this). Ensure that all pictures are a similar resolution and physical dimension.

STEP 2 Create a new document (File > New) with a transparent background to accommodate the picture elements. For example, if you are making a four-image Picture Tube, set the fields to 800 pixels wide and 200 high. Choose Transparent as the background color and then click OK.

STEP 3 Open PaintShop Photo Pro's Rulers palette (View > Rulers) and drag the guideline to the 200 pixel mark. Drag another to the 400 pixel mark and a third to the 600 pixel mark.

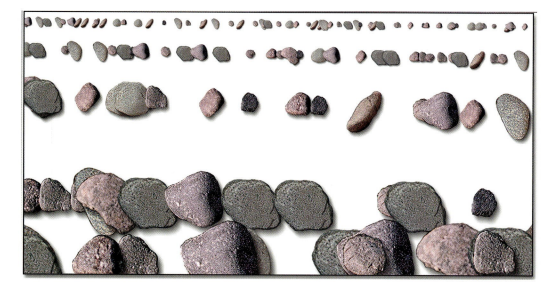

FIGURE 8.26 The Picture Tube icons can be of different sizes and randomness. Shift-clicking creates a point-to-point straight line.

STEP 4 You should now have a document with a transparent background (a checkbox pattern indicates transparency) with colored grid lines dividing a long, wide frame into four sections. Copy and paste (Edit > Paste as New Layer) the four pictures into this document. At this stage it's a good idea to save a copy of the file in case the resulting tube is no good. Give it a unique name and save it as a '.pspimage' (layered) file for later use.

STEP 5 Merge all the layers (Layers > Merge Visible) that PaintShop Photo Pro has created (don't flatten this as it will produce a default background color that is not required at this stage). Once merged, the four pictures should be sitting on a single layer that has a transparent background.

Tip

In the Picture Tube Tool Options palette, you can control the scale of the Picture Tube elements, the frequency of their placement and selection modes (how they are placed from the file).

STEP 6 Select File > Export > Picture Tube, and another dialog opens. Enter the amount of cells that you have made for the tube (in this case, four). Make a unique name for the tube and click OK. To test the tube, create a new document with a white background (any size and resolution will suffice) and select the Picture Tube tool. Open its Options palette and, after pressing the Image Selection tab, scroll through the preset tube files to find your alphabetically placed file. Select this and paint away to test the tube.

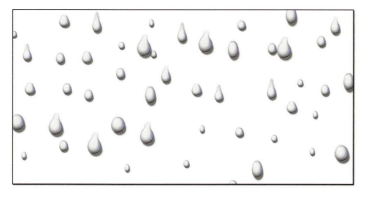

By setting the randomness to a high value and reducing the frequency you can use the tube to paint individual objects one at a time over the canvas.

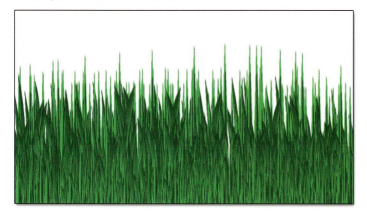

You can use the tube to create cartoon-like effects. Download new tubes from the Corel website's community page.

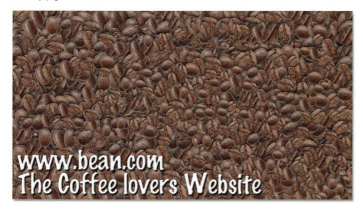

Another use for the tube is to create backgrounds. Lower the opacity on the layer so that text can be read more clearly over the top.

You'll soon discover whether the selections you made, the scale of the images, and their colors are attractive or not. If you are not happy with the result it's simple enough to open the '.pspimage' version again, make changes, save it over the previous tube file and try again.

Further Fun

While a few photo-purists might swear at the Picture Tube, there are still a heap of devotees that swear by it. So many that there are entire websites dedicated to its use, offering loads of free tubes. Start by visiting Corel's site for further resources and downloads at www.corel.com.

Technique: Adding Edge and Framing Effects

PaintShop Photo Pro gives you the power to not only add frames to any picture you import into the program, but also to add a great range of frame edges to the file as well, using the Picture Frame tool.

PaintShop Photo Pro's Picture Frame tool is fantastic, providing a great range of paint style edges (among others) that normally would take hours to create or several hundred dollars to buy. Why use edges? Photographers live in a rectangular world so it is great that we can now change that to recreate the look of a painted or sketched edge, film, crayon, and heaps more edges. If you habitually work with the program's specialist filter effects, you'll find this extremely useful.

Technique: How to Add an Edge or Frame to a Picture

STEP 1 Open the picture and choose Image > Picture Frame, and choose a frame or a picture edge from the dialog's many options. (There are not as many frames in this version as you'd get with an expensive third-party product; however, all the frames and edges here are changeable – you can flip, mirror and rotate each, making up to 60 extra choices and designs from which to choose. Not bad for a freebie.)

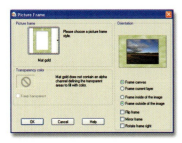

STEP 2 Once the Frame dialog is open, choose a frame or edge that you like the look of and click OK to add it to the full-resolution picture. If you don't want the frame to obscure detail at the edges of your photo, check the 'Frame outside of the image' radio button.

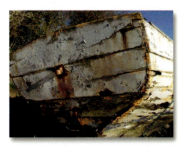
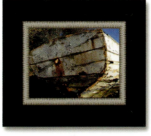
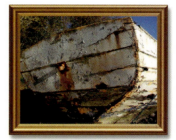

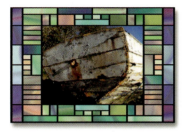
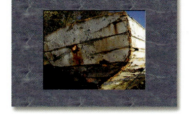
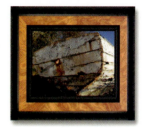

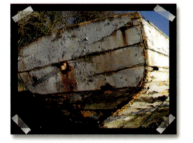
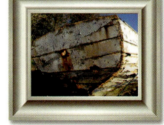
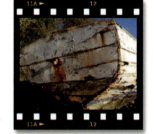

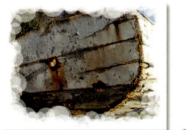
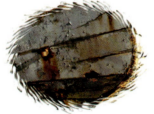
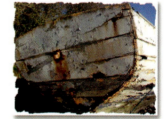

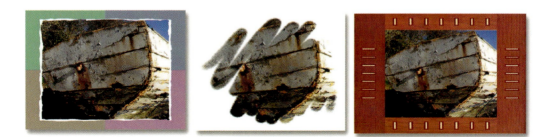

FIGURE 8.27 Just some of the frame styles available with PaintShop Photo Pro's Picture Frame feature.

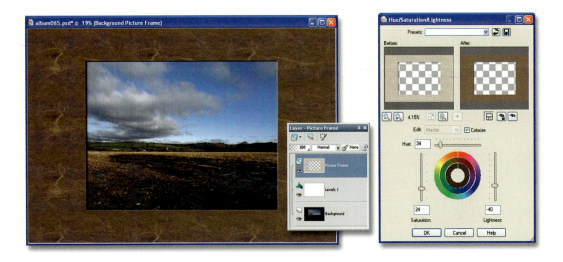

STEP 3 PaintShop Photo Pro puts the frame on its own layer, so you can apply adjustments to the frame, leaving the photo untouched. Here, I've used the Hue/Saturation/Lightness tool to change the frame color. You could just as easily change the Layer blend mode, transparency, or apply any of the Effects filters.

Technique: Using the Color Changer Tool

Changing colors in a photo is something you'll find yourself wanting to do all the time. Whether it's someone's shirt, a front door, or a car, PaintShop Photo Pro has the tools you need to make a neat job of it. In a previous edition of this book I showed how you can use the Color Replacer tool to change a front door from red to green. The Color Replacer tool remains a good choice for some color-change jobs, but PaintShop Photo Pro X3 has a tool that is much easier to use called the Color Changer tool.

One of the advantages of the Color Changer tool is that it works on the entire image. The Color Replacer tool is a brush tool – you paint over the parts of the image you want to recolor and, depending on the color of the original pixels and the Tolerance setting, the pixels the brush touches are changed to the new color. The Color Replacer tool remains the best option for fiddly detail, but to change large areas of similar color in a photo the Color Changer tool is the way to go. Here's how to use it to respray your car, or change the color of any other large object.

STEP 1 Right-click the Background layer in the Layers palette and select Duplicate from the Context menu. You can make your changes to the Duplicate layer and still have the original to fall back on if anything goes wrong. Select the color you want to change to on the Foreground color swatch in the Materials palette.

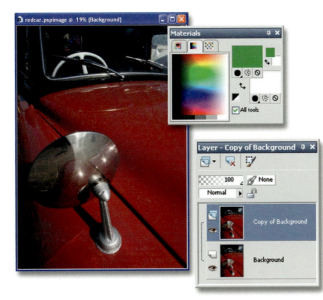

STEP 2 Select the Color Changer tool from the Flood Fill fly-out on the tool-bar. There are only two settings on the Tool Options bar for the Color Changer tool – Tolerance and Edge Softness – and you'll need to experiment with both to get the results you want.

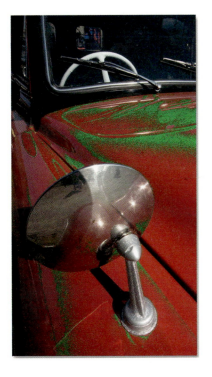

STEP 3 The Tolerance setting determines the extent of the color change. If you set a low value, only pixels that closely match the color of the pixel you click on will be changed. Here I've set a Tolerance of 10 and, although there's a lot of red, only the red pixels that are very close in terms of color to the red pixel I clicked on have been changed. One great feature of the Color Changer tool is that you can adjust the Tolerance after you've clicked to change pixels and the preview updates to color new pixels using the new Tolerance settings.

STEP 4 Rather than trying to get all of the red paintwork in one hit you can use the Color Changer repeatedly, clicking on different parts of the car to add to the original selection. Continue clicking with the Color Changer tool until most of the paintwork is the new color.

245

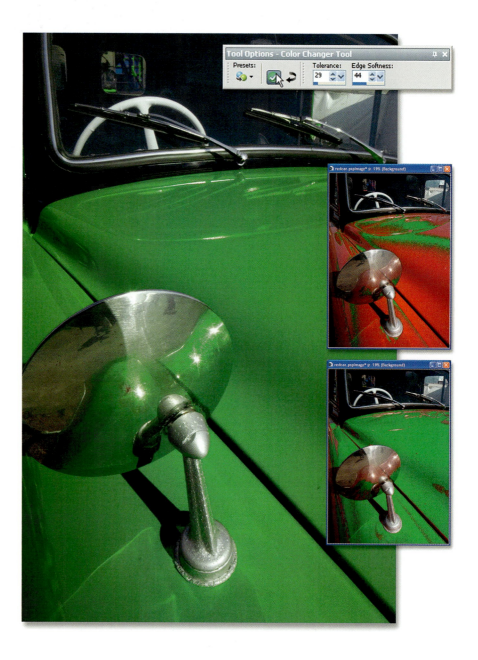

STEP 5 Incrementally increase the Tolerance setting until all of the red goes green. Incrementally increase the Edge Softness setting to produce a soft, more natural-looking edge to areas of changed color. When you're happy with the new paint job, press the Apply button to apply the color change.

CHAPTER 9

Printing

What's Covered in this Chapter

- This chapter is short, but it contains a lot of things worth knowing if you ever want to turn your photos into real physical things that you can hold in your hand rather than something you only ever see on a screen. What with web photo-sharing sites, email- and Wi-Fi-enabled electronic photo frames, most of your photos may never find their way on to paper. Believe it or not, though, not everyone owns a PC and, even among those who do, there are people who will always prefer a physical printed photograph over an electronic one. Some photo competitions still insist on you sending hard-copy prints, and if you want to exhibit your photos or just hang them on the wall you'll need to know how to print them.
- This chapter kicks off with a discussion about resolution and how it affects print quality, and if you read nothing else you should at least try and get your head around this concept as it's one of the most important factors affecting print quality.
- If you're having problems getting what comes out of your printer to match what you see on the screen you're not alone; it's one of the most common problems digital photographers face. Read the section on monitor calibration and color management to find out how to overcome the problem and stop wasting precious ink and paper.

PaintShop Photo Pro X3 for Photographers. DOI: 10.1016/B978-0-240-52165-7.10009-7

- Another way to save on expensive consumables is to print several photos on one sheet of paper. PaintShop Photo Pro's Print Layout application is designed to help you do just that. The step-by-step project at the end of this chapter shows you how.

Printing can be a frustrating business because there are many factors that affect final print quality – the quality and resolution of the digital image, the type of printer, the inks and paper used, color management, and printer settings. By following the advice provided here you'll be able to consistently produce the best results possible from your printer.

Image Resolution

In order to get good results when printing it's important to understand a little about image resolution. If you've bought an inkjet printer recently, one of the things that may have influenced your decision is the printer resolution. Your inkjet printer may boast a resolution of 1440 dpi or even more. Similarly, if you've recently bought a digital camera, somewhere on the box it will say 10 or 12, or even 18, megapixels.

Like printer and digital camera manufacturers, makers of flatbed scanners use resolution as a selling feature – the higher the better. But what do all these numbers mean and how are they related? Perhaps more importantly, how does the size of a camera's sensor affect how your photos will look when they are printed?

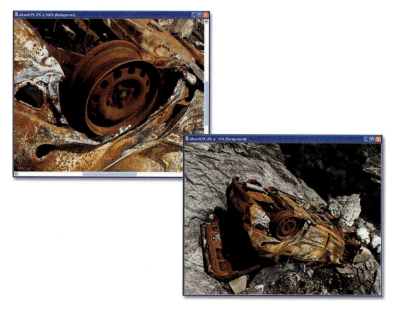

FIG 9.1 At 100% magnification only a small part of this 2592 × 3888 pixel image is visible; to see the whole thing it's necessary to reduce the magnification using Window > Fit to Window.

When it comes to digital images, cameras, scanners, printers, and PaintShop Photo Pro all deal in the same currency – pixels. The starting point with any digital image, therefore, is its size in pixels. Figure 9.1 has a size of 3888 × 2592 pixels, giving a total pixel count of 10,077,696. If you viewed this image in PaintShop Photo Pro at 100% magnification you would only be able to see a small part of it. As well as the number of pixels in an image we also need to take account of the resolution, measured in pixels per inch (ppi). The resolution of most screens in use today is around 100 ppi. If you divide the pixel dimensions by the resolution you get the physical size of the image. 3888/100 = 38.8 and 2592/100 = 25.9, so a 10-megapixel photo would measure approximately 39 × 26 inches on screen at 100% magnification.

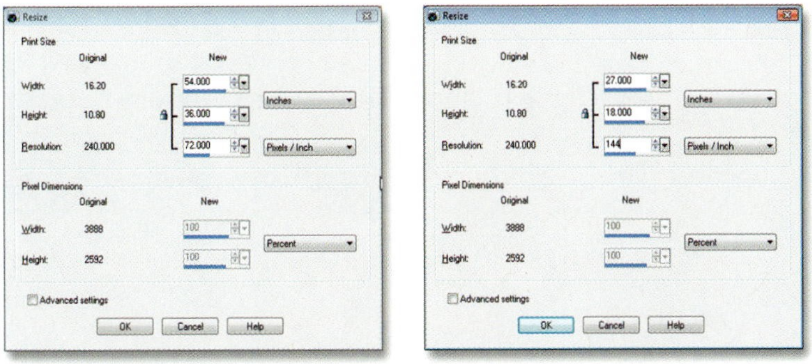

FIG 9.2 There's an inverse relationship between resolution and print output size – doubling the resolution halves the output size.

Shuffling Pixels

Open an image in PaintShop Photo Pro and select Image > Resize. The Pixel Dimensions pane in the Resize dialog box tells you the pixel dimensions of the photo, in this case 3888 × 2592 pixels. The Print Size pane shows the physical dimensions of the image at the specified resolution; at 72 ppi this image measures 54 × 36 inches.

Click the Advanced Settings box and make sure the Resample using box is unchecked and enter 144 in the resolution field; notice how the width and height print dimensions halve when you double the resolution. If you enter 288 in the resolution field the print size decreases again by a factor of 2. All you are doing here is rearranging the same information – the 10,077,696 image pixels – into a progressively smaller space.

On the screen at 72 ppi, the pixels are packed so closely together that you can't see them individually. But inkjet printing technology requires images of higher resolution to produce good-quality results. Generally, your photos should have a minimum resolution of 200 ppi to print well.

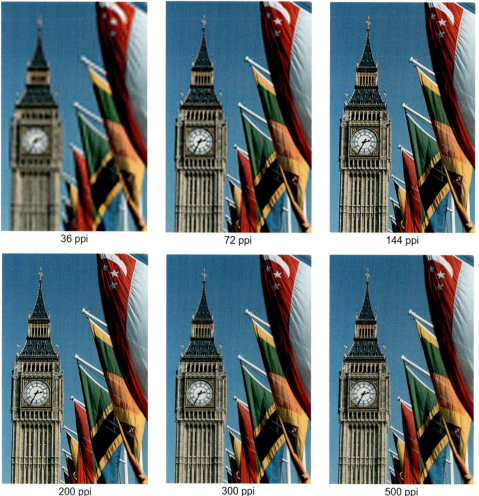

FIG 9.3 Though the commercial printing process used for this book is technologically dissimilar to inkjet printing, these images nonetheless provide a good example of what you could expect to see if you output images at these resolutions to a desktop inkjet. At low resolutions pixelation is clearly visible. A good-quality image is produced at 200 ppi, but at higher resolutions no improvement in picture quality is discernible. The minimum recommended resolution for the offset litho process used to print this book is 300 ppi, so you may see some improvement from the 200 ppi to the 300 ppi image above (look at the detail in the clock face), but this is unlikely to be the case with an inkjet printer. Try carrying out your own resolution tests to determine the point at which increasing the resolution produces no apparent quality improvement on your printer.

Resampling

Go back to the Resize dialog box and enter a value of 200 in the Resolution field. This gives a print size of roughly 10 × 15 inches. What if you don't want to make a print almost A3 in size? That's easy, just enter the size you want in the Width or Height box – changing one automatically changes the other to maintain the aspect ratio. Say you want to fit the photo on a 6 × 4 inch piece of photo paper, enter 4 in the Width field (for a portrait-shaped photo) and the Height field automatically changes to 6. Wait a minute, though, now our image resolution is 648 ppi, far higher than the 200 ppi required for inkjet printing. This doesn't really matter too much and it certainly won't affect the print quality, which will be no better and no worse than at 200 ppi. It will take longer, though, for your computer to send all that data to the printer and for the printer to process it. You can speed things up by downsampling the image – removing the extra pixels that aren't required for printing at this size.

Downsampling

Check the 'Resample using' box and select either Smart Size or Bicubic from the interpolation pull-down menu. Now enter a value of 200 in the Resolution field. This time, rather than changing the physical dimensions to accommodate all the image pixels at the new resolution, PaintShop Photo Pro has done something different. It has removed pixels to produce the requested resolution at the existing size (it hasn't done it yet, but it will when you press OK). Take a look at the Pixel Dimensions pane and you'll see the new pixel dimensions are 800 × 1200. If you do the math yourself you'll discover that this does indeed produce a 6 × 4 inch image at 200 ppi.

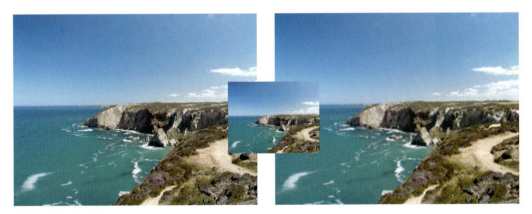

FIG 9.4 The photo on the left has been downsampled from an original 2560 × 1920 image to 6 × 4.5 cm at a resolution of 300 ppi – suitable for printing. Its pixel dimensions are now 717 × 538. The smaller middle photo was downsampled to 2 × 1.5 cm at 300 ppi, giving new pixel dimensions of 237 × 178. The middle photo was then upsampled to the original 6 × 4.5 cm size at 300 ppi (left). You can clearly see the loss of detail and sharpness caused by the interpolation, hardly surprising as only one-third of the pixels in this image are original. You can improve things marginally by unsharp masking, but there's no substitute for the original pixel data, so always make sure you keep originals backed up before resizing!

Removing pixels in this fashion will not affect the picture quality. This 4 × 6 inch print will be indistinguishable from one printed at 512 ppi, but you'll have it in your hand much sooner. But what if you change your mind and decide that an A3-sized print would look pretty cool after all (assuming you're lucky enough to own an A3 color inkjet printer)?

Upsampling

Open the Resize dialog box once more. (In PaintShop Photo Pro XI and earlier, when you open the Resize dialog, it applies the last-used settings to the current image. To get back to the current image size select Percent in the Pixel Dimensions units pull-down menu and enter 100 in the Width field.) Make sure the 'Resample using' box is still checked and enter the original pixel width of 2592 in the Width field (the Height box will automatically increase to 3888). Click OK and PaintShop Photo Pro will upsample the image, taking us back to where we started, right? Wrong!

Take a look at the new image and you'll notice it's not quite as sharp as it was to begin with. PaintShop Photo Pro has added new pixels in between the existing ones to bring the image up to size. The values of these new pixels are based on those of neighboring ones using a process called 'interpolation'. Interpolated pixels are OK if you're in a fix, like you need to make a large print from a small digital file, but they are no substitute for the real thing.

So, you can take pixels out of a digital photo with no loss of quality, and this can help speed up printing, but you can't put them back without things starting to look mushy. What are the implications of this for storing and printing your digital pictures? If you follow one simple rule you won't go wrong. Always keep a full-sized original copy of your digital photos backed up on removable media (i.e. CD or DVD). Then you can downsample your images for printing, emailing, uploading to the Web or whatever, but if you need to make a full-sized print that requires the maximum image resolution you'll always have the original to fall back on.

Printing with PaintShop Photo Pro

Having opened the picture, make sure that the quality is the best possible and choose Print Layout from the File menu. The Print Layout dialog shows the files selected for printing in the left margin. Click Open Template to view your options. The default template group is Avery. This group has over 50 templates that cover most everyday options, but you can also make your own and save them in the template library (File > Save Template).

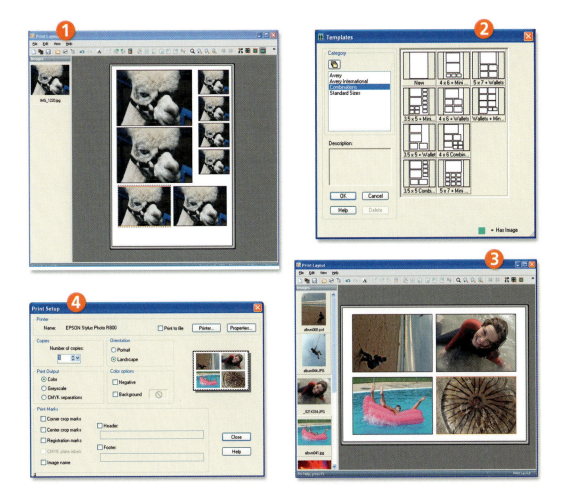

FIG 9.5 Clockwise from top left: (1) Print Layout provides an easy way to print multiple copies of the same photo or a selection of photos on a single sheet of paper, saving you time and money. (2) A range of templates is available, including Avery standard sizes so you can, for example, produce one large print for your album, or framing, and several smaller versions to send to friends. (3) You can print multiple photos by opening them in the Full Editor or selecting them from a Media tray and choosing File > Print Layout. The selected images appear in a strip on the left and are dropped in position on the template layout. (4) Click the Print Setup button to change the paper orientation and add captions (though this is better done in the Print Layout dialog box). Most of the settings here are for producing film separations for commercial printing.

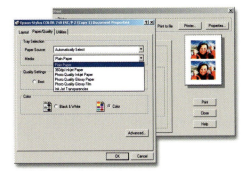

FIG 9.6 Don't forget to select the appropriate inkjet paper type. If you don't, the color may not come out as you'd hoped.

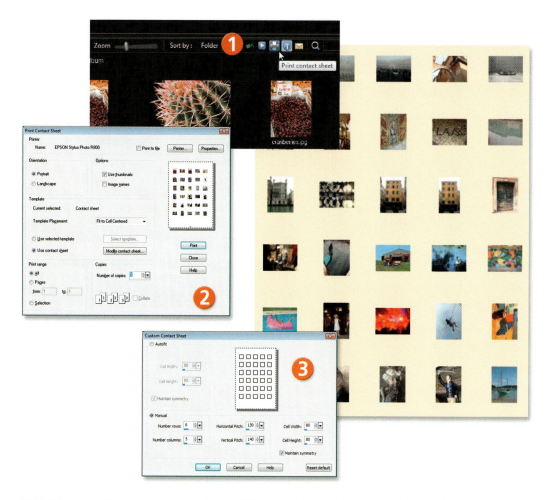

FIG 9.7 Click the Print Contact Sheet button in the Organizer (1) to quickly print a sheet of thumbnails for the current folder. This opens the Print Contact Sheet dialog box (2), where you can use the default template or choose another. Click the Modify Contact Sheet button to open the Custom Contact Sheet dialog box (3) and produce your own layout. Doing this with a folder containing a large number of images may take a while.

What Can You Use Templates For?

- Creating unique contact sheets.
- Customizing for specific jobs such as cards, receipts, invitations, business cards, etc.
- For making mini-stickers.
- For creating your own business and address labels.

Color Management

If you've ever asked the question 'why don't my prints match what I see on the computer display?' then you need to know about color management. A color management system (CMS) ensures that individual devices – digital cameras, scanners, computer monitors, and printers – all treat color in the same way so that you get consistent color from one to the other.

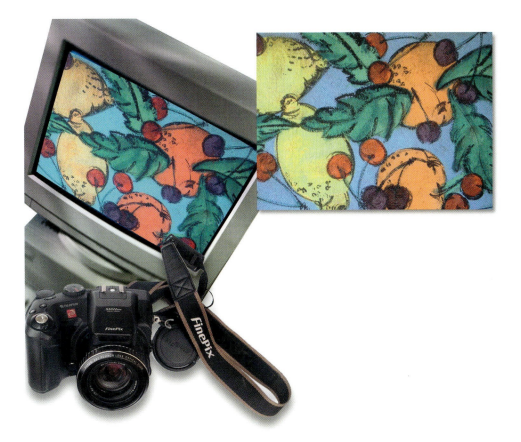

FIG 9.8 A color management system can help you avoid problems like unexpected variations in color from monitor to printer by ensuring consistent color from your digital camera to your monitor and finally to printed output.

To return to the original question, it is in fact impossible for your printer to reproduce exactly what's on your monitor as the two devices use different physical systems to produce color. The monitor transmits light using red, green, and blue phosphor dots (or, in the case of an LCD panel, a fluorescent backlight passing through a colored filter) and a color print uses pigment- or dye-based inks to reflect light. As we saw earlier in the chapter, color printers can use up to seven inks; even so, it is not possible for them to reproduce all the colors on your computer display. In color reproduction terms the two devices are said to have different gamuts.

It's not just different devices that vary in the way they handle color. As anyone who has visited the TV department of a high street electrical store can verify, no two TVs look the same. A picture viewed on your PC at home will quite probably look different on your work PC, and if you email it to your friends each one of them is likely to see a slightly different version, due to the individual color characteristics of their display.

Color Profiles

To try and sort out this mess, an organization called the International Color Consortium (ICC), which has as its members companies like Adobe, Apple, Agfa, and Kodak, developed a system of profiling for color imaging devices. Each device has a profile that describes its color characteristics and that can be read and understood by imaging software. Windows has built-in support for ICC-compliant color management.

Using ICC profiles a color management system can accurately convert color information from one device to another. In short, this means more accurate color from your camera to your monitor and finally out to your printer. It also means that, providing they use a CMS, what everyone else sees on their monitor is the same as what you see.

Calibration

In order for color management to work successfully, it's important that your monitor is correctly calibrated. To do this, select File > Color Management > Monitor Calibration and complete the Monitor Calibration wizard. Once your monitor is calibrated, the next step is to ensure you have profiles installed for all of your devices, or at least for your monitor and printer. These should have been installed automatically when you installed the devices but it doesn't hurt to check. To find out what profile your monitor is using in Windows XP, right-click on the desktop and select Properties from the contextual menu. Click the Advanced button on the Settings tab and then the Color Management tab. In Windows Vista right-click on the desktop, select Personalize, and select Display Settings. Click the Advanced Settings button, select the Color Management tab, then click the Color Management button.

If your monitor profile isn't listed, click the Add button and try to find it. All Windows color profiles are stored in the folder C:\Windows\system32\spool \drivers\color. If you can't find it here, check any disks that were supplied with the monitor, or the manufacturer's website.

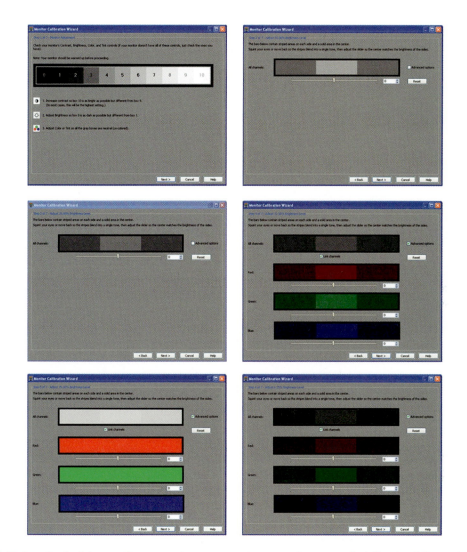

FIG 9.9 Monitor calibration is important for accurate color management. Let your monitor warm up for half an hour before running the wizard.

For your printer, select Printers and Faxes from the Start menu, right-click the printer icon, select Properties from the contextual menu and click the Color Management tab. It's not always easy to identify the correct color profile from its name. Windows should automatically assign the right profile, if it's available, though you can add it manually if necessary. As with monitor profiles, if one wasn't supplied with your printer the best option is the manufacturer's website.

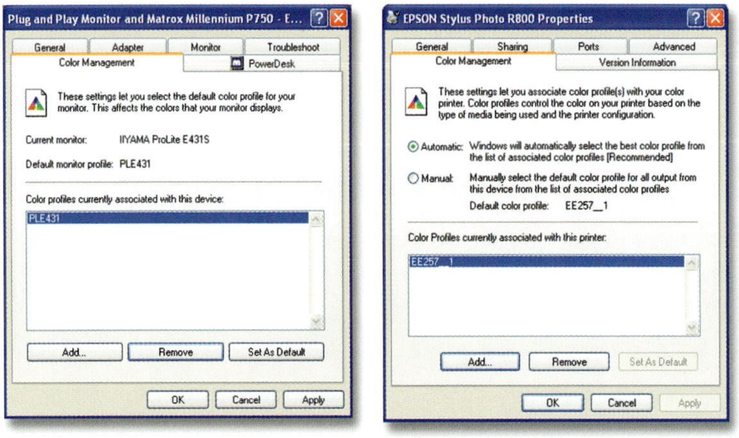

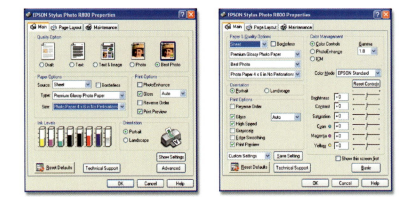

FIG 9.10 You can check the currently installed default profiles for your monitor and printer by opening the Display and Printer Properties dialog boxes.

Printer profiles are less straightforward than monitor profiles because they are designed to work with a specific combination of inks and paper. A profile generated for photo-quality glossy paper is unlikely to produce satisfactory results with matt paper. Furthermore, there is a wide variation in different manufacturers' paper characteristics, so a profile designed, for example, for Epson Premium Glossy Photo Paper will not provide good results with another manufacturer's glossy photo paper.

FIG 9.11 In Basic mode (left), the printer driver for the Epson Stylus Photo R800 helpfully indicates ink quantities remaining. Advanced mode (right) provides a range of color controls, but these should be avoided if you are using color management.

Color Management in PaintShop Photo Pro X3

PaintShop Pro X introduced support for ICC color profiles, which makes getting consistent color from your monitor to your printer that much easier. To turn on color management select File > Color Management > Color Management and check Enable Color Management in the Color Management dialog box.

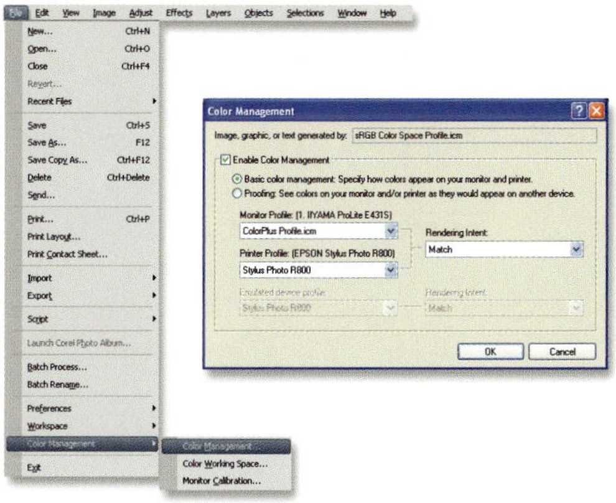

FIG 9.12 Use the Color Management dialog box to turn on color management and configure your display and printer profiles.

Select your monitor and printer profiles from the pull-down menus – unless you have several profiles installed there will be only one, the default profile for the device that you installed previously. That's nearly all you need to do.

If you have an image open, the color profile, if it has one, will be displayed at the top, after the message 'Image, graphic, or text generated by:'. Not all images are tagged with a profile, but if it's a photo from a digital camera it will most likely have an embedded sRGB profile.

Don't worry if the image has no embedded profile; you will still be able to see how it is going to look when printed. All of the elements for a color-managed workflow are in place and the color management system can correctly interpret the numbers in the profiled image and translate them for display on your monitor or printer using the profiles for those devices.

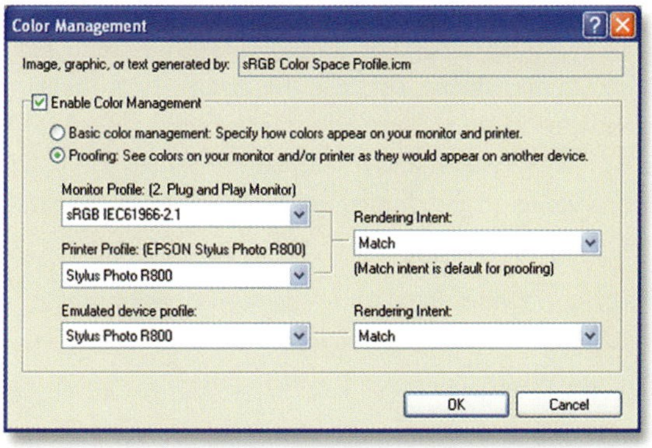

FIG 9.13 To produce a 'soft proof' – an on-screen view that accurately simulates output from your printer – check the Proofing radio button and select your printer profile from the 'Emulated device profile' pull-down menu.

Despite all of this, for the reasons explained earlier, it's still not possible for the image displayed on your monitor to match your printer. But PaintShop Photo Pro can show you on screen what an image will look like when printed on your desktop color inkjet, or any other printer for which you have a profile. This is called 'soft proofing', as opposed to 'hard proofing', which involves making a hard-copy print.

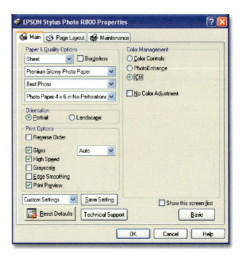

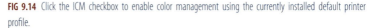

FIG 9.14 Click the ICM checkbox to enable color management using the currently installed default printer profile.

To display a soft proof on your monitor open the Color Management dialog box and check the radio button labeled 'Proofing'. To see colors on your monitor and/or printer as they would appear on another device, select your printer in the 'Emulated device profile' pull-down menu and click OK to view the proof.

Printing Using Color Management

How your Print dialog box looks will depend on the printer you are using and the driver software. The examples shown here use the Epson Stylus Photo R800 printer, but other printer drivers will provide similar options. Firstly, make sure your image is the correct size and resolution for printing on your chosen paper, as described earlier in this chapter. Select File > Print and click the Properties button on the Print dialog box.

The Stylus Photo R800 driver provides Basic and Advanced options. It also provides an extremely useful graphical representation of the ink levels. Click the Advanced button and select the paper type, size, orientation, and other print options.

On the right-hand side of the dialog box you'll find the Color Management settings. In Color Controls mode you can alter the brightness, contrast, saturation, and color balance of the print output using the slider controls. Only use these controls if you don't want to use color management. PhotoEnhance mode allows you to apply a number of effects to the printed output, including monochrome and sepia toning and soft focus, canvas and parchment texture effects.

The button we are interested in is the one marked 'ICM'. Click this and the driver will use the color management system to correctly interpret and print the colors in the image. Once you click the ICM button in the Epson R800 Printer driver dialog box, the other color controls disappear as you won't be needing them. Don't check the No Color Adjustment box as this is intended for use where the conversion to the printer color space has already been made in the image-editing software. There's a Save button that lets you save this configuration. I'd recommend you use it as it's easy to miss just one thing if you have to do all this manually each time you print.

No Profile?

If you can't get a color profile for your printer and ink/paper combination there are three options available to you. You can pay a company to produce a profile for your individual setup. The way this works is that the company supplies you with a set of images composed of color swatches, which you print out and return to them. They then analyze these using sophisticated spectrophotometry equipment and produce a profile based on the results. This kind of profiling is very accurate, because it is tailor-made for your specific printer, paper, and inks, as opposed to a generic profile. Epson provides a bespoke profiling service: details can be found on the Epson website at www.epson.co.uk. Two other companies that also produce printer profiles are Pixl (www.pixl.dk) and Chromix (www.chromix.com). These services aren't cheap, but if accurate color is important to you, and certainly if you are producing images for commercial use, they are well worth the cost.

The second option is to produce your own color profiles using a device such as the Datacolor Spyder 3 Express or the X-rite Eye-One display LT. These are spectrophotometer devices that you connect to the front of your monitor so that they can take readings and compile a profile. These monitor profiling devices used to be the expensive preserve of imaging professionals but are now very affordable.

If you are making prints for personal use and can't justify the cost of a profiling service or dedicated hardware, you can make your own printer adjustments. As I said at the beginning of this chapter, you will never get your printer to emulate exactly what you see on your monitor (even professional setups have to content themselves with soft proofing – getting the monitor to show what the print will look like), but you should be able to improve an existing unsatisfactory setup.

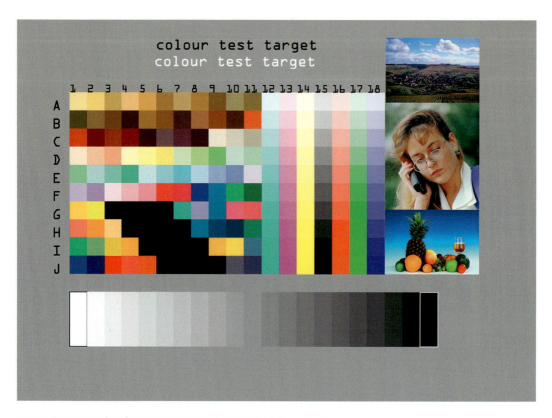

FIG 9.15 Use a target such as this one to compare printed output with what's on your screen.

You can do this in one of two ways. Either use the printer driver's color adjustment controls to alter the color balance, or use PaintShop Photo Pro's Adjustment layers to make temporary adjustments prior to printing. In either case you will need to compare printed output with what is on your screen and for this you should use a test calibration image that displays a wide range of colors, including naturally occurring hues like sky, foliage, and skin tones. Professionals use specially designed color targets for this, but you can easily create your own, like the one pictured here. If you haven't got time to make your own, you can download this target image from www.gopaintshoppro.co.uk

Step-by-Step Project

Technique: Printing Multiple Photos with Print Layout

Print Layout is a straightforward layout application that you can use to make multiple prints on an inkjet printer, saving time and money. Using Print Layout you can print several copies of one photo on a single A4 sheet of paper, cut them up, and send them to friends and family. You can print out multiple photos for passport or driving license applications, or you can use Print Layout to arrange different images on the same page for quick and convenient printing. There is a range of templates that you can adapt to fit your own needs and save for future use.

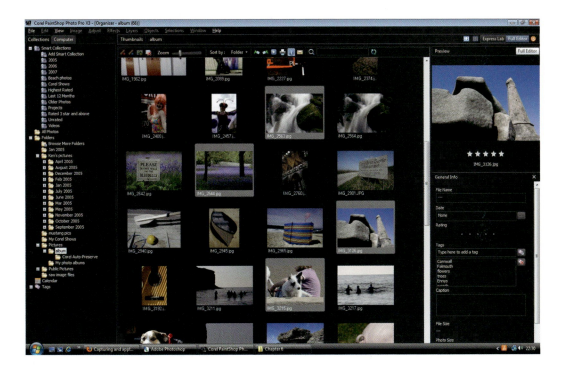

STEP 1 We're going to use Print Layout to print a selection of photos on to template pages. Select the images you want to print in the Organizer and click the Full Editor button to open them for editing. Alternatively, make your selection from a Media tray.

STEP 2 Select File > Print Layout. The photos you selected appear in the Images window on the left. The default template is 21.59 × 27.94 cm. Drag the images to the layout window and size and position them.

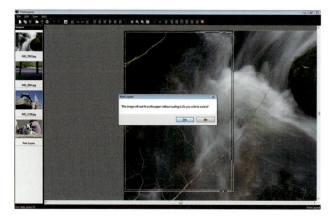

If you're printing multiple images on a page for cutting out, it helps to minimize wastage if you sort your photos into landscape and portrait format and print only one kind at a time. Don't mix land-scape and portrait format photos on the same layout.

STEP 3 If the images exceed the size of the template you will get an alert box telling you they won't fit and asking if you want to resize them. This can happen if you have not resized your image. Click OK and they will be scaled to fit the width of the default template. Drag a corner handle to make them smaller – the proportions are automatically retained so you don't need to worry about stretching or squeezing them.

STEP 4 Don't worry too much about neatly laying everything out at this stage, just get the pictures in the layout window at roughly the size you want them. If you want to get four pictures on a template, make them slightly smaller than a quarter of the page size to allow a border around them.

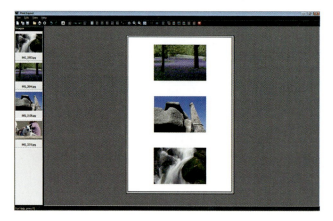

STEP 5 You can position the images manually, but Print Layout has a few auto positioning features to help out. The four buttons in the center of the toolbar will position an image in any of the four corners of the page or dead center. To the left of these, you'll find the Auto Positioning button. Roughly arrange your images on the page, click the Auto Arrange button, and they will be automatically sized and positioned for the best fit.

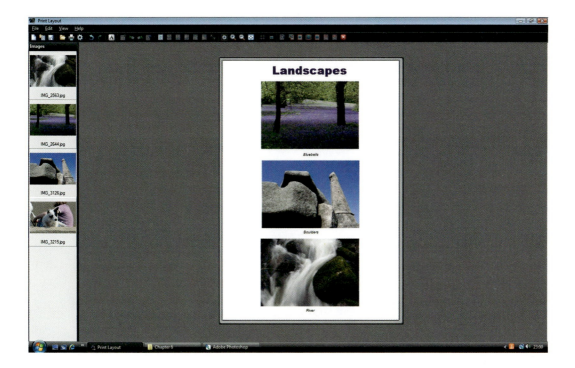

STEP 6 Manually arranging images like this is the best way to create poster layouts. Use the Text tool to add a headline at the top of the page and to put a caption under each image.

STEP 7 To choose a template layout, click the Open Template button on the toolbar or select File > Open Template. Select a category, click on one of the template thumbnails, and click OK. This will replace your previous layout so, if you want to keep it, save it first using File > Save Template.

STEP 8 To add photos to the template, just drag and drop them from the Images window on to the 'cells' in the template. If the image isn't an exact fit, you can drag a corner handle to resize it and drag it around within the rectangle to change the crop, or click the Fill Cell with Image button; there are buttons to help with this on the right of the toolbar.

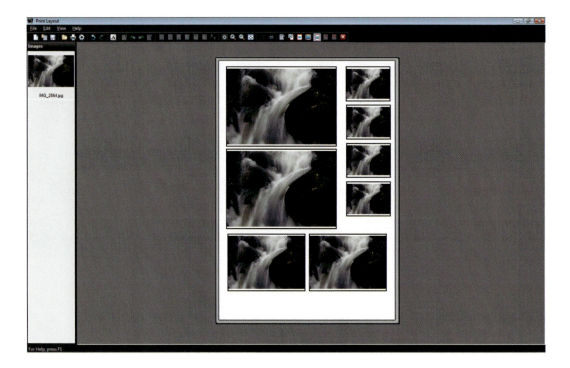

STEP 9 If you are making a page that contains only one image, click the Fill Template with Image button to copy the image to every cell on the template. Otherwise, drag the remaining images into position and resize them. Right-click on any of the images and select 'Apply placement to all cells' to have the positional changes you make to one image automatically applied to all of the others.

STEP 10 Add captions using the Text tool and click the Print button on the toolbar, or select File > Print to print the page.

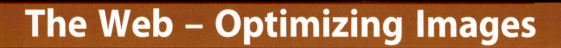

CHAPTER 10

The Web – Optimizing Images

- In this chapter you'll discover how to produce pictures for the Web. Whether you want a decent photo of your old camera to put on eBay, to email a few snaps to friends, or if you have something more ambitious in mind like an entire website, the following pages will tell you everything you need to know.

- If you're not sure of the difference between GIFs and JPEGs and when and how to make use of the different web image file formats, then read through the opening pages. Experiment with PaintShop Photo Pro's GIF and JPEG Optimizers, try to reproduce some of the examples shown here and you'll soon understand what optimization is all about.

- In these days of fast broadband connections it's tempting to think that file size doesn't matter, but even a broadband link can sometimes slow to a crawl. If your site downloads in a flash, regardless of connection speeds, you'll get and keep your visitors' interest.

- Towards the end of the chapter we take a look at specialized web graphics that make your site easier to build and maintain, and provide a more interactive experience for users.

PaintShop Photo Pro X3 for Photographers. DOI: 10.1016/B978-0-240-52165-7.10010-3

- The step-by-step projects show you how to produce a web navigation bar with rollover images and how to upload your images to a web server using Internet Explorer.

We take it for granted that websites integrate pictures and words seamlessly, but producing images for the Web requires a little knowledge of how the Web works as well as a practical grasp of digital image-making.

How the Web Displays Images

You're probably aware that web pages are written in HTML – Hyper Text Markup Language – and that your web browser interprets that code to display formatted text and pictures on your screen. To see what HTML looks like, in Internet Explorer select View Source from the Page menu. You don't need to be able to write or even understand HTML in order to produce web pages, as there are plenty of applications that will help you do this while keeping the code at arm's length.

Picture files are loaded into a browser page by HTML code, which looks something like this:

<img src = "images/pelican_02.GIF" width = 234 height = 53>

The HTML code tells the browser what the image is called, where to find it on the server and what size it is. Once the browser interprets this line of code it will download the image and display it.

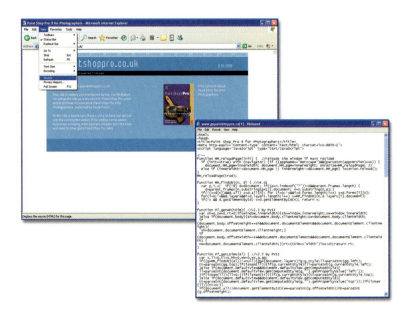

FIG 10.1 You can display the HTML code for the currently displayed browser page by selecting View Source from the Page menu in Internet Explorer. The source code is opened as a text file in Notepad, where you can edit and save it.

If it's a large image, or if the PC on which the browser is running accesses the Internet via a slow connection, it could take a while for the image to download and display, and trying to keep this delay as short as possible whilst maintaining good image quality is the main aim of web image editing.

The first, and most often overlooked, method of reducing image file size is to reduce the size of the image itself. The resolution of most display monitors is around 100 ppi, so the first thing to do is open the Image Resize dialog and change the resolution to 100 ppi. If you work at a higher resolution than this, your images will simply appear bigger on the web page. Because of this, most web designers prefer to work in pixels rather than other units and, if you are doing a lot of web work, you should try to get into this habit. If you make an image 100 × 100 pixels it will be roughly an inch square on screen.

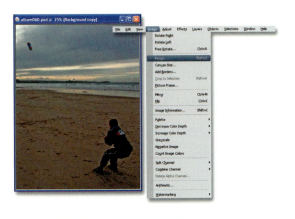

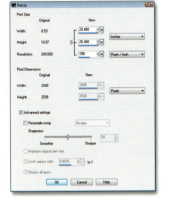

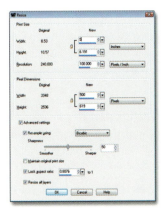

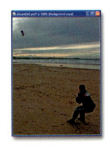

FIG 10.2 The Resize dialog box provides lots of options and it's important to pick the right ones. First, check the 'Advanced settings' box, uncheck the 'Resample using' box, and enter 100 pixels per inch in the Resolution field. This 5 megapixel image would be approximately 20 × 25 inches on a web page if we didn't downsample it. Check the 'Resample using', 'Lock aspect ratio' and 'Resize all layers' boxes, and enter the 100 ppi size in the width box of the Print Size pane. Click OK and view at 100% to see how it will look on the Web.

If you want to include big images, link them to a smaller thumbnail and give your viewers the option to sit through a lengthy download if they wish. Another effective but little-used file-shrinking strategy is to aggressively crop images. Get rid of extraneous background detail and crop right in on the subject.

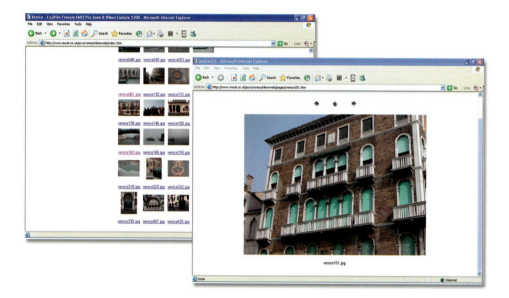

FIG 10.3 If you want to upload larger images, link them to a page of thumbnails so visitors can pick which ones to view, and not be overwhelmed with lengthy downloads.

Web File Formats

Nearly all images on the Web are saved in one of two file formats – JPEG and GIF. If you own a digital camera you'll know about JPEG even if you don't know much about the Web. GIF has been around even longer than JPEG and is used pretty much exclusively for web graphics. There's a rule of thumb that says you should use JPEG for photographic images and GIF for graphics with flat color and, like most rules of thumb, it's a good one 99% of the time, but there are situations when it's best ignored. As always with web images, the objective is to produce the smallest possible file size, whilst maintaining the best possible image quality. By experimenting with both JPEG and GIF compression, you'll soon learn which works best for particular images.

If you look hard enough, you'll find some web images that are saved in the PNG format. This relative newcomer was introduced in an effort to combine the strengths of JPEG and GIF and eliminate some of their shortcomings. Despite some advanced features, like drop shadows and support for layers, PNG has never really taken off, though you can easily create PNG files using the PNG Optimizer from PaintShop Photo Pro's Web toolbar.

JPEG in Depth

JPEG is actually a compression algorithm, a process that reduces the size of digital picture files, but it's come to be used to describe the file format that uses it. JPEG is a lossy compression method, which in plain English means that when you use it some loss in quality occurs and the compressed file won't look the same or as good as the original. Compression algorithms that maintain the exact same data and image quality are called 'lossless'. Although JPEG doesn't offer lossless compression, at low compression settings it comes pretty close. A newer version of JPEG, called JPEG 2000, provides a lossless option as well as other advantages, but, like PNG, hasn't gained widespread support.

JPEG is pretty good at removing quite of lot of picture detail, and thereby considerably reducing file size without anyone noticing, because the algorithm is designed to remove the kind of color information that the human eye doesn't perceive that well. You can compress image files by a factor of about 3 and you would have to look very hard to spot any degradation in image quality.

Using the JPEG Optimizer

Most image editors, and PaintShop Photo Pro is no exception, leave it to you to make the decision about how much compression to use. It's up to you to decide just how much image quality you are prepared to sacrifice in return for smaller file sizes.

To make this decision you need to know two things. What will the image look like if you compress it using a given JPEG setting? And how long will it take to download? The answers can be found in PaintShop Photo Pro's JPEG Optimizer, which you launch by clicking the JPEG Optimizer button on the Web toolbar or selecting File > Export > JPEG Optimizer.

The optimizer has three tabs – Quality, Format, and Download Times – and Before and After preview windows. Make sure the preview is set to 100% view so you can see the image exactly as it will appear on the web page; enlarge or maximize the dialog if necessary. Enter a number between 1 and 100 in the 'Set compression value to' box, or use the slider. The higher the value entered here, the more compression is applied, resulting in a smaller, lower-quality image: 1 is virtually no compression; you'll start to see the preview deteriorate at around the 20 mark, and beyond 60 things will start to look very bad indeed.

Bear in mind that these figures are not percentages, and if you enter the same values in a different Web Optimizer you're unlikely to get similar results. These values just represent PaintShop Photo Pro's maximum and minimum JPEG compression settings.

Tip

The most effective way to reduce the size of images is to crop them. A good-quality, closely cropped photo is always better than a highly compressed one with lots of extraneous detail, so get into the habit of making the Crop tool your first step in web image preparation.

271

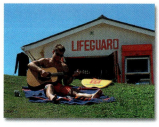

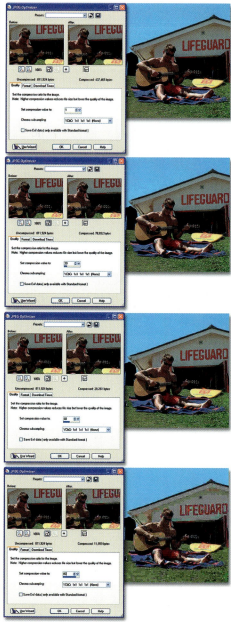

FIG 10.4 The more JPEG compression you apply to an image the smaller it gets, and the worse it looks. At a setting of 1 the compressed image (top) is indistinguishable from the original, but the file size is nearly halved. At a setting of 20 (second from top), you can begin to see JPEG artifacts creeping in – look closely at the lettering on the hut. Increase the compression setting to 40 (third from top) and the file size drops to a mere 25 Kb – down from an original 784 Kb. On a cable or DSL Internet connection this would take a fraction of a second to download, but the image quality has suffered badly, with JPEG blocking visible just about everywhere you look. If 40 is a step too far, 80 (bottom) is just ridiculous. It's interesting to note that, beyond a certain point, not only does the image quality suffer horrendously, but file size savings get correspondingly smaller. A setting of 20 slices 670 Kb from this file; increasing it to 80 gains you only another 53 Kb.

Judging Picture Quality

Just below the Before and After preview windows you'll see two figures. The left-hand one under the Before window says 'Uncompressed' followed by the file size in bytes and, on the right, the compressed size is given, again in bytes. Notice that even at the lowest compression setting of 1 the size of the compressed file is only about a half to one-third that of the uncompressed one. If you want the approximate file size in kilobytes, just divide by a thousand. Generally speaking, compression settings in the range of 10–30 will give acceptable quality images with high compression ratios, but let your eyes be your guide and as soon as the image becomes unacceptably grubby drag the slider back towards the low side.

Feel free to experiment with the various Chroma subsampling presets on the pull-down menu, though it's unlikely you'll achieve any improvement by changing this. Even the PaintShop Photo Pro Help file recommends leaving it on the default setting.

Use the Format tab to select either Standard or Progressive format; the latter preloads a low-quality preview into the browser so that the viewer has something to look at while waiting for the real thing. With Standard format nothing is displayed until the entire image is downloaded.

Estimating Download Time

The Download Times tab provides the answer to our second question. In actual fact it provides several answers, any one of which might be true, depending on the kind of link visitors to your website are using to access the Internet. Four download times are displayed. These provide a guide to the time it will take to download the optimized file on links operating at 56, 128, 380, and 720 Kbps (kilobits per second).

It's a little disappointing that Corel has passed up the opportunity to update the JPEG Optimizer for several years now, with the result that the download speeds in the JPEG Optimizer are looking pretty archaic. 56 Kbps is the speed at which someone using a modem connects to the Internet. 720k would be the speed of a very slow broadband connection. These days, most web connections are broadband ones operating at speeds measured in megabits per second (Mbps) rather than kilobits and, depending where in the world you live, average broadband speeds are in the 5–20 Mbps range and getting faster all the time.

Of course, a 10 Mbps line doesn't guarantee 10 Mbps transfer rates. Speeds could be affected if the line is shared via a network router, or if there's Internet congestion, or if the server can't cope with the level of traffic so, regardless of the increase in the speed of net connections, it still makes sense to optimize your images.

> **Tip**
>
> You can increase the JPEG compressibility of images by blurring them slightly before compressing them. A small degree of blur softens the contrast in edge detail, which is where JPEG artifacts are most noticeable. Use the Gaussian Blur filter with a radius of between 0.5 and 1 before JPEG optimizing.

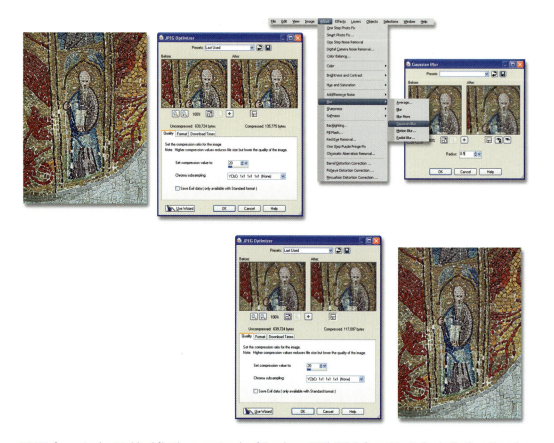

FIG 10.5 Compressing the original (top left) with a compression value of 20 produces a 135 Kb JPEG. By first applying the Gaussian Blur filter with a radius of 0.5, compressing with the same settings produces a file 20 Kb smaller. The resulting image is slightly softer, but perfectly acceptable.

It's good practice to ensure that most people can access your site without having to wait all night for the images to download, so if the JPEG Optimizer is telling you that just one of the many images that may end up on your home page will take several seconds to download on a 720 Kbps link, you need to think about how you are going to speed things up. As a general rule, you can use the 720 Kbps readout to provide an estimate of the worst performance someone on a broadband connection is likely to experience.

Once you're happy with the quality and size of the Optimized file, press the OK button to save the file.

GIF in Depth

Whereas JPEG images are full-color 24-bit files, GIFs make use of an indexed color palette to help keep file size down. Each pixel in a JPEG file needs 24 bits (or 3 bytes) of data to describe it. But the same pixel in a GIF needs only 8 bits and in some circumstances even fewer. GIF does this by refer-encing each pixel to a color lookup table, or palette. The palette has 256 colors. The first color is numbered 0, the next 1, and so on all the way up to 255; to describe the color of a pixel all you need is its number and, as there are only 256 possibilities, 1 byte is sufficient to describe them all.

One shortcoming of this approach is that, compared with the 16 million or so colors that a 24-bit format like JPEG can display, 256 seems a bit meager. This is one of the reasons GIF is recommended for graphics images that often contain very few colors. Indeed, some graphics contain far fewer than 256 colors and in such cases it's possible to make further file size economies by reducing the color palette to as few as four, or even two, colors. A four-color palette can be defined with 2 bits. That's 2 bits for every pixel in the image compared with 24 for JPEG – a massive saving.

Although 256 colors may not sound like a lot, it's surprising how little image quality suffers when you convert even complex photos containing lots of colors into GIF format. GIF can also expand the palette of perceived colors using a process called 'dithering', in which colors are combined to produce intermediate hues.

Once the palette has been defined, GIF further reduces the file by applying a lossless compression algorithm called 'LZW'. So GIF has two methods of reducing image file size: color palette reduction and LZW compression. Typically, LZW compression reduces the file size by a factor of 2, in other words halves it, so most of the work involved in reducing GIF size involves making careful choices about how the color palette is created so you can represent all the colors in your image with the smallest possible palette.

Using the GIF Optimizer

To open the GIF Optimizer, click the GIF Optimizer button on the Web toolbar or select File > Export > GIF Optimizer. Expand the window so you can see the previews at 100% and click the Colors tab. The first input field, 'How many colors do you want?', lets you specify, well, just that. The maximum and minimum values depend on the method of color selection and there are four choices here: Existing Palette, Standard/Web-safe, Optimized Median Cut, and Optimized Octree.

The Existing Palette option will be grayed out unless the image was an 8-bit indexed image to begin with, or you converted it prior to opening the GIF Optimizer. The Standard/Web-safe option uses a palette of standard colors devised to provide the best viewing experience for those using Internet Explorer or Netscape on an 8-bit display, but now that 24-bit color displays are commonplace this isn't such an important consideration and you can safely ignore this setting, unless of course it provides better results than the others.

> **Tip**
>
> Avoid using drop shadows on images that you intend to convert to GIF. It's impossible to render subtle gradations of tint with a limited color palette.

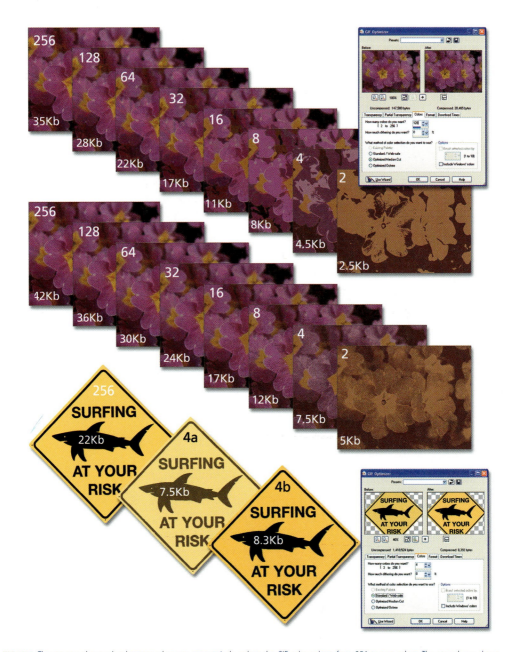

FIG 10.6 The top row shows what happens when you progressively reduce the GIF color palette from 256 to two colors. The second row shows the same process with 100% dither selected. GIF is best suited to graphic images like the bottom one. Reducing the palette to four colors produces little noticeable quality loss because there were few colors to begin with. The GIF Optimizer doesn't always select the best color palette (4a). In this case choose Image > Decrease Color Depth > X Colors, then optimize using the existing palette (4b).

Optimized Median Cut and Optimized Octree are two different algorithms designed to derive the most representative palette of 256 colors from all of those in the unoptimized 24-bit image. If your existing image contains only a few colors use Optimized Octree and if you want to reduce the image to fewer than 16 colors use Optimized Median Cut.

For now, select Optimized Median Cut and drag the slider under the 'How many colors do you want?' box as far as it will go to the left until the box contains the value 2. This is what your image will look like if it's displayed with 1 bit per pixel, allowing two colors. Unless there were only two colors to begin with, the odds are it will look terrible. Highlight the 'How many colors do you want?' box with the mouse and enter the value 4. Things will look a little better, but not much. Double the number of colors to 8, then 16, 32, 64, 128 and finally 256, taking a look at the compressed preview each time.

Dare to Dither

Assuming your original image was a color photo, it probably will have begun to look something like normal when you got to 16 or 32 colors. Even so, some of the colors may not look right and you may get 'banding' – discrete bands of color where the original showed subtle gradations – in skies, for example. What's happening is that the original colors in the image are being mapped to the closest one available in the palette and it's one of the reasons GIF is a poor choice if your original contains lots of colors (but a good one if it only contains a few).

There is something you can do about banding. Enter 100 in the box marked 'How much dithering do you want?' This will considerably reduce and perhaps even eliminate the banding and posterization, but it also introduces a speckly graininess into the image that you may find no more acceptable than the banding. Another drawback is that dithered files are slightly larger than undithered ones. By dragging the Dithering slider you should be able to reduce the graininess to an acceptable degree without reintroducing the banding.

Try Transparency

One very useful feature of the GIF format is that it supports transparency. You can tell the Optimizer to use the existing image or layer transparency, or define a color from within the image as transparent. The advantage of including transparent areas in the GIF is that you can place irregular graphics – logos or text, for example – over different backgrounds on your web page and the background will show through. The Partial Transparency tab of the GIF Optimizer provides sophisticated controls to deal with semi-transparent pixels (for example, those around the edges of anti-aliased text), which can cause problems.

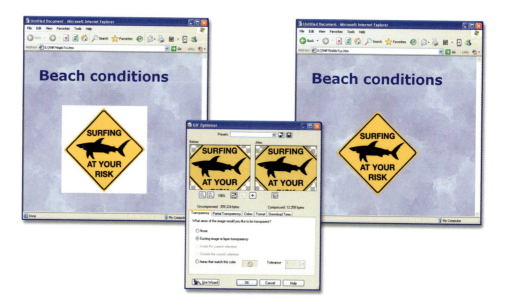

FIG 10.7 The Transparency tab of the GIF Optimizer allows you to use existing layer transparency, or specify a color from the image (usually the background). Use the Partial Transparency tab to specify a blend color for the edge pixels that is similar to the background on your web page.

Whatever file format you choose, optimization is a trial and error process. Every image is different, and while you can Batch Process similar images using the same settings, if you want to get the best possible quality at the smallest file size you will need to give each one individual attention, selecting the settings you think will provide the right balance between quality and download times, and then fine-tuning depending on what you can see in the Optimizer preview window.

Special Internet Graphics

We've seen that lengthy download times are anathema to web designers, and PaintShop Photo Pro's Optimizers provide some useful tools that enable us to reduce images' file sizes considerably. HTML provides some other ways of efficiently using images to avoid the necessity for lengthy downloads and PaintShop Photo Pro provides specialized tools to help you take advantage of them.

Image Slicing

As we've seen, large images on a web page can take a long time to download, and lengthy downloads are to be avoided at all costs. But what if you sliced a big image up into more manageable chunks? Of course, if the sliced-up image contained exactly the same content as the original, it would take just as long to download the bits as the whole thing but, as we shall see, there are some big advantages to be gained by image slicing.

Let's suppose the image you want to put on your site contains a photo and some text (like the one below). By slicing it you can apply the most effective optimization to each segment. For example, you can use the JPEG Optimizer to compress the photo and the GIF Optimizer to compress the text, which has only a few colors, and if the image contains white areas you can leave them out altogether.

Reassembling the slices is done using an HTML table. Like a spreadsheet this is simply a grid of cells. Each slice occupies a cell in the table; the slices abut one another and appear as a single image. Sometimes, entire web pages are composed of sliced images reassembled in a table in this way. PaintShop Photo Pro's Image Slicer allows you to slice the image and apply optimization to individual slices, and takes care of image naming (this can be complicated if there are a lot of slices) and creating the HTML table. You'll find the Image Slicer on the File > Export menu and on the Web toolbar.

Rollovers

As the name suggests, rollovers change appearance when you roll over them with the mouse pointer. Generally (but not exclusively), rollovers are used for buttons, so that the viewer knows something will happen when they click on the button. Some websites use rollovers in a clever and sophisticated way to change content on one part of the page when you roll over another part.

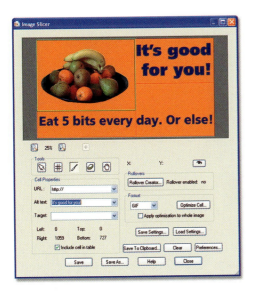

FIG 10.8 The Image Slicer lets you apply different Optimization settings to areas (or slices) of an image. In this example you'd use JPEG for the fruit bowl slice and GIF for the others. You can also specify HTML attributes like Alt tags, link URLs, and target windows.

Rollovers display different images according to their state, and their current state depends on what's happening with the mouse. You can create and edit rollovers in PaintShop Photo Pro's Image Slicer by pressing the Rollover Creator button. The dialog provides no fewer than six rollover states to which you can assign images – 'Mouse over', 'Mouse out', 'Mouse click', 'Mouse double click', 'Mouse up', and 'Mouse down'. In practice, most people get by with three – 'Normal', 'Mouse over', and 'Mouse click' – and in fact even the last of these could be considered extraneous, as once a user has clicked on a button, they're usually linked to another page and don't see what happens to the button.

Rollovers and image slicing really come into their own when used together to produce website navigation bars, the kind you commonly see with a row of buttons arrayed along the top or down the side of the home page. The entire navigation bar can be divided so that each button has its own slice. When a user mouses over one of the buttons, only that slice needs to change, not the entire image. If it has been properly optimized, that means a file size of just a few bytes and almost instantaneous download.

Image Maps

Image maps are almost the reverse of image slices; they allow you to add hotspots to an image file that, when clicked, link to other web pages. You might, for example, have a map of the world with red spots at various

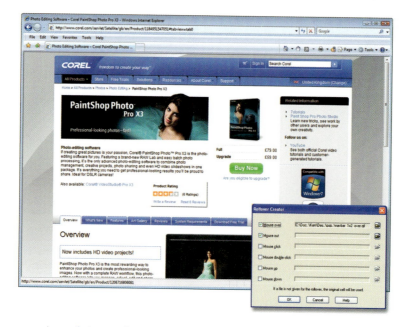

FIG 10.9 Rollovers are a popular way of animating web navigation elements, seen here on the Corel website. Use the Rollover Creator dialog box to specify files for the various rollover states — 'Mouse over' is the only one you need for most situations.

locations to indicate international sales offices. Using PaintShop Photo Pro's Image Mapper, you can cover each of the dots with an invisible hotspot, together with a URL link to the page on your site giving contact details for that office. The Image Mapper tools aren't restricted to regular shapes and as well as rectangular and circular hotspots you can define irregular ones. The image is available from the File > Export menu and the Web toolbar.

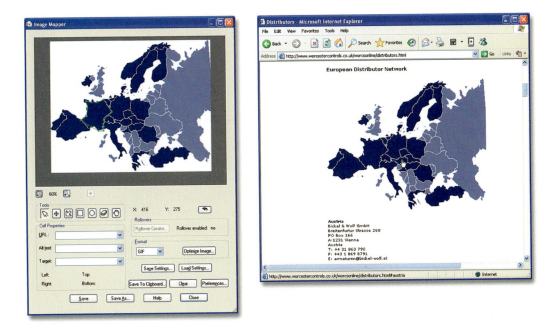

FIG 10.10 Use image maps to assign multiple links to areas of an image. Here an image map is used to link individual European countries to pages containing distributor details.

Step-by-Step Projects

Technique: Creating a Rollover Navbar

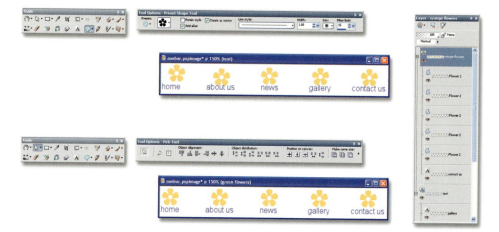

STEP 1 As we saw earlier, rollovers are a useful way of signaling active links on a website and PaintShop Photo Pro's Web toolbar provides all the tools you need to create them. Using layers simplifies the process because you can put the original graphic elements on one layer and the changed elements – that will appear when the viewer mouses over the graphic – on another.

The first step is to create the graphics. For this navbar, we've used the Preset Shapes tool to create a series of flower graphics. After drawing the first flower, select it with the Pick tool and press Ctrl + C to copy it. Then select Edit/Paste/Paste as New Vector Selection to place a copy of the flower on the same Vector layer as the existing one; you can click the plus sign to the left of the layer to expand it and see the individual vector objects.

Just press Ctrl + G to paste further copies of the flower object into the layer. When you have as many as you need (don't let your navbar get too long and complicated), select them all by Shift-clicking with the Pick tool and use the Object Alignment and Distribution buttons on the Tool Options palette to align them vertically and space them equally horizontally. When that's done, add a text label underneath each one to describe its destination.

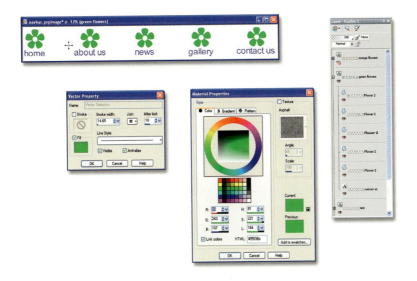

STEP 2 Now it's beginning to look like a navbar, but we need to produce the rollovers. The yellow flowers are going to turn green when you mouse over them (and back to yellow when you mouse out), so we need to create a new layer with green flowers. Right-click the yellow flowers layer, select Duplicate from the contextual menu and double-click the newly created layer. In the Layer Properties dialog change the layer name to 'green flowers' and click OK. Now turn off the yellow flowers layer by clicking the Visibility toggle (the eye icon to the right of the description in the Layers palette) and Shift-click or drag with the Pick tool to select all of the flowers on the green flowers layer. Double-click within the bounding box to bring up the Vector Property dialog and change the fill color to green.

STEP 3 On the Web toolbar click the Image Slicer button; you'll see the navbar displayed in the preview window at the top. The next job is to optimize the GIF nav buttons that you're about to produce using the Image Slicer and Rollover controls. Select GIF from the Format pull-down menu, check the 'Apply optimization to whole image' box, and click the Optimize Cell button. Using what you've learned earlier in this chapter, optimize the color palette to achieve the best balance between image quality and download times. For this GIF navbar a 16-color palette provides good image quality with a file size of just over 2 Kb for the entire navbar.

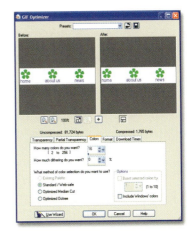

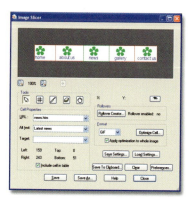

STEP 4 Select the Slice tool (the one that looks like a knife) and create an individual slice for each button. Position the tool equidistant between two buttons, drag a short distance up or down until a vertical line appears, then release the mouse button to create a vertical slice. When all the slices are created select the first one using the Arrow tool. In the Cell Properties panel enter the URL of the page that this button links to. You can enter either the entire URL, e.g. http://www.mysite.com/news.htm, or a relative link to the page. For example, if all of your website pages are in the same folder all you need enter here is 'news.htm'. Anything you put in the Alt text box will display in a small box next to the graphic, so put a description of where the link goes in here for those using browsers that can't display graphics. You can use the Target box to have the linked page open in a window other than the current one, or for advanced handling of sites that use frames.

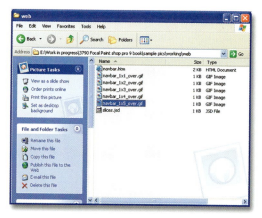

STEP 5 Click the Save As button to save all of the slices to a folder on your hard disk. The name you enter in the Filename field will be given to the web page that's created, and one file will be produced for each slice, with the original document filename, together with a row and column suffix. The five slices created here are called 'navbar_1x1.GIF', 'navbar_1x2.GIF', 'navbar_1x3. GIF', and so on. Before you close the Image Slicer you need to save the position of the slices so you can use them again for the main buttons. Click the Save Settings button and save the settings in the same folder as everything else with the filename 'slices.jsd'. It's important you do this because PaintShop Photo Pro doesn't automatically keep the slice positions and next time you open the Image Slicer the position of the slices will be lost. The slices for the main menu and rollover graphics have to be in exactly the same positions, as any difference will show up as movement when you mouse over – we only want the color to change, everything else must remain exactly as it was.

STEP 6 In Windows Explorer, find the folder you saved the web page and rollover images to and rename all of the GIFs, adding the suffix '_over' to each one. For example, rename the first file 'navbar1x1_over.GIF'.

STEP 7 Go back to PaintShop Photo Pro, turn off the green flowers layer visibility and turn on the yellow flowers layer visibility, then click the Image Slicer button on the Web toolbar to reopen the Image Slicer dialog. Click the Load Settings button and select the 'slices.jsd' file to reload your original slice settings. Select the first slice with the Pan tool and click the Rollover Creator button.

Each of the fields in the Rollover Creator dialog allows you to specify the image you want to appear when that particular event occurs; we are only interested in the first two – 'Mouse over' and 'Mouse out'. Check the 'Mouse over' box, click the Browse button to its right, and navigate to the folder where you saved the web page and image files in Step 5. Select the 'nav-bar_1x1_over.GIF' image and click the Open button, which will return you to the Rollover Creator, where you can see the path to the file you just selected in the 'Mouse over' field.

Next, check the 'Mouse out' box. There's no need to enter a filename here because, as it says at the bottom of the dialog box, 'If a file is not given for the rollover, the original will be used', which is exactly what we want. Click OK to close the Rollover Creator.

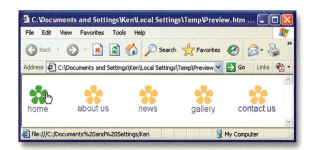

STEP 8 Now that you have a working rollover for the first button you can preview it in your default browser by clicking the Preview button (the eye icon). If you are using Internet Explorer 6 and Windows XP with the SP2 service pack you may get a message saying 'Internet Explorer has restricted the file from showing active content'. If this happens click the message and select 'allow blocked content' from the pop-up menu. Position the cursor over the first button and the flower will change color from yellow to green; move the cursor off the button and it will change back to yellow. Don't try clicking on the button, as the links won't work at this stage.

STEP 9 Create the remaining rollovers by assigning the rollover images created in Steps 5 and 6 to each of the remaining slices. When you've done them all click the Save button. Use the same filename (navbar.htm), as you want to overwrite the original web page file with the new one. Don't worry about overwriting the rollover images you created earlier, as you renamed them. A check of the folder contents will reveal the new navbar.htm web page and 10 graphics images – five for the initial web buttons and five rollover images. Double-click on the navbar.htm file to view it in Internet Explorer and check everything is working properly.

To use the navbar on your site you will need to use an HTML editing application to add the code to your pages, although it is possible to create entire pages in PaintShop Photo Pro and use the Image Slicer to optimize and tabularize them.

Technique: Uploading Web Files to a Web Server

Most Internet Service Providers allocate server space that you can use to host your own website. You will need to check your documentation to find out how to access this; you'll need a host name and password. Files are uploaded to the web server using a protocol called 'File Transfer Protocol', or 'FTP', and you'll need FTP client software to upload your web pages and images.

There are a number of shareware and inexpensive FTP clients that you can download from the web – WS_FTP, FileZilla, and CuteFTP being just a few.

FTP client software is simple to use. Once logged on, the application displays local and remote files in two windows and you simply select the local files for uploading and the remote folder you want to transfer them to. Another simple way to upload files via FTP is to use Internet Explorer.

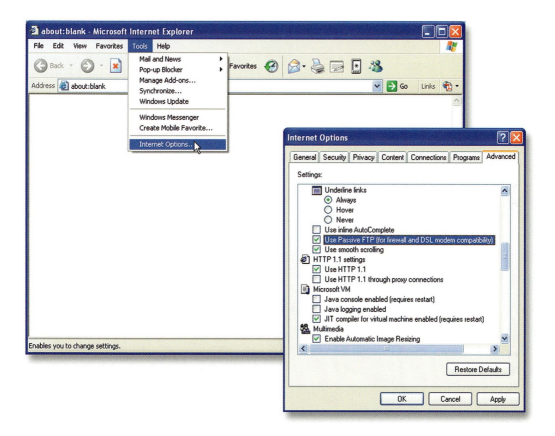

STEP 1 If you have a firewall you will need to configure Internet Explorer's Passive FTP feature. Open Internet Explorer and select Internet Options from the Tools menu. Click the Advanced tab and check the box marked 'Use Passive FTP', then click OK.

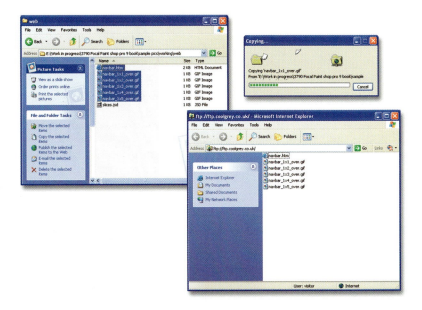

STEP 2 In the address bar type the host URL – this will be something like ftp://myserver.com/– and press Enter. The Log On dialog box will appear and you will now need to enter your user name and password in the appropriate fields. Some sites that are configured for public access, such as shareware software download servers, allow anonymous access, which doesn't require a user name and password. If you are logging on to one of these servers, click the 'Log on anonymously' checkbox, enter your email address in the password field, and click OK.

STEP 3 Now you are logged on and can see the contents of the remote server, you can drag and drop files to and from any other open windows in exactly the same way as with local files. To upload files to the remote server locate them in Windows Explorer and drag them on to the remote window – you can drag folders as well as individual files.

Appendix 1
Jargon Buster

Use the jargon buster to increase your understanding of the digital techniques discussed in this book.

Adjustment layer A special layer that permits users to change a wide range of things in the picture (tone, etc.) without affecting the rest of the layer data. Ideal for experimentation, as you can have as many Adjustment layers as you have the time for and they never change the integrity of the original image data.

Batch (processing) Technique for applying the same photo-editing action to more than one file at a time.

Bezier curve A type of line used to draw vector objects. The shape of the line is altered using control handles making it possible to draw any irregular shape. See **Vector image**.

Bit The smallest unit of computer information.

Bit depth The number of bits used to represent each pixel in a digital image. A 16-bit image can hold more information (and therefore tonal detail) than an 8-bit one.

Bitmap Term describing a digital image made from pixels laid in a grid pattern.

Blend mode Blend modes alter the way pixels react with each other. Especially useful for creating effects between layers in a picture. Many tool actions can also be heavily influenced by changing their respective blend modes before applying them to the canvas.

Blown highlights Term used to describe highlights (most usually skies) that have been overexposed and lack any detail, i.e. are totally white.

Burn (tool) Brush-driven technique for increasing the local density in a picture.

Canvas The entire picture area. Enlarge the canvas of a picture and you add pixels to its overall dimensions, although the picture itself never changes size.

CCD Charge-coupled device – the digital sensor (the 'film' equivalent) found in a scanner or digital camera. CCDs are made up of light-gathering pixels. The more pixels in the CCD, the higher its resolution.

Chromatic aberration A lens defect that causes (often purple) colored fringes to appear on high-contrast edges. PaintShop Photo Pro's 'One Step Purple Fringe Fix' deals with it.

Clone (tool) Cloning is used simply to copy and paste pixels from one part of a digital image to another so that it can be repaired, retouched, or replaced.

CMYK A system of color representation that uses cyan (C), magenta (M), yellow (Y), and black (K) to produce all colors. CMYK is the basis for most commercial color printing.

Colorize Effect that changes the color image to monochrome and then adds a single color tint. Similar to a duotone.

Color management system (CMS) A means by which color can be consistently displayed across a range of devices, e.g. from your camera or scanner to your monitor and printer. A CMS 'translates' color data using color profiles for each device.

Color Profile A file describing the color characteristics of a device such as a camera, scanner, display, or printer.

Contrast A measure of the tonal values in a picture between black and white. The fewer the tones, the higher the contrast.

Cropping (tool) The Crop tool is used to remove or cut pixels from a digital image. Cropping reduces the total file size.

Curves Sophisticated tool for adjusting image contrast and brightness.

Deformation (tool) Technique used for distorting, rotating, turning, and bending objects on a layer.

Dialog (box or window) A generic term describing the window that displays certain controls or options within the photo-editing program.

Displacement map A greyscale image that is used to displace pixels in a photo to give the appearance that the photo has been projected on an uneven or textured surface. Displacement maps can be used effectively to make text look like it has been painted on to an object.

Dither A technique used to provide the illusion of additional colors in low-bit-depth images such as GIF files. See **Indexed color**.

Dodge (tool) Brush-driven technique for reducing the local density in a picture.

Dots per inch (dpi) System of measuring the pixel spread in an image. The higher the dpi value, the clearer the detail in the photo.

Driver Small software program that controls scanners, printers, and other third-party plug-in devices.

Feather Process of softening, or blurring the edges of a selection. Feather is typically used to produce a 'vignette' effect where the edges of a photo fade away rather than having a well-defined, crisp edge. Feathered selections are also used to soften the boundary of effects filters.

File format The form in which a computer, scanner, or camera saves digital data. Each file format has slightly different characteristics. For example, '.jpg' files are ideal for storing many pictures in a small space as they can be compressed, while '.tif' files are there for preserving the best possible image quality.

Filter A preset software action that applies a certain effect to a digital file, layer, or selection. Most filter effects can be adjusted through their respective dialogs. Examples include Digital Camera Noise Removal, Gaussian Blur, Soft Focus, and Unsharp Mask.

Flat (contrast) Term used to describe a photo with low contrast levels.

Flatten (layer) Command used to 'squash' all layers into one document so that it can be resaved in another, non-layered, format, like JPEG.

FTP File Transfer Protocol, a method of transferring files to a web server. A program that does this is called an FTP client.

Gamma (adjustment) Term given to the brightness values in the image.

Gaussian Blur A type of blur filter. Can be used to soften the edges of shadows and to produce out-of-focus effects.

GIF (file) A special file format used for saving and displaying graphics on the Internet.

Greyscale An image type that contains only shades of black and white. An 8-bit greyscale contains 256 tones from black (0) to white (255). Greyscale images can't contain color data, so to add, for example, colored text they must first be converted to 8-bit RGB.

Grids/guides Lines that can be overlaid on a photo to aid positioning of elements (e.g. text), but which do not print. Snap to Grid/Guides pulls dragged objects on to guides like a magnet when they get close.

Halftone A method by which photos are prepared for commercial printing that involves applying a screen. The screen enables the range of tones and colors to be reproduced on a printing press using different sized dots. PaintShop Photo Pro has a haftone filter, but this is purely for effect and is not suitable for preparing photos for commercial printing.

High Dynamic Range (HDR) A composite image made from several photos taken with different exposure settings and capable of displaying the entire dynamic range of a high-contrast scene from dense shadows to bright highlights.

Highlights The brightest tones in a photo, represented on the right-hand side of a histogram.

Histogram A graphic representation of the tones captured in a scan or digital photo. Represented as a mountain range where the darkest tones lie to the left-hand side of the range and the highlights to the right.

Hue Another word for color (values).

Hue/Saturation/Lightness A system of representing colors using three values – one each for hue, saturation, and lightness. Also the name of a PaintShop Photo Pro feature that allows you to change the hue, saturation, and lightness values for all, or a specific range of, colors in a photo.

Indexed color A system that allocates color in an image using a palette usually consisting of 256 colors that can be referenced in a single byte (8 bits). Indexed color images (e.g. GIF files) are usually smaller than equivalent 8-bit file types like TIF or JPEG and are therefore well suited for Web use. See **GIF**.

Interpolation The process of changing image resolution by adding pixels. The new pixel values are based on those of neighboring pixels.

JPEG (file) A type of file used to save and store scanned images. JPEG files can be compressed (squashed) so that you can get more pictures on to a disk drive. Once opened again they revert to the original proportions. Too much compression introduces errors or ugly 'artifacts'.

Layer A second (or more) level within a single digital picture. Layers add editability to a file. Text, multiple images, masks, and special effects can be applied to separate layers and these in turn can be edited for greater creative control. Layered documents must be saved in the '.pspimage' file format. But they can be flattened (layers are squashed together) so that they can be reconverted into any other picture file format like TIFF or JPEG.

Layer mask Used to hold back parts of an underlying layer to create a blended or merged effect. Layer masks are simple black and white layers that can be edited using any of PaintShop Pro's paint or drawing tools.

Levels Sophisticated tool for applying changes to image contrast and brightness.

Metadata Text information included in a photo either by the camera when the picture is taken, or added later. Metadata can include exposure information, date and time, title, caption, and keyword tags. The standard format for camera-recorded metadata is called EXIF and another standard for added metadata is IPTC.

Midtones The mid-range tones in a photo, represented by the central section of a histogram.

Moiré The odd, checkerboard pattern displayed when you scan a commercially printed document like a magazine page. Use a softening filter to remove or to soften this detrimental effect.

Noise Ugly speckling apparent in underexposed digital camera images. Setting your camera to a high ISO rating also introduces excessive noise. PaintShop Pro ships with a number of filters designed to minimize this problem.

Opacity Density or translucency of an image or layer. All tools and layers have opacity settings (default at 100). This value can be lowered for more subtle effects.

Palette A dialog window that relates to a specific photo-editing tool. Palettes give access to a wide range of controls that permit you to fine-tune that feature. Palettes can be docked or floating.

Platen The glass scanning bed on a desktop scanner.

Plug-in A piece of specialist software that operates from within a host software program such as PaintShop Pro.

PNG A slightly newer file format for displaying photographic data on the Internet. While PNG files are not supported by all web browsers, the format does exhibit superior features over the more widely used JPEG format.

Posterization Drastically reduces the amount of colors used in a picture – typically to fewer than eight colors. Produces an Andy Warhol-type visual.

Print resolution Typically this is about 300 dpi for inkjets, although equally good quality is attainable from resolutions of 200 dpi and sometimes even lower. Commercial print devices like Fuji Frontier labs require slightly different settings – check with the manufacturer.

Raster Same as **Bitmap**.

Red-eye An undesirable effect where subjects' eyes appear red as a result of flash reflecting off the eye's retina. PaintShop Photo Pro's Red-Eye Tool fixes it.

Resampling See **Interpolation**.

Resolution Typically a measurement of the number of pixels in a digital image. The more pixels there are, the more detail is visible and therefore the higher the resolution of the image.

RGB A color system used to represent all colors by combining red, green, and blue light. When combined in equal quantities, red, green, and blue light make white, so these three colors are known as the additive primaries. Nearly all digital photo hardware and software, including your digital camera and PaintShop Photo Pro, are based on the RGB model. See **CMYK**.

Saturation Term used to describe the intensity of color. A fully desaturated picture, though still technically a color image, appears black and white.

Scripting Technique for recording certain PaintShop Pro actions (rather like using a video recorder). Can then be replayed on other files for batch processing techniques.

Selection Isolating part of a digital photo for the purposes of additional editing or the addition of special effects. Selections can be made automatically, freehand, or geometrically. Selections protect everything outside of the selection marquee.

Shadows The darkest tones in a photo, represented by the left side of a histogram.

Sharpening A software technique used to apply the effect of making an image crisper by applying specific contrast adjustments. Too much sharpening causes an ugly, brittle texture to the file.

Solarization Similar effect to film solarization – highlights turn to shadows and shadows to highlights. Particularly effective in color photography.

Thumbnail This is a small representation of the original picture file. In PaintShop Photo Pro thumbnails are displayed in the Organizer.

TIFF A file type typically used to save and store high-resolution digital scans or camera files. Unlike JPEG files, TIFF files are not lossy. This means that, though they can be compressed slightly (up to 30%), they do not suffer from image degradation or artifacts.

Toolbar Generic term for the part of a software program that displays certain functions. Accessed through the mouse cursor or through keyboard shortcuts. Toolbars can be docked or left 'floating'.

Twain This is the bit of software that allows you to operate a scanner through a plug-in in a host program such as PaintShop Photo Pro.

Unsharp Mask A filter that makes photos look sharper by enhancing edge contrast. Most digital cameras have built-in unsharp masking; even so, most photos benefit from application of PaintShop Photo Pro's Unsharp Mask filter.

Vector image Unlike bitmap or raster images, vector images are represented by mathematical formulae, rather than pixels as, for example, a circle might be described by a pi-based formula specifying the radius. In PaintShop Photo Pro text is produced using vectors, as are objects created using the Preset and Symmetric Shape tools.

Warp (tool) Effect used for bending and distorting the pixels in a digital file.

Appendix 2
Keyboard Shortcuts

Keyboard shortcuts are probably the last thing on your mind when learning a photo-editing program – there are too many other considerations to take on board. However, learn a few of these keystrokes and you'll not only increase the speed at which you can perform basic actions with PaintShop Photo Pro, but you'll also have more time to do other things – such as experiment more with your photos.

General

Open a file	Ctrl + O
Save a file	Ctrl + S
Delete	Ctrl + Del
Undo previous keystroke	Ctrl + Z
Repeat previous keystroke	Ctrl + Y
Repeat New File	Ctrl + Shift + Z
Cut	Ctrl + X
Load New Workspace	Shift + Alt + L
Save Workspace	Shift + Alt + S
Delete Workspace	Shift + Alt + D
Start Screen Capture	Shift + C
Print	Ctrl + P
Copy	Ctrl + C

Paste

As a New Image	Ctrl + Shift + V
As a New Layer	Ctrl + L
As a New Selection	Ctrl + E
As Transparent Selection	Ctrl + Shift + E
Into Selection	Ctrl + Shift + L
As New Vector Selection	Ctrl + G

View

View: Full Screen Edit	Shift + A
View: Full Screen Preview	Ctrl + Shift + A
View: Rulers	Ctrl + Alt + R
View: Grid	Ctrl + Alt + G
View: Brush Variance Palette	F11
View: Histogram	F7
View: Layers	F8
View: Learning Center	F10
View: Materials	F6

View: Overview	F9
View: History	F3
View: Tool Options	F4
View: Magnifier window	Ctrl + Alt + M

Image

Flip Image	Ctrl + I
Mirror Image	Ctrl + M
Free Rotate Image	Ctrl + R
Resize Image	Shift + S
Crop to selection	Shift + R
Image Information	Shift + I
Load palette	Shift + O
Decrease Color Depth > 2 color palette	Ctrl + Shift + 1
Decrease Color Depth > 16 color palette	Ctrl + Shift + 2
Decrease Color Depth > 256 color palette	Ctrl + Shift + 3
Decrease Color Depth > 32k Colors	Ctrl + Shift + 4
Decrease Color Depth > 64k Colors	Ctrl + Shift + 5
Decrease Color Depth > x Colors	Ctrl + Shift + 6
Increase Color Depth > 16 color palette	Ctrl + Shift + 8
Increase Color Depth > 256 color palette	Ctrl + Shift + 9
Increase Color Depth > RGB – 8 bits/channel	Ctrl + Shift + 0

Adjust

Adjust Color Balance > Red/Green/Blue	Shift + U
Adjust Brightness and Contrast > Brightness/Contrast	Shift + B
Adjust Brightness and Contrast > Equalize	Shift + E
Adjust Brightness and Contrast > Gamma Correction	Shift + G
Adjust Brightness and Contrast > Highlight/Midtone/Shadow	Shift + M
Adjust Brightness and Contrast > Histogram Adjustment	Ctrl + Shift + H
Adjust Brightness and Contrast > Histogram Stretch	Shift + T
Adjust Hue and Saturation > Colorize	Shift + L
Adjust Hue and Saturation > Hue/Saturation/Lightness	Shift + H

Layers

New Mask Layer > Hide All	Shift + Y
Select All	Ctrl + A
Select None (Deselect)	Ctrl + D
Make Selection > From Mask	Ctrl + Shift + S
Make Selection > From Vector Object	Ctrl + Shift + B
Invert Selection	Ctrl + Shift + I
Hide (Selection) Marquee	Ctrl + Shift + M
New Window	Shift + W
Duplicate (Window)	Shift + D
Fit to Image	Ctrl + W

Index